THE POLITICAL IDEAS
OF THE ENGLISH
ROMANTICISTS

The
Political Ideas
of the
English
Romanticists

by
CRANE BRINTON

Ann Arbor Paperbacks
THE UNIVERSITY OF MICHIGAN PRESS

20,938

First edition as an Ann Arbor Paperback 1966
All rights reserved
Published by special arrangement
First published by the Oxford University Press 1926
Published in the United States of America by
The University of Michigan Press and simultaneously
in Toronto, Canada, by Ambassador Books Limited
Manufactured in the United States of America

TO MY MOTHER

PREFATORY NOTE

I wish to thank Mr. H. J. Laski for suggesting the subject of this study. At Oxford I am especially indebted for advice and encouragement to Mr. R. W. Chapman, to Professor Gordon, to Mr. P. E. Matheson, and to Mr. L. G. Wickham Legg. At Harvard I have to thank Mr. Penfield Roberts, Mr. E. S. Mason, and Mr. C. J. Hill, for assistance with manuscript and proofs.

CONTENTS

INTRODUCTION

A VAST change came over England during the hundred
years which separate the mid-eighteenth century from
the mid-nineteenth. In 1750 politics were ruled by the
methods of Walpole and the aristocratic traditions of
the Revolution of 1688 ; formalism was as strong as it
was ever to be in English letters ; ' Gothic ' was a term
of reproach ; Shakespeare had faults, and Pope was
a peer of the great poets ; religion, like philosophy, was
comfortable and rational, scornful of uncertainties ; agri-
culture was the mainstay of the State, and the parish
the centre of common life ; enterprise was engaged
rather in commerce than in industry, and the mercantile
theory had not yet encountered Adam Smith. In 1850
England had already progressed far in that political
transformation which has produced a suffrage as general
as ever Jacobin desired ; in letters, standards and canons
had been banished from the finite world of law to take
precarious refuge in the soul of the artist ; Shakespeare
was enthroned above suspicion ; Pope had become a
minor poet, and Keats and Shelley were well on the way
to becoming great ones ; Gothic churches had long been
springing up all over England in the wake of a religious
movement which had small consideration for Right
Reason ; the abolition of the Corn Laws had meant the
final destruction of the old landed aristocracy ; in an
urban industrial civilization rural life had become an
anomaly or a distraction.

This is a revolution. A century is a small thing in
a nation's life. The true revolution is not a matter of
guillotine and barricades, *coups d'état*, and conventions.
It is simply a transformation, rapid only by comparison
with the long unfolding of human history, in the ideas
that govern men's minds. And so material change alone
is no measure of revolutions. The aeroplane, the sub-

marine, and a dozen other recent inventions are mechanically at least as much superior to the early steam-engine
as the steam-engine was to the water-wheel. To conclude from this, however, that we have lived through
changes greater than those that came over the England
of George III would be a great error. For again, the
true revolution is worked not in means of communication, in methods of production and distribution, but in
the way men think and feel. The industrial revolution
was not made by machines, but by the men who invented,
the men who set up, and the men who ran machines. It
is true that in England were to be found coal and iron
side by side, that England was geographically suited for
commercial expansion, that political organization and
social tradition left the Englishman, in comparison with
his continental neighbours, free to give rein to his
creative and acquisitive impulses. But none of these
factors could have produced the industrial revolution
had they not been accompanied by a contagion of
enterprise, a desire for expansion, a willingness to experi-
ment—in short, by a revolution in the minds of men.

A just and complete historical survey of this century
of English life would weigh all these movements : would
appraise machinery and evangelism, romance, and the
theory of rent, in the same scale ; and would refer all
things to the activity of human intelligence, which
alone attempts to give unity and meaning to a chaotic
world. This study is to be devoted to the consideration
of a restricted portion of human activity during a part
of the period, which, for lack of a specific name, we shall
call the Revolution. Now, it is pretty generally agreed
that, on the literary side, the Revolution should be
termed the *Romantic Revolt*, the *Romantic Movement*, or
simply *Romanticism*. Many literary critics, however,
object to such scholastic labels. A distinguished man of
letters has recently put the objection emphatically :

' I think, if you will look into " classicism " and " romanticism "
for yourselves, with your own open eyes, you will find—though

the whole pother about their difference amounts to nothing that
need trouble a healthy man—it amounts to this : some men have
naturally a sense of form stronger than their sense of colour ;
some men have a sense of colour stronger than their sense of
form. . . . All things considered, I advise that it may help our
minds to earn an honest living if we dismiss the terms " classic "
and " romantic " out of our vocabulary for a while.'

Professor Quiller-Couch is clearly right in telling his
classes that loveliness exists in works of art rather than
in text-books about them. A glance at the stiff row of
' naturalisms ', ' realisms ', and ' romanticisms ' within
which pedantry so often attempts to confine the abun-
dance of English literature is almost enough to convert
one to Professor Quiller-Couch's delightful anarchy of
taste. Yet it is hard to see how the historian can do
without the term ' romantic '. A very simple instance
will show just how necessary it is.

Suppose Percy Bysshe Shelley born in 1692 instead of
in 1792. Suppose him the same animal being, with the
same quivering sensibility, the same frailty, the same
passion sublimate. It is obvious that he could not have
been the same poet. The thing is inconceivable ; and
that not for any physical reason, but because such poetry
could not possibly have endured the literary atmosphere
of England in 1720. Actually Shelley, as we are told
often enough, was little read and much calumniated
during his lifetime. But the way had been broken for
him by a century of steady transformation of literary taste ;
and what is far more important, by a spiritual change
which had accustomed men to the search for emotional
novelty, to the endless discontent which is romance. The
literary atmosphere of England of the Regency was such
that the poet Shelley was at least not suffocated by it.

It is perhaps misleading to call this essential condition
of all literary activity ' atmosphere ' or ' background ' ;
for it is not impalpable and vague. It is nothing less
than an imaginative interpretation of the facts of life
held in common by men. Thus, it has the reality of

a loyalty, a faith ; it is a social bond, a common thing, a Church or a State in its way. In old-fashioned language it was known as a ' school ', and this word does bring out the associative character of such literary movements. Now the authors of our period, whatever their bickerings, were certainly a ' school ' in this sense ; and, since the world has for a hundred years or more fastened on them the epithet ' romantic ' we shall do well to retain it.

Granted, then, that romanticism is no schoolmaster's bogey, but as much a fact as Methodism or Socialism, it is perhaps not clear what it has to do with politics, or why it should interest the political historian. In the first place, romanticism as a way of thought is a part of that vast change in men and things, the Revolution, and as such has many links with the political changes of the Revolution. But the writings of the English romanticists can also provide the political historian with valuable material for reconstruction of the actual politics of the time. This is possible because, almost to a man, the English romanticists were actively interested in politics. Men of letters, from Aristophanes to Mr. Shaw, have often busied themselves with politics. But it is seldom—and this in itself is a significant fact—that a whole generation devotes itself to politics as fervently as did that of 1800 in England. Indeed, among the romantics Lamb and Keats alone seem to have escaped the contagion. There thus exists a great mass of political writing which, from the circumstances and character of the writers, has a peculiar value to the historian of political ideas. This value springs largely from the role men of letters can play in politics. Roughly their activity falls into three divisions.

In the first place certain men of letters like Plato, Burke, and Rousseau have been profound political philosophers, makers of creeds, and leaders of men as well as artists of the finest sort, a distinction to which many great political thinkers, like Bentham and Aristotle, can have no claim. With the great example of this type who falls within our period we shall not directly concern ourselves. Edmund Burke had certain romantic traits ; but he was so much more than a romanticist, so much more indeed than a man of letters, that it would be presumption to include him here. In the second place men of letters who fail to attain to original thought often play an important part in the dissemination of the ideas of others. We who are contemporaries of Mr. Galsworthy and Mr. Wells need not be reminded that men of letters can be very active agents in the spreading of political doctrines. Finally, the politics of men of letters can frequently give us an insight into the reality behind that fiction, the ' average ' man. In order to get at the realities of politics, and especially the politics of a nation governed in some measure by public opinion, like the England of the Georges, it is necessary to know not only the intrigues of the governors, the currents of professional political philosophy, the details of government machinery and the organization of economic life, but also the political mind of the average man. We have records enough of all the rest, but the ' man in the street ' leaves no record behind him. At best a few letters to newspapers and periodicals of the day, signed ' Pro bono publico ' or ' Britannicus ', and he is gone. We can form no connected knowledge of his state of mind from such vagrant fragments. For us he is less than the shadow of a name. Yet if the study of political philosophy cannot somehow be run to ground in popular consciousness, it may merit the reproach of impracticability so often brought against it by the hard-headed politician.

It is just here that the political opinions of men of letters become especially valuable. For men like Scott and Southey, although exceptionally gifted in their proper sphere of activity, were politically very close to the ordinary plain citizen. Like most men they did not create their political standards, but took them from circumstances, from leaders and thinkers, from the spirit of the age. It is not that literary men are distinguished for common sense in politics. Indeed, they are often enough quite visionary. But they have ideas ; they are articulate ; and they are neither professional nor academic. They do not run in the ruts of political routine, nor do they skip uncontrolled along the open paths of professorial abstraction. You will find among them neither a Creevey nor a Kant. They look at the political scene from an angle quite their own ; but it is an angle that much more nearly coincides with that from which the vast inarticulate mass of spectators sees it than any of which we have a consistent record.

Since politics is a spectacle which is itself inevitably modified by the effect which it has upon its spectators, this fact has its importance. The whole record of the political consciousness of a number of our fellow-men is there for our inspection, not fragmentary, but thanks to the labours of many students as complete as one could wish. For not only are there the works of the romanticists ; there are richly documented biographies, vast numbers of letters and journals, industriously garnered ' Belesenheit ' and ' Einwirkung ' theses from Germany.

Much of this material is untouched by the historian of serious political thought. Yet if our premises are correct it ought to throw light upon some aspects of a period which, close to us though it be, we can see to have been a turning-point in English and European history.

Our first task must be to search out from the mass of the writings of the romanticists their political ideas. Next we must attempt to judge, by reference to the biographies, periodicals, newspapers, and letters of the period, how far these ideas had currency. Since the number of these journals and letters, and other sources is legion, we must select those which will most satisfactorily give us an anchorage in facts. Finally, we must attempt to understand the part played by the political ideas of the romanticists in the Revolution.

Such an attempt will have its dangers. But danger is the salt of thought, as of any other adventure ; and history is an adventure in thought. It is not after all a chronicle, nor even a précis of State Papers. Such simple registers of fact as these, like all things mechanical, are perfectly safe. Indeed, machines never fail, though the men who control them may ; nor do they ever succeed. Only things that are alive know failure and success. And surely history is alive ?

I

JACOBIN AND ANTI-JACOBIN

I

It was the great concern of the mature and militant romanticists of the early nineteenth century to destroy the poetic pretensions of the school of Pope and of ' one Boileau ' ; and so successful were their efforts that, in the peaceful time of Wordsworth's laureateship, cultivated people agreed that Pope was no poet—and that Boileau, being a Frenchman, was rather less than none. Wordsworth and Keats, however, merely completed the task of destruction. For the best part of a century, men had been at work to undermine the classic edifice of Augustan letters. Some knowledge of the nature of this edifice, and of the reasons why men found it inadequate, is essential if we are to understand the feelings of a later generation, who saw in it a stronghold of poetic tyranny, a very Bastille of literature.

The tritest of paradoxes informs us that in literary and historical criticism distance is an aid to the perception even of details ; and so this edifice is no longer to us quite the simple, ugly barrack it was to Wordsworth and Keats. It is, in fact, a labyrinth. We cannot hope to understand its plan, nor that of any other social structure. We shall have done enough if we can but find our way through it.

Unfortunately, the influence of our romantic predecessors has been so great that we are still frequently told that the eighteenth century was after all, as Keats and Wordsworth thought, intellectual, aristocratic, contented, and dull. It had a reasonable attachment to the idea of God, but no faith. Nature it dissected, distrusted, or ignored ; skylarks and daffodils moved it to no ecstacy. Men suppressed their emotions under the

contemptuous name of enthusiasm. Their political life
was a series of sordid intrigues within a Venetian oligarchy
of great families. Here, too, no hearts were moved. It
is true that in this placid England there are certain
intruders, who become increasingly numerous as the
century nears its end. These are none other than the
' pre-romantics ', prophets of the coming storm. Their
names are sufficient : the Wartons, Shenstone, Blair,
Collins, Gray, MacPherson, the Wesleys, Whitefield,
Berkeley, ' Capability ' Brown, and Brown of the *Estimate*, the rebel Wilkes, and many another. They were
lovers of mystery in a society that thought the unknow-
able not worth knowing ; they were sensitive men in
tune with the infinite and out of tune with their age.
Above all they were iconoclasts, destroyers who made
room for the new civilization that was to come in the
next century.

Such is the common or text-book pattern of English
civilization in the eighteenth century. Surely it has
truth enough to merit a juster correction than caricature
can give. A facile dualism runs through the whole
pattern. Now dualism is one of the commonest vices of
human thought. It may well be born of the ineluctable
antithesis between the individual and the external world.
It has certainly persisted throughout human history, and
forms the basis for most of the schemes with which
thought cheats life. This dualistic exaggeration has often
found a corrective in art and in common sense. Its
schematic simplicities have, however, flourished in the
modern world unchecked by the subtleties of truth, for
neither common sense nor art has had much share in
popular education.

It is true enough that in 1750 most educated people
admired Pope, and that an increasing number of iconoclasts did not admire him. What is not true is that there
was an abstract Age of Pope, which contained within
itself an abstract Pre-Romantic Opposition. English
letters and English civilization had not this death-like

simplicity, like that of an exhibit in a museum of natural history. They were alive and much too occupied with living to try to catalogue themselves. Shenstone undoubtedly was much concerned with himself as a gentleman, an amateur gardener, a wit, a poet, and an Englishman—but not as a ' Pre-romantic '. For just this reason, none of the sweeping statements too commonly made about the eighteenth century can stand alone. De Foe, Richardson, and Johnson hardly live up to the epithet aristocratic. Moreover, with Grub Street and with publishers like Lintot and Tonson, men of letters were passing from their servitude to noble patrons to their modern servitude to their own popularity. The world of Hogarth is not dull, formal, nor orderly ; and while it is true that there was no shallow cult of obscure Elizabethans, Shakespeare was admired even before Garrick made him adored. Nor did Pope feel less the woes of Heloise and Abelard because he crammed them into heroic couplets. All feeling need not take on the form of Shelley's *Indian Woman's Lament*. There is indeed not much great poetry more filled with emotion than Pope's lines on Addison. And if by emotion we mean sentiment, how can we forget *George Barnewell*? Nor were the greatest men of this age persuaded that the human intellect could compass all things. Pope wrote, indeed,

> Say first, of God above or Man below,
> What can we reason, but from what we know ?
> Of Man, what see we but his station here
> From which to reason or to which refer ?

This Man, however, ought surely to have been recognized by the romantic poets as a brother :

> Chaos of Thought and Passion, all confus'd ;
> Still by himself abus'd, or disabus'd ;
> Created half to rise, and half to fall ;
> Great Lord of all things, yet a prey to all,
> Sole judge of Truth, in endless Error hurl'd
> The glory, jest, and riddle of the world.

There was room for doubt, mystery, and infinity in the mind of Pope. It is a very small mind that has no room for these.

In politics the same difficulty is to be found. M. Halévy has remarked that in the eighteenth century England was regarded throughout Europe as 'le pays classique de l'émeute'; the history of the early Methodists reveals the miseries of a class afflicted not only with physical but with spiritual poverty; the victories of Marlborough at the beginning of the century, and those of Nelson at its end, are not the victories of peace. Indeed, the delightful little war of Jenkins's ear was begun under the peace-loving Walpole. Neither Chatham nor Wilkes quite fits into the Venetian oligarchy; and the vivid pamphleteering of the time fits no better into a scheme where politics are the personal concern of a few. Finally, the modern movement for parliamentary reform originates with such sons of the eighteenth century as Major Cartwright. There were Jacobins before the name was coined.

A rigid distinction between 'classic' and 'preromantic' cannot be applied to men any more than to movements. Pope, Swift, Bolingbroke, Walpole, Chatham, all escape it. Was Edward Young an Augustan? At any rate, Keats would hardly have recognized him as a fellow Titan. Gray may seem to be a true romantic born too soon. But he was enough of a conformist to be a don at Cambridge. As for the unnatural taste imposed on him by his time there is at least as much nature in unlyrical abstractions like

> Pale Grief, and pleasing Pain,
> With Horror, Tyrant of the throbbing breast

as in the meaningless and crudely lyrical *Ullalume* of the romantic Poe.

> As the lavas that restlessly roll
> Their sulphurous currents down Yaanek
> In the ultimate climes of the Pole—
> That groan as they roll down Mount Yaanek
> In the realms of the boreal pole.

Then there is Thomas Warton, who generally appears among the pre-romantics. In some verses on *Sir Joshua Reynolds's Painted Window at New College, Oxford*, he confesses that

> Long enamoured of a barbarous age,
> A faithless truant to the classic page,

he had loved to wander about among the remains of old splendour ; had responded to the wildness and exuberance of Gothic architecture ; and had feared that Reynolds's new window in the modern style would spoil the mystic beauty of the fourteenth-century New College Chapel. He sees the window, however, and at once addresses the painter :

> Thy powerful hand has broke the Gothic chain,
> And brought my bosom back to truth again ;
> To truth, by no peculiar taste confin'd,
> Whose universal pattern strikes mankind.

Warton, evidently, can be assigned neither to the sheep nor to the goats. Again, this same failure to fit into a dualistic classification is observable in politicians. One is inclined to hesitate whether to assign Wilkes to the eighteenth century for his aristocratic vices, or to the nineteenth for his democratic virtues ; and then one thinks of Mr. Horatio Bottomley.

The text-book pattern of the eighteenth century must, therefore, be discarded ; but it is no easy task to construct a new one in a dozen pages. Something must be done, however, for it is unhistorical, or worse, to approach the romantic revolt without considering that from which it was a revolt. To say that the romanticists revolted against a misconception of their predecessors not unlike that which we have just outlined would be true, but it would be a sorry way out for the critic. For had the eighteenth century really been what Wordsworth and his fellows thought it, their victory would have been more catastrophic and less satisfactory. England might have had an *Hernani* instead of a *Prelude*.

Perhaps it is best to approach the problem by a detour. The too simple view from which we started might well be represented after the manner of the statisticians, with a line standing for ' classicism ' sloping downward as the century goes on, and another line for ' romanticism ' climbing upward to meet and pass above it at some such dramatic date as the year of the publication of the *Lyrical Ballads*. We cannot in decency adopt this device, for statistics and history are not yet one. But were we to do so we should have a very involved diagram indeed ; not two lines, but many, tracing through the century the changing fates of deists, Methodists, mystics, rationalists, Whigs, Tories, Jacobites, lovers of Gothic, lovers of classical antiquity, imitators of France, ballad-writers, satirists, pamphleteers, old authors and new ones, old thinkers and new ones, merchants, inventors, adventurers, and many others. Each of these lines would rise or fall with fashion or accident, interwoven in a strange and apparently meaningless pattern. Yet, if all possible human activities had been carefully represented, certain conclusions could be drawn about the relative place of these activities in the life of the century. The century would, in short, be real, yet have a meaning. At least, one must hope so ; for if there is no change even in the elements of human life then there is no romance and no revolt, and there is no use writing a book about these things.

We have, of course, merely stated the problem. The diagram itself we can hardly attempt, but we must at least consider briefly what sort of picture of the century ought to result. In the first place there would no doubt be certain underlying racial or national qualities fairly constantly at work. However much the more hopeful of this generation may be inclined to deny that national differences are worth fighting for, only those whose hope has turned to madness will deny that there are such differences. That London and Paris are physically different is hardly more apparent than that Shakespeare and Racine are spiritually different; in both cases, two different sorts of imagination have been at work. After all, Milton's phrase about the ' native wood-notes wild ' is at least as true as it is condescending. Something which at one point is eccentricity or even madness, at another extravagance, at another the imagination that makes known the unknown, and that always has a little of the ' desire of the moth for the star ' has never dropped out of English letters and English life. Further to define this is a difficult task, for it is at the very centre of the romantic movement. It is almost always accompanied by a distrust of anything exact, completed, regular, planned. Life is conceived as a force that is weakened and eventually destroyed by any kind of constraint. Life must ever attempt the impossible, and fail; for the alternative to the attempt and the failure is death. Law, reason, and convention try to set bounds to human activity, and make life impossible. Therefore those who are on the side of romance will be for Nature against Art, for all that *grows* against all that is *made*.

Now, there were many in eighteenth-century England who sought in literature this wildness. Pope protests that in his polished world

> Chaucer's worst ribaldry is learn'd by rote
> And beastly Skelton Heads of Houses quote.

The ' pre-romantics ', too, are generally moved by a similar spirit to seek for the unusual, to cultivate irregularity, to feel more than can be put into words, and certainly more than can be put into heroic couplets. Hardly a nineteenth-century poet would have disowned Collins,

> And hamlets brown, and dim-discovered spires.

Woods, fields, flowers, and gardens play quite as large a part as drawing-rooms in the literature that has come down to us. Surely this is not wholly because we ourselves prefer woods and fields to drawing-rooms? In this place, too, in our scheme of things must come the old familiar romantic portents—the ballad, the novel and play of sentiment, the beginnings of the Gothic revival, the cult of Ossian. The significant things about these literary innovations, and the whole movement to which they are attached, is their ready acceptance by the reading public. Thus absorbed into a public mind already full of much inconsistent matter, these innovations ceased to cohere and form a system. Quarrels over such abstractions as ' romanticism ' and ' classicism ' are always limited to schools. In eighteenth-century England systematic education and the periodical press had not yet converted the middle class into a school.

This element of romance is not limited, however, to the mere forms of polite literature. It is an attitude toward life, a philosophy. What is worth while in life is the unexpected. But the rationalizing intellect rejoices above all in the suppression of the unexpected. Therefore those who are on the side of romance will turn away from the intellect, and cultivate their emotions. Emotion is ever fresh, and uncursed with the memory that desiccates. Civilization, it is evident, attempts to substitute certainty for uncertainty, and to suppress the affective elements in human life. It succeeds only partially, and produces what is called evil. Now if man could cast aside the restraints of civilization, it is evident that he would be more happy, for then these affective elements would have complete power, and evil would be unknown. Here the eternal fable of the Golden Age gains a new force; for it is assumed that the Golden Age knew not law, convention, and other social restraints, that in it man's natural goodness was given free play. What has once been can surely be again. Man is good and will prove his goodness if kings, priests, and nobles will let him.

To love Nature in man, then, was to hate what was unnatural in him, to hate social distinctions, commercial prosperity, cities, polished society, governments, and artificial poetry. The nobleman is to be condemned, the peasant to be praised. Urban life is vicious, rural life virtuous. The idylls of the century are many. In most of them the myth of a Golden Age is presented in engaging fullness. Thomson's *Spring* and Warton's *Enthusiast* contain long passages of this sort. Cowper has succeeded in giving an epigrammatic turn to the idea, which usually does not tempt the epigrammatic mind :

> God made the country, and man made the town.

It follows, of course, that man should be freed in the name of his own natural goodness from the badness of institutions. Fielding in one passage has stated this belief that man is bad only because of his environment as clearly as Rousseau ever did.

' The nature of man is far from being in itself evil ; it abounds with benevolence, charity, and pity, coveting praise and honour, and shunning shame and disgrace. Bad education, bad habits, and bad customs debauch our nature, and drive it headlong as it were into vice. The governors of the world, and I am afraid the priesthood, are answerable for the badness of it.'

Later, Shelley was to announce that through the magic power of poetry men were to be freed from their long dependence on their governors, and restored to their primitive natures, as the poet had been who sang to them. So colourless and moderate a man as Edward Young is not free from this idea of the poet-legislator :

> Not far beneath the hero's feet,
> Nor from the legislator's seat
>   Stands far remote the bard.
> Though not with public terrors crown'd
> Yet wider shall his rule be found,
>   More lasting his reward.

This same Young, no doubt unintentionally, has added the final touch to this process of freeing man from all restraints save those he would *naturally* impose on himself. He writes of England,

> Where empire's wide-established throne
>   No private master fills ;
> Where, long foretold, the People reigns :
> Where each a vassal's humble heart disdains ;
> And judgeth what he sees ; and, as he judgeth, wills.

Godwin's whole philosophy is but an expansion of that last line.

Over against this quality of extravagance, which is evident enough in eighteenth-century England, and which inspired the cult of Nature and of the natural man, one must put the quality of common sense, which has never been absent from English life, and has often been present in English letters. In spite of its name and origin common sense is a vague quality. Perhaps it has most of the characteristics of critical intelligence, except detachment. At any rate it is conservative, accepts limitations, and distrusts generalizations. Common sense composed all such wisdom as 'The burnt child shuns the fire '. Therefore it is against romance. To Campbell's description of the Pennsylvania valley where

> aye those sunny mountains half-way down
> Would echo flageolet from some romantic town

common sense would simply remark that there are no romantic towns in Pennsylvania. In its desire to put a halter on life common sense may well go too far, and make life unliveable. Certainly common sense founded neither Peru nor Massachusetts ; nor did it write *Hamlet*, nor discover the law of gravitation. But then, neither did it inspire the Children's Crusade, nor compose Blake's epics.

Literature never quite surrenders itself to common sense ; for like any other form of art literature arranges material which common sense is content to use as it finds. The rather stupid eye of the camera is after all the eye of common sense. But if common sense is not quite taste it can tell a monster when it sees one. There is much of it in English letters from De Foe to Johnson. Aided by good taste it produced the conversation of Dr. Johnson, at once witty and sober, energetic and restrained, profound and urbane, and never touched with that only real and unforgivable mannerism which is insincerity. There is, of course, much in Johnson that does not belong to the eighteenth century as it is commonly misunderstood. He liked the wild scenery of Scotland and the Peak of Derbyshire. He was not polished. He had a most unreasonable fear of death. He spilled his food on his clothes. So we might go on, without, however, quite losing the impression that Johnson belonged to his age and not to the ' pre-romantics '.

Just how much there was in Johnson of this restraint, which we have perhaps misnamed common sense, must be evident on a comparison of the man as he appears to Macaulay and to Boswell. There is something in Boswell's Johnson that escapes Macaulay ; that, indeed, is no small part of what we mean by the eighteenth century. For Macaulay has caricatured his subject— not a difficult task, since caricature is no more than the ability to neglect what we do not understand. Macaulay saw the eccentric in Dr. Johnson, saw what made him superficially different from his fellows, suspected perhaps the depths of his religious feelings. But he did not understand how the doctor hated humbug, whether that of Ossian or of Wilkes, how he distrusted emotional optimism, how he set truth above rhetoric though not above art. Above all, he did not know how humble Johnson was, how sure that life was a trial, how doubtful whether he had undergone that trial with credit. For Macaulay—like many of the Victorians, one suspects— was pious, but not humble. His life was not a trial, but a triumph.

This feeling for the limitations of earthly things, so strong in Johnson and so weak in Macaulay, is by no means uncharacteristic of the Age of Reason. The rasher hopes of a Condorcet or a Godwin are the products of a rationalism divorced from common sense at least, if not from higher qualities. In general reason, in the eighteenth century, refused to abandon the earth. The most rational of poets could sing

> Quelque sujet qu'on traite, ou plaisant, ou sublime,
> Que toujours le bon sens s'accorde avec la rime.

With Boileau we have come to the group of wits who most nearly conform to our text-book pattern. No doubt this group was polished, aristocratic, distrustful of ' enthusiasm ', incapable of mystic belief. No doubt its brilliance was heartless enough. In the language of the schools, it glittered, but did not glow. Yet there are touches of pain in *The Way of the World* as there are in *Le Misanthrope*. Millamant is quite as human as Beatrice Cenci. She is, it is true, a daughter of her age. There was no one quite like her in the next century. Such women were all turned into Becky Sharps.

To sum up, there was in eighteenth-century England a fairly constant endeavour to break away from ' classic ' restraints in the name of national tradition and individual freedom. In addition, a certain feeling that life is greater than intelligence penetrates everywhere, and certainly into the consciousness of great men like Pope. There was, however, a strong upper middle class, not yet spoiled by unlimited power, which possessed too much common sense to go all the way in anything like a romantic revolt. The same Fielding who seems to have stated the dogma of the natural goodness of man as clearly as Rousseau, was forced by qualms of common sense to question it in other passages. Mr. Square, who ' held human nature to be the perfection of all virtue ', is satirized in *Tom Jones* ; and Fielding admits in another place that some rather dubious arts are natural gifts. For Sophia, it seems, ' wanted all that useful art which females convert to so many good purposes in life, and which, as it rather arises from the heart than from the

head, is often the property of the silliest of women '.
This same middle class imitated in many ways an aristocracy of reason, in itself not without a healthy connexion
with common sense.

In politics there was a similar state of affairs. At the
very top there was a Whig aristocracy which had things
pretty much its own way. This aristocracy was never
without links with the commercial classes ; it did not
become a mere group of courtiers. It assumed that its
privileges were a matter of course, not merely a matter
of right. It was sober, contented, country-loving. Only
in the very highest circles did life sparkle. In the shade
of this aristocracy there reposed a middle class that was
apparently contented with a respectable if not glorious
existence. It had its malcontents, however, and it could
be affected by dangerous contagions of mob-emotion
over wars, and even over the excise. Below there was
a great mass whom Enclosure Acts were preparing for
fullest usefulness in the industrial revolution. The
Methodists had proved the possibilities of discontent in
this mass. All in all it is astonishing on what a small
foundation the peace of the eighteenth century was
built. The rationalist found it easy enough to see
faults in society. The prosperous *bourgeois* was contented with old ways only because the inventive genius
of other men had not yet shown him new ones. The
imaginative rebels, the Shelleys and the .Byrons, were
biding their time. The poor and the dispossessed were
finding compensation in religious ecstacy and catalepsy.
A few cultivated noblemen, some of the lesser gentry,
and a few of the more prosperous commercial classes
make up the contented group for whom life was moderation, politics conservatism, morals good sense, art a form
of reason and nature

Those RULES of old discovered, not devis'd.

We are back in a sense to our text-book pattern. But
text-books are dangerous only for those who misuse
them, as dogmas are dangerous only for dogmatists.

There is an eighteenth-century English civilization as real and as recognizable as English eighteenth-century architecture. But no more than any other civilization was it perfect, static, and supreme over its members. The physical qualities of human beings seem curiously independent of civilization. It is not improbable that as a mere animal the modern Italian peasant is as good a specimen as his Roman ancestor ; and he is certainly as satisfactory an animal as the British working-man. But as a human being, as a soldier, a citizen, a workman, a supporter of civilization, he is inferior to his ancestor ; and, even making allowance for race-prejudice, he would seem inferior to the Englishman. For civilization depends on law, morals, custom, faith, on a spiritual discipline which cannot be assimilated to the study of man as an animal. Great nations have lived and died, not indeed wholly independent of such natural factors as climate and soil-exhaustion, but largely so ; following another law than that which governs material organisms. So too the physical basis of aesthetic enjoyment would seem to be fairly constant. The reader of lyric poetry in Queen Anne's days got the same sort of imaginative impression as the reader of the Regency. Men must have been in 1800 what they were in 1700. The difference lies in the poetry, not in the reader. Hence all the genuine problems of aesthetics, as of politics and morals, lie in the mutations of forms or modes that are somehow outside the individual. These forms seem to impose themselves by contagion, and civilization is like an infectious disease, in that it is spread in human beings but not wholly by them. Or in a more hopeful way it may be said that civilization has something of the nature of a corporation, and must always maintain and develop itself through groups and ' schools '. These groups, as they are more than human, are not subject to the same laws of growth and decay that apply to the human organism. Hazlitt wrote sorrowfully in the 1820's that *The Beggar's Opera* was about to succumb to the spirit of the age, and that it could never be played again. A new spirit has seized his grandsons and falsified the prediction. Or is it the old returned ? This at least must be admitted : there has been no considerable physical change in Englishmen to explain so great a spiritual change.

In the great confusion of life certain of these forms of civilization, these group-contagions, recur, and give to it a sort of order. Sometimes they encourage an aggressive, but restless and disordered life ; sometimes they encourage a quiet, well-ruled and unadventurous life. At times they tend to suppress man's animal instincts in one way, and to open new outlets for them in another. Our desires are rarely strong enough to defy fashion ; and fashion is but civilization in its less ponderous moods. We may now return to our dualism, a dimmed and qualified dualism, and say that those forms of civilization that invite men to indulge their animal beings are romantic, and those forms that invite men to restrain their animal beings are classic. Neither of these forms could possibly exist in completeness. They neutralize each other, and they are vastly modified by the exigencies of the world. They are always present in any civilization. Homer is in some ways romantic, and Scott is often classic. If French drama of the great age was classic in its regularity, court morals were romantic in their irregularity. It is by no anomaly that Hume and Law were contemporaries in the England of the eighteenth century.

The Augustan Age in England was then a classic age. There is a sense in which English civilization had attained the rule of classic standards of moderation, self-restraint, order, decorum. The Augustan Age is not all of eighteenth-century England, however, nor were the Augustans supreme over their fellows. The fine balance of the classic ideal was always precariously maintained in England. There is a sense in which this civilization is a transition to the restless civilization of the next century. It is with this new civilization and with the intricacies of its evolution that we are now concerned.

2

The year of the *Lyrical Ballads* is generally considered by historians of literature as marking the inception of the Romantic Revolt. Actually, however, the *Lyrical Ballads* made no great stir in the world of letters, and certainly not in the world of politics. At most they gave Canning and Frere a better mark for *The Anti-Jacobin*. If we do not begin our study until 1798 we must omit a decade filled with political strife. It will be well, then, to look more closely at the work of the many forgotten poets and novelists who were writing when the first generation of revolt, that of Wordsworth, Coleridge, and Southey, came to intellectual maturity.

First, as to the poets. They were all very minor people, for the best work of Cowper and most of that of Burns had been done. So far as this throng of verse writers can be sorted, they appear to be of three different complexions: the extravagant, the didactic, and the satirical. The extravagant have acquired a certain immortality of scorn under the name of Della Cruscan. Their leader was Robert Merry, a man not without intelligence but quite without taste. He signed his poetry with the name of the Florentine Academy of which he was a member (already expatriate English poets were living in the land of romantic desire), and the satire of Gifford fixed it on the school. Merry took up the cause of the French Revolution with a warmth we are constrained to believe sincere, since it involved his ostracism from the fashionable world in which he had once shone as a poet and a dandy. His disciples were mostly women, and like himself wrote *vers de société* until the French Revolution inspired them to join the crusade against kings and lords. For at least one of them, the actress, Mary Robinson, ' Perdita ' to the ' Florizel ' of the Prince of Wales, this crusade was surely not unjustified. The didactic poets also owe their survival as names not wholly unmeaning chiefly to satire—to that poetry of *The Anti-Jacobin* that gave Canning his fatal reputation for brilliance. Erasmus Darwin, a scientist of distinction who was led into verse by the unfortunate taste of the age, is perhaps best known to us now. Then there were Richard Payne Knight, poetaster and art critic, who may be dismissed in the latter capacity with the statement that he advised against the purchase of the Elgin Marbles ; Thelwall, Jacobin lecturer and a figure in the State Trials of 1794 ; and William Hayley, dullest of his generation, and a friend of Cowper. Thelwall was a bit too enthusiastic for the others. They are mostly without strong feeling, without strong thinking, devotees of a spurious and mechanical ' golden mean ' which sinks extremes in the mind without overcoming them in reality, Whigs of course, and mildly in favour of the French Revolution. The satirists, on the other hand, are mostly Tories, like the self-made Gifford, once a cobbler, and destined to edit the *Quarterly*, the clergyman Mathias, an academic wit who thought himself an heir of Pope and who really was an heir of Settle, and, finally, the brilliant group of politicians who edited *The Anti-Jacobin*. This Tory satire is chiefly valuable for the light it throws on the ideas of their opponents, men who are very evidently attempting to make literature a vehicle for the propagation of ideas hostile to the existing order. In itself, even in its masterpiece of serious-mindedness, the *New Morality* of Canning, it hardly affords a missionary gospel of its own. In spite of the ardour of its attacks it is really on the defensive ; it is besieged in its own castle. What the Tories are defending is the state of things created by the revolution of 1688 by the Whig aristocracy and the wits and philosophers of Queen Anne's reign. One of the ways in which this state of things was attacked was through the literature we are to consider.

The starting-point of this attack can be discerned in

some lines of Merry's, which are not as meaningless as they seem.

> And has not kind, impartial Heav'n
> To every rank an *equal feeling* giv'n?
> Virtue alone should vice subdue,
> Nor are the MANY baser than the FEW.[1]

The phrase *equal feeling* is the root of the matter. Man is by nature good. He is by nature the equal of any of his fellow men ; that is to say, equality among men is really an equality of goodness. Now men have come to differ obviously in outward circumstances, in wealth and power. That in which they still preserve a rough sort of equality is *feeling*. Our desires are surely more nearly common than anything else about us. If then we assume that feeling, instinct, desire, are in themselves good, we have brought equality into the practical world. We have gained a powerful means of persuading people that inequality is not in the nature of man. We have put inequality, and the whole problem of evil, into the accidents of things ; that is, into our environment. A little freewill can work wonders with environment. We have solved the problem of evil, and that with one assumption—that man's feelings are naturally good. That men have similar feelings observation shows. Therefore men have similar goodness. Hence something unnatural, something foreign to man's real self, has produced badness and inequality among men.

But if all man's desires are naturally good how is he to choose between them? The answer is simple. He has a natural gift of reason which invariably chooses the right desire for gratification. Now all men would reason alike, just as all men feel alike, were it not for the purely external conditions of life. You cannot greatly affect a man's capacity for feeling, but you can affect his capacity for thinking by forbidding him his share in the tools of thought. If the many were educated they would think as the few do. Had not the philosophy of

[1] Merry, *Ode on the Fourteenth of July* (1791).

the enlightenment produced an extraordinary agreement among educated men ? It is thus that rationalism destroyed itself. It is not merely, as is commonly thought, that the rationalist criticism of men like d'Alembert found defects in everything, took away respect from institutions, and thus opened the way for the destructive forces of the Revolution. What is far more important, the geometrical perfection of reason helped to strengthen, and indeed, to form ' Nature's simple plan '. Destructive criticism in itself rarely destroys. M. Anatole France was in his way quite as bitterly critical as d'Alembert ; but it is difficult to believe that the blame for a new French Revolution will ever be imputed to him.

A virtuous and rational man of nature is thus easily set up against the corrupt man of civilized society. But his makers must have felt that he needed something more of the earth in his composition. Hence they strove to find somewhere a state of things corresponding to their deal. There was always, of course, the ' golden age ', a former state of happiness to which men might return. This notion of *saturnia regna* is as old as man's imagination ; but it was never more rife than in the time when it had received a fresh glamour from the writings of Rousseau. It was not, however, sufficiently real ; the natural goodness of man had, if possible, to be placed in a contemporary setting. Ignorance could still happily find that setting in America. Washington became the perfect copy of virtue, an example of the way man developed away from civilization. The fairy tale of the golden age had come true in the United States.

> There social order first began
> And man was reverenc'd as man.
> All were obedient, all were free,
> And God's own law—equality—
> Dispensed its blessings with a lib'ral hand,
> And banished vile oppression from the land.[1]

---

[1] Samson, J., *Oppression, or the Abuse of Power*, a poem (1795), p. 14.

Or again, this perfect state could safely be placed in the
future, as in the following bit of Della Cruscan prose, in
a letter from Merry to Rogers :

' Still am I troubled by the Revolutionary struggle ; the great
object of human happiness is never long removed from my sight.
O that I could sleep for two centuries, like the youth of Ephesus,
and then awake to a new order of things ! But alas ! our existence
must be passed amidst the storm ; the fair season will be for
posterity.' [1]

The natural goodness of man thus strengthened by
projection into the historic past, the New World, and
the future, is next to be brought into actual politics.
It must, of course, work through feeling. For this feeling,
the one effective channel through which men could be
brought back to nature, the word ' philanthropy ' came
into general use. Here was a sentiment that could break
the set forms of artificial society and rescue men from
their evil environment. Thelwall celebrates it warmly :

> That thus, as with all I alternately blend,
> The *mind* may expand and the *heart* may amend ;
> Till, embracing Mankind in one girdle of Love,
> In Nature's kind lesson I daily improve,
> And (no haughty distinctions to fetter my soul)
> As the brother of all, learn to feel for the whole.[2]

But this brotherly love must not be subject to restraint or it
will be turned into selfishness. Payne Knight warns us that

> If abstract reason only rules the mind,
> In sordid selfishness it lives confin'd ;
> Moves in one vortex, separate and alone,
> And feels no other interest than its own.[3]

Love is a mighty force for good, but it is a free force.
Modern marriage laws are too unyielding for it, since

> . . . fix'd by laws and limited by rules,
> Affection stagnates, and love's fervour cools.[4]

[1] Clayden, P. W., *Early Life of Samuel Rogers* (1887), pp. 284–5.
[2] Thelwall, J., *The Peripatetic* (1793), vol. ii, p. 228.
[3] Knight, R. P., *The Progress of Civil Society* (1796), Bk. II, 452–5.
[4] Ibid., Bk. III, 150–1.

The same necessity for freeing the virtuous man from
the rule of law is obvious in religion.

> Religion's lights, when loose and undefin'd,
> Expand the heart, and elevate the mind.
>
> .   .   .   .
>
> But in dogmatic definitions bound,
> They only serve to puzzle and confound.[1]

One more quotation we must have, though forbidden by
the piety that reminds us of our own sins, and of our
nearness to our fathers. Love must be free in all things,
since love, not law

> In softer notes bids Libyan lions roar,
> And warms the whale on Zembla's frozen shore.[2]

This claim of the individual to emancipation from outward restraint by reason of a natural grace inherent in
us all is one of the constant themes of the romantic
movement. It is significant that the mere admission of
benevolence should lead a sober gentleman like Knight
into a radical protest against the marriage laws.

Love, then, must remake the world in its own image.
Benevolence must drive out the restraint that has somehow come to blight all things. These versifiers were
neither historians nor metaphysicians, and troubled not
at all about the origins in nature of this unnatural
restraint, this vicious system of law, society, and civilization. In this they were not unwise, for poets and
reformers, as men who wish to get something done,
should always avoid the problem of the origin of evil.
It was very clear to them that something in society
opposed the rule of love they found it so easy to imagine.
This something could not be natural, for nature is love.
It must therefore be artificial, man-made. But what
more artificial and man-made than kings and nobles,
bankers, priests, and lawyers? Existing governments,
then, are unnatural; that is, they put limitations on

---

[1] Knight, R. P., *The Progress of Civil Society* (1796), Bk. IV, 456–67.
[2] Ibid., Bk. I, 97–8.

the expansion of men who are impelled by a benevolent
nature to expand. Away with them then. Have not
Frenchmen already learned

> That when they have the *will*, the strength's their own,
> That *Right* returns where Union is begun,
> That *Ninety-nine* can ever conquer *One*.[1]

Men of feeling must unite, and then indeed, as Mrs.
Robinson has said in a line which her typographical
sense has made emphatic :

TYRANTS SHALL FALL—TRIUMPHANT MAN BE FREE.[2]

We ought not to expect our poets to explain what
triumphant man is to do when he shall be free at last.
The actual framing of a polity is the hack-work of
political philosophy, a task to be left to the Benthams of
this world. Besides, the Della Cruscans never thought
as far as the composition of the New Society. As
ordinary men with a weakness for verse-making they
versified their own experience, their own desires. If the
result reminds us of *The Anti-Jacobin's*

> Reason, philosophy, fiddledum, diddledum ;
> Peace and fraternity, higgledy piggledy,[3]

does it not indicate that the main ideas of the revolutionary movement, the natural goodness of man, equality,
philanthropy, the evils of institutions, were mingled
somewhat vaguely in the brain of the average English
'Jacobin'? There is nothing remarkable about this.
Clear ideas do not make popular revolutions.

[1] Merry, R., *The Laurel of Liberty* (1790), p. 28.
[2] Robinson, Mary, *Poems* (1791), vol. i, p. 209.
[3] *Poetry of the Anti-Jacobin* (1799), p. 20 ('The Soldier's Friend ').

3

The novel is a better vehicle for a political programme, for communicating something more than mere political enthusiasm, than is poetry ; and prose tempts less to affectation than verse. The propaganda of the Jacobin novelists is more substantial than that of their poetical brethren. It has more body and no less spirit. It is designed, as Godwin innocently puts it in his preface to *Caleb Williams*, to spread political truth ' among persons whom books of science and philosophy are never likely to reach '. And, indeed, most of the novels of the last years of the century are inspired by political and social ' purpose ' ; even a novel of mystery like Mrs. Radcliffe's *Romance of the Forest* is filled with natural virtue, rustic simplicity, and aristocratic depravity.

A complete list of these Jacobin novelists would be intolerably long. But even a partial one must make room for two men who wrote before the French Revolution, and who would certainly have disliked the epithet ' Jacobinical ' had it existed in their time. These are Thomas Day, author of *Sandford and Merton*, and Henry Brooke, author of *The Fool of Quality*. Both books are eloquent in praise of the simple, manly virtues of the workers of the world, and quite as eloquent in denouncing the vices of the drones. The popularity of *Sandford and Merton* as a boy's book in the Victorian Age shows how completely Day had expressed some of the fundamental social ideas of the later epoch. *The Fool of Quality* is an interesting work, which a modern reprinting has not saved from oblivion. It is long and rambling, filled with homilies on all sorts of social questions. We must, however, pass it by with a significant quotation. Love, says Brooke, is ' a giving, not a craving ; an *expansion*, not a *contraction* ; it breaks in pieces the condensing circle of self, and goes forth in the delightfulness of its desire to bless '.[1]

Among the novelists who wrote during the French Revolution we may distinguish Bage, Holcroft, Godwin, Mrs. Smith, and Mrs. Inchbald. Bage is a sort of inferior Fielding who has read Rousseau. Between 1781 and 1796 he produced some half dozen novels which are not without a curious wit of their own, as if the writer's Fielding self were laughing at his Rousseau self. Holcroft, jockey, actor, dramatist, political agitator, could hardly be expected to refrain from writing novels. Godwin, to put the speculations of his *Political Justice* within the understanding of unphilosophic minds, wrote his not quite forgotten novel, *Caleb Williams*. Charlotte Smith wrote numerous novels in order to reform society and support her husband. Finally, Mrs. Inchbald, actress and dramatist as well, produced a gem of purest Rousseauism, her novel *Nature and Art*.

There is happily no need to go into the details of all these novels. An analysis of a few representative ones, however, will help to set forth more tangibly than in their poetry the political ideas of the English Jacobins. An excellent starting-point is afforded by Bage's *Barham Downs*, published in 1784, and especially interesting because it shows how far Bage had gone in Jacobinism before events made possible the coining of the word. The hero is a respectable young merchant of great sensibility who has failed in business through the treachery of friends, and has, at the opening of the story, retired from the base intrigues of city life to the idyllic quiet of Barham Downs. As a foil to his sensibility we have his correspondent and confidant, a shrewd, misanthropic lawyer, who jeers at sentiment. The hero does not remain long in absolute solitude. He meets the lovely daughter of the village squire during a rural stroll. The squire is a narrow Tory, a domestic tyrant, and a snob.

---

[1] Brooke, H., *The Fool of Quality* (ed. E. A. Baker) (1906), p. 261. The italics are mine.

He will have no merchant as a son-in-law. His choice is
Lord Winterbottom, ' a young nobleman ', says Bage,
' whose integrity—has been at court '.[1] Being a nobleman he is vicious and stupid. But the heroine is a lady
of virtue, and the combined sensibilities of the lady and
her lover eventually triumph over the heartless calculations of the father and the perfidy of the noble suitor.
All ends happily. There are occasional topical remarks
on politics, but in general it is only in its social tone that
the novel seems to be preaching a way of life. Throughout there is a strong dislike for the upper classes, a conviction that their vices are incurable ; and there is also
a note of rather vulgar defiance, a glowering self-assertion
that was to melt in the next century into respectability.

' Sir, you know my rank and state in life—— '
' I do, thou art the son of an earl, and, I know not why, they
call thee honourable.' [2]

When Holcroft's *Anna St. Ives* appeared in 1792 the
French Revolution had entered into English politics.
The novel is based on a situation made popular by the
Nouvelle Héloise. Anna St. Ives, a lady of wealth and
family, is loved by a young man of obscure birth and
humble circumstances. Henley is virtuous and intelligent
by reason of his condition. Anna, surmounting the difficulties of her position, appears to us a perfect female,
full of sensibility, yet guiding herself always by the ruling
principles of benevolence and equality. She admires
Frank, but her reason forbids warmer feelings, first, on
account of her duty to her father, but chiefly because
marriage with Frank would be a dangerous example to
females less well-balanced than herself. She knows the
true worth of Frank ; but the danger is that other
young girls would see only the romantic side of the
match, would be encouraged to accept the addresses of
adventurers, and marry beneath themselves morally as

[1] Bage, R., *Barham Downs* (1784), vol. i, p. 9.
[2] Ibid., vol. i, p. 330.

well as socially. She decides to marry and convert Clifton, a young man of fashion who possesses, however, an ' enlarged understanding '. Clifton is an Epicurean, a man of the world, a gentleman who abuses the privileges of his station and provides a living justification for the Revolution. He ultimately decides that it is not worth his while to marry Anna, but that he ought to seduce her to justify his hedonism against her humanitarianism. To accomplish this he is driven to all sorts of criminal attempts, culminating in abduction of Anna and her seclusion in ' a lonely farmhouse near Knightsbridge '. But in the crucial moment the lady's innocence proves in itself alone an unconquerable defence. Hedonism yields to benevolence. Frank and Anna marry ; Clifton is reclaimed and turns social reformer.

The difference between this novel and the *Nouvelle Héloise* is instructive. Julie, virtuous though she be, is always toying with her virtue. There is in the *Nouvelle Héloise* a cloying, sensual quality of emotion, something carnal, and (since it is generally concealed and always disavowed), unhealthy. In Holcroft's novel there is none of this. Anna St. Ives has acquired most of Julie's philosophy, but none of her more human qualities. This difference is by no means a national one. Keats can create quite as well as Rousseau an atmosphere of warm, fragrant sensuousness with just that touch of vicariousness that makes romance. The real difference is that the *Nouvelle Héloise* is a novel and *Anna St. Ives* an ethical and political manifesto. Holcroft's characters are not human beings, but principles ; they live not lives, but formulas. Therefore the book is forgotten, and rightly, by the lover of literature ; but it remains a curious monument to an era when an interest in theoretical politics seems to have penetrated into a certain number of English heads.

Mrs. Inchbald's *Nature and Art* did not appear until 1796 ; but it shows no lessening of faith in the natural goodness of man. The groundwork of the story is formed

by the contrast between two cousins, one brought up
as a pampered only son of rich parents, the other fortunate
enough to have been wrecked on a tropical isle while
yet an infant, and to have been brought up by the
savages. When the story begins this lad has been rescued
and brought back, at the age of fourteen, to his uncle's
house in England. In spite of his youth he is a very
acute social critic, and works havoc in the respectable
family circle. When he asks his uncle why gentlemen
wear wigs he receives the answer :

'As a distinction between us and inferior people, they are worn
to give importance to the wearer.'
'That', replies the boy, 'is just as the savages do. They hang
brass nails, wires, buttons, and the entrails of beasts all over them,
to give them importance.'

From this reply we can possibly understand better
than Mrs. Inchbald why little Henry was not liked by
his family. He grows up misunderstood and virtuous.
His spoiled cousin falls into evil ways and seduces a village
maiden, who is forced to expose her child in a wood.
Henry is blamed as the seducer, for his family refuse to
believe his perfectly true story of how he found the child
in the wood, and took it to the village to save it. The
plot is finally untangled so that every one has his deserts,
except the young woman, who comes to a tragic end
through the harshness of society. Henry decides for a life
of voluntary poverty. Riches are esteemed because they
are a mark of distinction and power, and not because
they provide mere sensual pleasures. When, however,
the poor shall cease to venerate the rich this magic
power of wealth will disappear, and all will be well.
Henry will help to prove to the poor how useless are
riches.[1]

There is no need to go further into the structure of
these novels ; the three we have chosen will stand for
all of them. In general it is true that they aim rather

---

[1] Inchbald, E., *Nature and Art* (1796), p. 404.

to spread a sort of emotional revolutionary contagion than to define a political programme. They are not, however, wanting in specific suggestions. There is, of course, the usual attack on hereditary rank, of which Holcroft furnishes us a delightful example, sketched no doubt from Lord Chesterfield : ' What is a peer of the realm, but a man educated in vice, nurtured in prejudice from his earliest childhood, and daily breathing the same infection as he first respired ? '[1] In this same novel, *Hugh Trevor*, we find a long and unfriendly criticism of Oxford as a stronghold of Toryism and vice, and another on the system of English law, which is compared unfavourably with the justice of a ' Turkish Cady '.[2] Godwin in *Caleb Williams* discourses on the cruelties of the English prison system, and quotes Howard in a foot-note.[3] In the same novel he preaches at length against the barbarous custom of duelling. Bage in *Hermsprong* pays tribute to Mary Wollstonecraft, and urges that faulty education alone has made woman inferior to man.[4] He, as well as Payne Knight, disapproves of modern marriage, and looks forward to a time when ' the commerce of the sexes shall be pure and unmixed, flowing always from the heart, unshackled and unrestrained '.[5] Holcroft is almost a good Socialist :

' Who are the tillers ? Who are the manufacturers ? The poor. Without their labour, the earth itself would be barren. The foundation of the laws of property is that each man is affirmed to be entitled to the produce of his own industry. If all these original laws therefore were executed, with all the rigour with which it is pretended they ought to be observed, the poor and the poor only would be entitled to eat.'[6]

That with which these novelists chiefly concerned

---

1 Holcroft, T., *The Adventures of Hugh Trevor* (1794), vol. i, p. 209 ff.
2 Ibid., vol. ii, p. 109; vol. iv, p. 181.
3 Godwin, W., *Caleb Williams* (1794), Chap. XXIII.
4 Bage, R., *Hermsprong, or Man as he is not* (1796), vol. ii, Chap. IV.
5 Bage, R., *Man as he is* (1792), vol. ii, p. 273.
6 Holcroft, *Letter to Windham* (1795), p. 46.

themselves, however, was the search for some means to
help the people to a richer life. They find that means
in the bosom of the individual. Somehow that mysterious
part of man must be freed for action, and then evil will
cease. ' Men are rendered selfish and corrupt ', writes
Holcroft, ' by the baneful influence of the system under
which they live. . . . They are not in love with baseness,
it is forced upon them.' [1] Man, left to himself, need but
consult this inner prompting, and he will act morally.
Now this inner prompting, whether it be called instinct
or feeling or reason, is certainly not the accumulated
wisdom of human experience as manifested in law or
tradition or a code of ethics. It is quite opposed to all
these, as products of a vicious civilization. It is, in fact,
the beginning of anarchy. Godwin was driven by logic
from his premise of natural reason to conclusions that
have formed the basis for modern European speculation
in anarchy.

Most of our writers stopped long before anarchy, and
contented themselves with an irrational mixture of convention and revolt, of adherence to traditional propriety,
and faith in natural goodness and the inner voice. This
is what Canning called the ' new morality '. It was
really nothing but the expression, as a very individualist
ethics, of the old human desire for expansion, for a better
place in the sun, for a more varied life than old social
conditions permitted. It was as old and as new as
romance.

4

The drama had gone into a decline in the England of
1790 ; but, unlike other forms of literature, it rose no
higher in the following age. Nor has it as much political
interest as poetry and the novel. The *pièce à thèse* was
an invention of the next century. The Jacobin theorists
did not have the advantage of a modern realistic technique

---

[1] Holcroft, *The Adventures of Hugh Trevor*, vol. vi, pp. 102–3.

for the dramatizing of their ideas, nor of a modern audience accustomed to listen to them in patience. Blank verse tragedy was too dignified and too remote for their purposes, so they were forced to make use of a form more suited to social satire than to political propaganda. Yet by making the comedy of manners thoroughly sentimental, they made it a means of spreading abroad some of the most important doctrines of the ' new morality '. Its range is narrow ; but within that range it is emphatic enough.

The old comedy of manners had long been suffering infusions of sentiment, and the process continues with increasing rapidity after the French Revolution, until with the rage for Kotzebue, the manners disappear and only the sentiment remains. The Jacobin drama is like the novel and verse in its scorn for the rich. Holcroft delights in displaying caricatures of the newly enriched, like Goldfinch in the *Road to Ruin*, and in proving the emptiness of aristocratic pretensions by exhibiting the emptiness of the heads of his aristocratic characters. The following dialogue is typical of a hundred attacks on the fashionable world :

Lady Taunton. Oh, ho, you romantic creature ! Ha, ha, ha ! Pure undivided hearts ? Do you think our handsome fellows and fine women trouble themselves about pure, undivided hearts ? Lord ! They know nothing about hearts. They have no hearts.

Olivia. Nor heads neither, perhaps ?

Lady T. Oh, no ! They have no use for them. Thinking and feeling are out of fashion.[1]

Restoration comedy had indeed made fun of the vanities of the world of fashion ; and *The Beggar's Opera* contains some bitter remarks on lords. But the difference between the attitude of comedy to the faults of the upper classes at the beginning and at the end of the century is so great that it helps to measure the change which came over English thought. There is in the later

[1] Holcroft, *Man of Ten Thousand* (1796), Act II, Sc. i.

comedy a constant undercurrent of sentiment totally
lacking in the earlier. You will find no talk of ' pure
undivided hearts ' in *The Way of the World*, no remarks
like ' a feeling fool is better than a cold sceptic '.[1]   The
Jacobin comedy has an animus against the whole upper
class, all of whom seem to it corrupted by their very
position ; the comedy of Congreve and Vanbrugh is
perfectly content with aristocracy, and only makes a butt
of a few individuals belonging to it.   The Jacobins contrast their fops and pompous fools with an imaginary,
but very vivid natural man, uneducated and unspoiled.
Their predecessors had referred them to the standard of
the cultivated man of good sense and good manners.
The restoration dramatists have for country people
a shallow contempt which would not be wholly out of
place in a modern music-hall.   For the Jacobins, the
countryside is sacred, its inhabitants priests of Nature.
But chiefly, the writers of the earlier comedy did not
hate the characters they ridiculed, and certainly did not
wish to rid the world of them.   One even suspects
Vanbrugh of a sort of liking for his Lord Foppington.
At the utmost, if these writers had a moral purpose, it
was limited to the mild correction of the absurdities of
rank and of fashion.   Not so the Jacobins.   They would
sweep their noble fools and villains from the face of the
earth.   They have what their predecessors had not, an
idea of the better world that would result from this
riddance.   They are not criticizing manners ; they are
preaching a crusade.

It is the same crusade to the holy land of Nature
which we have heard preached before.   The natural life
is simple, joyful, peaceful, and physical.   The peasantry
is nearer to Nature than any other class.   Hence, the
Jacobin drama turns to the domestic life of the humbler
classes as the concrete representation of a moral world,
as an illustration of the workings of man's natural goodness.   In this light, it is worth while analysing one of the

----

[1] Kotzebue, *The Stranger* (trans. by B. Thompson, 1801), Act I, Sc. i.

most famous of the hybrid German dramas that overwhelmed the London stage in the last years of the century, Kotzebue's *Das Kind der Liebe*, adapted by Mrs. Inchbald as *Lovers' Vows*.

Agatha, poor, of humble birth and good character, was in youth seduced and abandoned by Baron Wildenheim, who has married in his own class, and has a daughter, Amelia. When the play opens, Agatha, ill and starving, is succoured by her illegitimate son, Frederick, who has never known his father the baron, now a widower. To get money for his mother Frederick has to resort to begging. The baron refuses him alms, and goads him into a desperate assault. He is secured by the baron's servants before any harm is done, and thrust into the manorial dungeon. Meanwhile the baron's virtuous daughter Amelia is wooed at her father's request by the worthless Count Cassel. She, however, loves her tutor, Anhalt, although—or perhaps because—he is only a poor clergyman. She tells him so in a sentimental scene that shocked Jane Austen. Frederick is about to hang for his attack when he providentially discovers that the baron is his father. Tearful, tender explanations follow. The baron, horrified at his narrow escape from hanging his son, is converted to virtue. He dismisses Cassel, marries off his daughter to the humble clergyman, acknowledges Frederick as his heir, and throwing class distinctions to the winds, marries the peasant-woman he had wronged. A touching and motley family reunion ends the play.

The moral of this is clear. Rank is a source of evil. Pride in rank leads us to disown natural acts, and to treat them as if they were unnatural. If the baron had in his youth married the girl he loved in spite of class prejudices, if he had followed his affections and his conscience, instead of his lying reason, the evil in which we see him involved would never have occurred. Society—cultivated society—is always wrong. The individual who has courage to act against it is always right. We shall hear

more of this from the author of *The Giaour* and *The
Corsair*. For the present we can take leave of the
Jacobin dramatists, persuaded that they too demand
liberty and equality in society for the natural man
within all men.

5

It is difficult to estimate the place of these literary
Jacobins in the life of their time. As in a very
similar problem, that of the influence of the French
Revolution in England, one is often tempted to take
the articulate few for the inarticulate many. This
remark, however, is almost as true for Burke as for Tom
Paine. The temptation to declare that good English
common sense completely rejected French ideas, or indeed
all new ideas, and that the English Jacobins were in
a pitiful minority, is equally to be avoided. Clearly, it
is worth while examining into the nature of the public
that gave its support to these writers.

There are many signs that this public took its prophets
seriously, even when they were men of letters. In 1799,
Dumont, the Genevan disciple of Bentham who did so
much to straighten his master's contorted English into
good French, discovered that so innocent a boys' book as
Sandford and Merton could be dangerous, since it gave
' le beau rôle au petit fermier, et le mauvais au petit
gentleman '. ' On conviendra ', he continues, ' qu'il ne
serait pas trop bon entre les mains des petits fermiers.' [1]
Of the novels of Bage we hear little, although a pencilled
note, ' Hermsprong, or man as he is ' in the *Commonplace
Book* of Coleridge affords an interesting comment on the
sort of nourishment Coleridge found for his early political
hopes.[2] Charles James Fox, we are told, read ' all the
novels ' ; [3] and judging by the announcement of Lane,

---

[1] *Memoirs of Samuel Romilly* (1840), vol. ii, p. 70 (Letter from Dumont
to Romilly, 1799).

[2] Coleridge, *Commonplace Book*, B. M. Adds, 27901, f. 84.

[3] Rogers, S., *Recollections* (1859), p. 11.

the publisher, he cannot have lacked moral and political edification. It is hardly necessary to go beyond the titles of some of the seventy volumes in press—*Man as he is, The Carpenter's Daughter, Child of Providence, The Errors of Education, Mentoria.*[1] We live to-day in an age when literature is in many ways didactic ; but no one would now dare to publish novels with titles like these.

Nor were the Della Cruscans as obscure as would seem from the attacks of Gifford. The University of Glasgow thought sufficiently highly of the merits of Robert Merry to bestow an honorary M.A. upon him.[2] Merry must have felt himself an important personage when, at a dinner for fifteen hundred gentlemen at the Crown and Anchor on the 14th July 1791, his *Ode to Liberty* was sung, and the following toast delivered : ' The literary characters who have vindicated the Rights of Man ; and may genius ever be employed in the cause of Freedom.'[3] Merry's poetry appears to have turned the heads of these friends of the French Revolution, for they drank the rash toast, ' Thanks to Mr. Burke for the discussion he has introduced.' Mrs. Robinson, another Della Cruscan, was considered important enough by *The Times* to be insulted.

' Mrs. Robinson composes with such expedition that she is obliged to employ an *amanuensis*. She has now ready for the press an Epic Poem of 1,200 lines, a Romance in four volumes, and a moral essay on the Frailties of Fashionable Life. The motto of this last is " Quorum pars magna fui ".'[4]

That then Jacobinical newspaper, the *Morning Post*, made up for this, however, by indiscriminate praise on several occasions.[5] The redoubtable Mathias, whose forgotten satire, *The Pursuits of Literature*, was once on

---

[1] Lane's notice in the *Morning Chronicle*, 10 January 1793.
[2] *World*, 13 July 1790.
[3] *Public Advertiser*, 16 July 1791.
[4] *The Times*, 16 September 1797.
[5] *Morning Post*, 5 March 1794, 11 January 1798.

every gentleman's table, thought her worth attacking, along with other female novelists.

'Mrs. Charlotte Smith, Mrs. Inchbald, Mrs. Robinson, Mrs. etc., etc., though all of them are ingenious ladies, yet they are too frequently whining or fretting in novels, till our girls' heads turn wild with impossible adventures, *and now and then are tainted with democracy.*' [1]

Holcroft, affording in his own career a perfect illustration of the limitless possibilities of perfection in the very lowest classes, was an especial object of veneration to hopeful enthusiasts. Lovell, one of the Bristol pantisocrats, and a friend of Coleridge and of Southey, thus wrote to him for advice on the pant-isocratic scheme : 'From the minds of William Godwin and yourself, our minds have been illuminated ; we wish our actions to be guided by the same superior abilities.' [2]   Holcroft's action in voluntarily giving himself up to be tried for treason in 1794—nay, in forcing himself on the government officials—was certainly a courageous act, but it was also the act of a man acutely conscious of his position as a political oracle, and anxious to live up to it.   That he employed the drama as a means of spreading his political convictions was clear to his audiences and to the press.   Thomas Green, an obscure diarist of the time, has this note :

'Attended, in the evening, the representation of Holcroft's "Deserted Daughter". H. is here very busy at his purpose ; his aim, to those who are conversant with the tenets of his sect, is sufficiently manifest ; but he manages to conceal it with a discretion not very consistent, surely, with his principles.' [3]

No less a person than Henry Crabb Robinson has testified to the political influence of Holcroft's work. After declaring that a reading of Godwin's *Political Justice* had directed the whole course of his life, he adds : 'I

---

[1] Mathias, T., *Pursuits of Literature* (1794–97), Pt. I, p. 14 *n.*

[2] Hazlitt, W., *Life of Holcroft, Works* (ed. Waller and Glover) (1902–4), vol. ii, p. 279.

[3] Green, T., *Diary of a Lover of Literature* (1810), p. 19.

was in some measure prepared for it by an acquaintance with Holcroft's novels.' [1]

Political Justice itself, of course, made a great stir, and went through three editions in spite of Pitt's remark about its high price. Mathias attacked it at once and did not fail to warn his readers against *Caleb Williams*, ' written in evident allusion to his work on Political Justice'.[2]   It was the intellectual starting-point of two minds as different as those of Malthus and Shelley. Benjamin Constant thought it one of the master works of the age.[3]   It became, as the respectable *Gentleman's Magazine* is forced to admit, ' so popular that the poorest mechanics were known to club subscriptions for its purchase '.[4]   But we have a more sober witness than these in Francis Place, a man who is nowadays accepted as one of the most important collaborators in the practical work of preparing for the Reform Bill of 1832.   He writes to Joseph Hume :

' The *Enquiry concerning Political Justice* should be carefully read by everybody. Some of its speculations are pushed nearly to absurdities, but as the reader is informed that they are only to be considered as speculations, advised to examine them for himself, and recommended to take nothing for granted, even these speculations deserve more indulgence than it has been the fashion to bestow on them. . . . The abuse showered on Mr. Godwin's book was mainly caused by its propagating Utilitarian doctrines—it was disliked by the democrats on account of its mildness, its tameness, it was hated by the aristocrats on account of its violence, and was abhorred by the saints as anti-religious.' [5]

There is no lack of attention to the rest of our Jacobin writers. The pages of the *Gentleman's Magazine* are filled with complaints against the evil principles spread abroad in plays and novels. One contributor writes :

' We will, for a moment, leave mankind to follow their own *feelings*, or, if our readers prefer the term, *instinct*. But we will

[1] Robinson, H. C., *Diary* (1869), vol. i, p. 31.
[2] Mathias, *Pursuits of Literature*, Dialogue III.
[3] Robinson, H. C., *Diary*, vol. i, p. 181.
[4] *Gentleman's Magazine*, June 1836, p. 667.
[5] *Place Papers*, B. M. Adds. 35145, f. 109.

cease to wonder at the consequences of such extravagant departure from all that Reason and Duty, we had almost added Self-Interest, dictates ; or that the followers of Nature are completely unhappy in their choice and their connections.' [1]

Another gives a long list of shocking things to be found in the German theatre, and concludes : ' If there be any other perversion of human reason, or of those venerable ties which have long bound society together, the plays of Kotzebue will afford a thousand instances.' [2] Lord Holland assigns a similar influence to these minor writers, who helped ' to reconcile men's minds to approaching changes, and to shake the received manner of thinking on religion and politics '.[3] Even poor Thelwall, who travelled about the country lecturing on brotherly love and the Revolution in nonconformist chapels, seems not to have been unheard, to judge from this paragraph in *The Times* :

' At Derby Assizes, six persons against whom Bills of Indictment were found at the last Assize for riotously assembling and breaking the windows of the Baptist chapel at that town, at which Mr. THELWALL was lecturing, pleaded Guilty. They were fined *One Shilling* each, and discharged.' [4]

Thelwall's doctrines had certainly not corrupted the magistracy.

Every one who ventured to oppose Pitt's Government was immediately labelled Jacobin ; and literature was often blamed as the effective bond between Jacobins. Some bad newspaper verse will show how the Conservatives saw a non-existent unity among their opponents.

> Careless of late, I danced the ways
> Of *Godwin's* metaphysic maze,
>   And laughed at ties of honour ;
> From *Paine* I learn'd my rights to know,
> And plighted faith with *Fox and Co.*,
>   *Fitzgerald* and *O'Connor*.[5]

[1] *Gentleman's Magazine*, June 1798, p. 502.
[2] Ibid., May 1800, pp. 406–7.
[3] Holland, *Further Memoirs of the Whig Party* (1905), p. 380.
[4] *The Times*, 15 August 1797.   [5] Ibid., 8 November 1798.

It is easy for us, who know how divided the opposition to Pitt was, to smile at this joining of Fox, Paine, and Godwin. But it is also easy for us to fall into the error of underestimating the latent opposition to Pitt because the effective opposition is now seen to have been so slight. The vogue of the more respectable advocates of new ideas in literature certainly seems to indicate the existence of a class willing to tolerate Pitt in a crisis, but already almost ripe for Reform Bill agitation. Although many of the most influential of these people turned against the French Revolution in 1793–4 they did not turn to conventional Toryism. They kept their faith in expansion. They forswore Tom Paine, but they flocked to see plebeian virtue triumph in *Lovers' Vows*, and they devoured the novels of Mrs. Radcliffe and Monk Lewis. They continued all through the French scare to dislike lords and to admire their own domestic virtues, to long for a pleasanter life and a more important position in society. The sort of Jacobinism reflected in many of the novels, plays, and poems we have considered—much milder and more respectable than the Jacobinism of Tom Paine—is an indication of the existence of such a feeling, and must have had a share in maintaining it.

6

It has been possible to find in the long-forgotten writers of verse and prose in the last decade of the eighteenth century a forecast of a new order of society. No inconsiderable amount of the literature of the time, as we have seen, is filled with expressions of contempt for the old unprogressive, aristocratic society. The source of this discontent lies deep in the human heart —in that energy which drives us all to try to expand our own activity, to get more goods, more power, more consideration from our fellows, to live, in short, a richer life. This energy exists in a measure in all men. It is essentially a craving, an instinct which seeks uncriticized self-satisfaction. He would be a bold psychologist who should deny its existence. The external world provides a certain limitation to this expansive energy of the individual: and organized society is one of the facts of the external world. But society is after all a human thing, and does not seem to be of the same fixed, necessary character as other things in the external world. Men feel that they have voluntarily surrendered something to society, for which they ought to receive a return. This is the psychological truth that lies behind the social contract theory. Society, through its organ, government, can command the continued allegiance of its members only if they feel that society pays them back for the restraints it puts on their desire for expansion in one way by permitting them to expand in another. For men's desires, baulked of a direct and tangible realization, have a way of realizing themselves vicariously in an imaginative world of their own creation. This is the world of faith, where, by some mysterious magic of the human soul, desire feeds upon desire, and is requited. If men accept subordination in society, it must be because they are themselves dignified by the achievements of that society, and because they can throw over the limitations of their lot the veil of a mystic attachment to something greater than themselves, yet of which they are an integral part. No society can endure without this mystic faith. In a political society we commonly call it loyalty. It is essentially not rational, not a calculation of interest, but a feeling which finds in itself its own justification.

Now in the England of the eighteenth century there were fewer of these loyalties to act as restraints on individual expansion. The Civil Wars had lessened respect for authority in general, and the English had that reputation for political instability and unruliness later attributed to the French—so much so that Mackintosh writes with surprise of the taking of the Bastille that ' Paris exhibited the tumult and clamour of a London mob '. Religion, which in the Middle Ages had been a means of social restraint and an object of emotional attachment, had been greatly weakened by repeated schisms and by an apathetic deism. Methodism did indeed develop as a protest against religious apathy ; but Methodism is a part of the Revolution. Patriotism was doubtless a genuine emotion among a people who had been at war so often as the English in this century ; but it was not yet the all-absorbing passion that was to rule the next age. Jane Austen is surely an Augustan ; and her novels show no signs of the fever of the Napoleonic wars.

In these circumstances, then, there were fewer checks on the natural expansive desires of men. All that was needed was a social belief in which these desires, in themselves anarchic and incoherent, could be centred. The natural goodness of man was this belief. In it all discontent, however eccentric and even unsocial, could find a rallying point. It was vague enough to correspond to every one's dream ; yet real enough to make a positive contrast to actual conditions. Here was embodied the best life philosophy could devise, the life in perfect accord with the workings of the human mind. But this philosophic scheme was seen through an emotion that transformed it from an object of cognizance to an object of affection. It left the philosopher's closet to bestow itself on the common man. The literary Jacobins undoubtedly thought of themselves as important agents in the bestowal. But that is a minor point ; we must ask ourselves what the common man made of the gift.

II

THE FIRST GENERATION OF REVOLT

WORDSWORTH, Coleridge, and Southey in their later years, used to protest against the effacement of their strongly marked personalities in the common epithet of ' Lakist '. Modern criticism, ever distrustful of group labels, has accepted them at their own valuation, and it is now generally agreed that the term ' Lake School ' was an unfortunate misnomer. Yet these poets had much in common—far more than they, in their pride of poetic creation, were willing to admit. All three wrote poetry inspired with the deep conviction that there is for men a life higher than that of calculating, meddling reason. Wordsworth lost in pantheism above Tintern Abbey, Coleridge living more in Xanadu than in Somerset, Southey writing strange epics about strange lands, are certain that the creations of their imagination are all the more real because they appear fantastic to Right Reason. All three in their youth held religious opinions that had at least unorthodoxy in common; and in their maturer years, all three became firm adherents of the Church of England. When they first began to write they were all Jacobins of one shade or another; and by the time they had entered old age they had become unmistakable Tories. This is an agreement far too complete, and on facts far too important, to be a coincidence. The truth is that Wordsworth, Southey, and Coleridge, along separate but never widely divergent courses, were making for the same port. Their political thought, which bears no small proportion to the rest of their work, illustrates the unity that makes them after all a ' school '.

I

Wordsworth relates in *The Prelude* how he was led to a tardy interest in the affairs of mankind by the gentle teachings of Nature. From such a teacher in the last years of the eighteenth century he could learn but one lesson. He became almost too apt a pupil, for he conceived, and very nearly put into execution, the plan of securing a seat in the French Convention as a follower of Brissot. Biographers have now made us familiar with the facts of his early political career, his long residence in France, his connexion with the patriot Beaupuy and his stay in London as a disciple of Godwin. They have further analysed with much patience the long process of his conversion to more orthodox politics. Very soon, we are told, he began to suspect that the Nature which had taught him wisdom on the Cumberland hills was not the guiding spirit of the French Revolution, and certainly had not assisted in the composition of *Political Justice*. He began to suspect that love of country was natural and instinctive, that it was a part of the mysterious power that was in hills and trees, in rocks and in himself. In this temper he retired to the West Country, to Coleridge and the *Lyrical Ballads*, and began a revision of his politics in the mood of the sonnets dedicated to political liberty. With the more delicate psychological aspects of this change we need not concern ourselves. We can turn—indeed must turn if we honestly put ideas before men—to what the young revolutionary wrote and said.

Wordsworth was a sensuous young man, who wrote of his mistress that she

> Impressed upon all forms the characters
> Of danger or desire; and thus did make
> The surface of the universal earth
> With triumph and delight, with hope and fear
> Work like a sea.[1]

[1] *Poems of William Wordsworth*, ed. N. C. Smith (1908) (hereafter *Poems*), *Prelude*, Book I, 471–5.

Thus Nature to the young man. Rocks and fells and mountain mists were a stimulus to his senses; they set in motion a whole train of pleasant emotions, of thoughts 'steeped in feeling', of mystic approaches to 'bliss ineffable'. This life of the emotions is in itself a selfish life. Wordsworth grew up a lonely and unsociable boy,

> taught to feel, perhaps too much,
> The self-sufficing power of solitude.[1]

Although he later rose to a juster conception of the fullness of human life, he never quite grew out of this early disposition. His whole career is an illustration of the anarchic basis of the return to Nature.

When this self-centred and unworldly youth was compelled to enter into the civilization of Cambridge, Paris, and London, he was, of course, driven into active revolt. Had he been less unworldly he might have been willing to turn his unsocial passions to the acquisition of material wealth; had he been less self-centred he might have been content with civilization. As it was, college and drawing-room seemed to conspire to suppress that mysterious expansiveness within him that made life worth living. It was not so in Cumberland. There he had seen the simple shepherd at his task, gathering some of the glory of his surroundings to himself

> As of a lord and master, or a power
> Or genius, under Nature, under God,
> Presiding.[2]

There men did not gather to make life miserable for one another, as they do in cities. The peasants of Cumberland and Westmorland were members of a simple and almost democratic society, with no extremes of wealth and poverty, with few resident nobles, with strong traditions of independence and self-respect. Wordsworth hardly knew these people, but what he thought about

---

[1] *Poems*: see previous page, note 1, *Prelude*, Book II, 76–7.
[2] Ibid., Bk. VIII, 258–60.

them went into the making of his political ideal. Was
it not to be expected

> That one tutored thus should look with awe
> Upon the faculties of man, receive
> Gladly the highest promises, and hail
> As best, the government of equal rights
> And individual worth ? [1]

Thus, as Wordsworth wrote, love of Nature led to love
of man. His early education gave him a glimpse of
a world where feeling could flow on without interrup-
tion. When he sought to carry this world with him into
the confusion of urban life, he found he must share it
with other men. He found, indeed, that he must impose
it on other men. He very naturally became a revolutionary. Various Jacobinical programmes, a whole series
of measures and theories, lay at hand for his use ; and
use them he did. But the fundamental belief in his
social creed he had arrived at himself ; and he holds it
with a far greater fervour than could those townsmen to
whom it was but a growth of fashion. He believes in
the natural goodness of man, in

> his noble nature, as it is
> The gift which God has placed within his power,
> His blind desires and steady faculties
> Capable of clear truth, the one to break
> Bondage, the other to build liberty
> On firm foundations. [2]

These firm foundations of the new liberty Wordsworth
has outlined in his *Letter to the Bishop of Llandaff*. In
this pamphlet, which was not published until the poet's
prose writings were collected in 1876, he boldly launches
into abstract political theory. A government is the
creature of the General Will of a society. It is at best
a necessary evil, caused by the existence of a few re-
fractory individual wills in that society. The problem
is to assure that the acts of the government correspond as

---

[1] Ibid., Bk. IX, 238-42.   [2] Ibid., 355-60.

exactly as possible to the General Will. This implies universal suffrage. But a representative assembly, once elected, may act contrary to the General Will. The electorate—that is the General Will—must assert its authority by holding regular elections at frequent intervals, and by applying the principle of rotation in office to its representatives. The people are by nature capable of this high office. If the masses are now ignorant, if they burn Priestley's house, it is because they are debauched by the unlawful holders of power, by the *particular* wills of royalty and aristocracy. Power is too great a temptation to be trusted to one man or to one set of men. A democratic republican government must be the goal. But Wordsworth would proceed slowly towards the republic, and by way of parliamentary reform.[1]

It is evident that Wordsworth is indebted to the Rousseau of the *Contrat Social* for the material and even the vocabulary of this pamphlet. The notion of the General Will dominates all. But it must not be forgotten that the *Contrat Social*, although designed to realize the world of the *Nouvelle Héloise*, is not in itself a revolutionary conception. Taken at its lowest terms, it is a political truism. The General Will of a society is more than a sum of all the particular wills that make it up : it is a whole greater than the sum of its parts. It has an independent collective being of its own. The particular will (that is the will of any individual) merges itself in the general will, yet gains added force and independence from this act of submission. This is so because the submission is essentially an emotional one, an act of faith in a mystical relation that ties the believer to a more than human ally. In this sense any living corporate body may be said to have a general will. It is simply the concrete, living, emotional reality of what to the intellect is an abstraction, a class concept. It is that which makes a collection of individuals a society.

[1] *Prose Works of William Wordsworth*, ed. Grosart (1876) (hereafter *Prose Works*), *Letter to the Bishop of Llandaff*, vol. i, pp. 3–23.

Wordsworth, like Rousseau, is in the end a very social anarchist : that, indeed, is the usual plight of the conscientious anarchist. The good life is to Wordsworth an indefinite expansion of self as in a void. But the world is not a void. He must come into contact, not only with an impersonal external world, but with other personal units like himself. The shock of the collision with other persons is diminished and made bearable, however, if he encounters them, not as roving, independent spirits, but as members of a society. He encounters not other men, but other citizens. The essential freedom to expand is not curtailed by any mere personal unit, or number of personal units, like himself, for such a curtailment would be only too comprehensible, and therefore unbearable : it is curtailed by an impersonal, incomprehensible force, by society. Man is still free, if he does not understand why he is enslaved.

Thus, if we submit ourselves to the restraints imposed by a society to which we are in that mystic relation known as faith, or loyalty, we remain essentially free. But the trouble is that societies do not always give enough scope to the irrational and anarchic individual energies which have been imprisoned within this mystic loyalty. For societies are forced to carry on their affairs by means of governments and laws which are only too evidently human and therefore open to criticism. Contented people commonly identify a society with its government. Discontented people can hardly hope to alter the deep-seated emotions that bind men in society ; indeed, such discontented people are almost always convinced that they share the emotions that are really universal among men in society. They therefore turn against the existing government, and make a new pattern of government for themselves—in theory, if they are fortunate ; otherwise, in practice. But society and government are in no merely formal relation ; they are as closely bound as heart and head, body and soul. To Wordsworth the revolutionary, the French republic and the system of

Godwin came to stand for that pattern of government that even the anarchist must set up for himself. Society continued to mean something which had a general will and to which he might surrender himself, receiving emotional satisfaction in return for loyalty. But his pattern of government began to fail him. The French republic was as bellicose and as unjust as the old monarchy had been. As for Godwin, that philosopher would rather rescue Fénelon from a burning house than his own brother, because Fénelon was more worth saving. That was not the sort of thing a Cumberland peasant would do. Wordsworth became aware of the fact that this pattern of government would no more fit the society to which he was instinctively loyal than the old English government had fitted it. For the moment he gave up in despair all his high hopes of politics.

But he could not abandon so pleasant a thing as hope for long. It is scarcely necessary here to trace the course of what he came later to consider his moral convalescence from this dangerous fever of Godwinism. It is not desirable—indeed it is not possible—to mark when old beliefs in direct election, in short parliaments, rotation in office, abolition of hereditary titles, necessity, and all the apparatus of his former philosophy were definitely given up. Suffice it to note that he had never really abandoned that essential part of his whole being, a belief in the natural goodness of man ; and that at Racedown and Alfoxden, and in his own Lake Country, he was forging a new anchor for that belief, a new means of fixing it in the material world outside himself. The result of these labours was the greatest of his political writings, the political sonnets and the *Tract on the Convention of Cintra.* Hence, although ' periods ' in a man's life are even more artificial and unsatisfactory as ultimate truths than periods in history, we are forced to give the next fifteen years of Wordsworth's political activity some such title as the ' patriotic period '.

A purely speculative system of politics, without fleshly

bonds of feeling, could no longer satisfy Wordsworth's longing to identify himself with a living society ; nor could he longer put his trust in tyrant-ruled France. Indeed, he already sees in consular France the incarnation of the calculating, logical, prosaic spirit that is the negation of Nature. France is to be despised and hated, not merely because she is the enemy of England, but because, through the whole course of her history, she has stood for a polished, artificial, aristocratic, vain, superficial, and unnatural culture.

> Perpetual emptiness ! unceasing change !
> No single volume paramount, no code,
> No master spirit, no determined road ;
> But equally a want of books and men.[1]

It is uncertain, from the context of the poem, whether Wordsworth meant this to be a *résumé* of the history of France or merely a description of her state in 1802. Nor does it greatly matter, for in any case it is absurdly untrue. What does matter is the instinctive aversion from the French mind, which Wordsworth now felt had always been dominated by qualities quite antithetical to those which beneficent Nature had implanted in his own mind. England, on the other hand, was a home worthy of him, as it had been worthy of Shakespeare and Milton. England came more and more to embody, in her past achievements and in her present possibilities, that spiritual and natural life which was to him the good life. Wordsworth thus evolved love of country, if not precisely from love of self at least from a conscious self-examination. Patriotism did not come to him, as it does to most men, so much a part of education and social experience as to seem quite external and involuntary ; it was the fruit of long introspection.

This does not, of course, imply that Wordsworth's patriotism was artificial or *voulu* ; it sprang from feelings that were all the deeper, because rooted in his abnormally

---

[1] *Poems*, vol. ii, p. 46.

introspective youth. His sonnets catch and bring to
a focus all the scattered emotions of patriotism. Like
the *Marseillaise* or a poem of Körner's, they are symbols
into which history and association have packed so much
that men will fight under them as under a banner. No
doubt this is the highest sort of political poetry. But
like all great lyric poetry it is simple, and centred on
a single emotional moment. Wordsworth's sonnets dedicated to liberty are supreme expressions of the passion
and faith of patriotism. But for this very reason they
are less suitable subjects for a study of the assumptions,
the principles, the desires that go into the making of his
mature political philosophy. For this we must look into
the *Tract on the Convention of Cintra.*

The immediate burden of Wordsworth's argument in
this tract is simply that Napoleon can be beaten only by
arousing the dormant national spirit of the subject
nations of his empire. The convention signed by
Dalrymple and Wellesley, by which Junot and his army
were allowed to go scot free from Portugal with all
their booty, was the act of unimaginative soldiers, who
failed to see how heavy a blow they had given to the
inspired popular movement in the peninsula. Wordsworth is concerned, however, with things far deeper than
this Convention of Cintra. There is throughout the
tract a steady attempt to define the moral basis of
nationalism, to show that nationality has a mystical
justification that makes it the true outward mark of the
general will of a society, and that renders the nation-
state the ultimate political result of the return to Nature.

Patriotism springs from the common homely feelings
that fill the hearts of all men. From this lowly ground
of ' the sentient, the animal, the vital ' Wordsworth
finds that our higher principles of benevolence soar into
being.

  ' The outermost and all-embracing circle of benevolence has
inward concentric circles which, like those of the spider's web,
are bound together by links, and rest upon each other ; making

one frame, and capable of one tremor ; circles narrower and narrower, closer and closer, as they lie more near to the centre of self from which they proceeded, and which sustains the whole.' [1]

The central problem of politics is to give man play for this sentient part of his being ; to provide *social* life for intensely *personal* instincts. Wordsworth puts it clearly :

' The vigour of the human soul is from without and from futurity—in breaking down the limit and losing and forgetting herself in the sensation and image of country and of the human race ; and when she returns and is most restricted and confined, her dignity consists in the contemplation of a better and more exalted being, which, though proceeding from herself, she loves and is devoted to as to another.' [2]

The nation is such an exalted being, made of common men but somehow better than its makers. Unlike the service of reason and humanity in the narrow and false sense of Godwin and his followers the service of the nation demands no break with natural, homely affections. Indeed, as the events in the peninsula show, it draws upon these affections, and breathes into them the very spirit of humanity. The Spanish patriot not only has a country to love ; he has a country to save from foreign tyranny. He has a common cause for action with millions of his fellow-men. Well may he feel that ' the whole courage of his Country is in his breast ',[3] for his breast is no longer his own, but his country's. He is no passive worshipper but a crusader. He lives in no ordinary time, for ' these are times of strong appeal—of deep-searching visitation ; when the best abstractions of the prudential understanding give way, and are included and absorbed in a supreme comprehensiveness of intellect and passion ; which is the perfection and the very being of humanity '.[4]

That which is to-day the strength of Spain is potentially the strength of all nations. Patriotism, though

[1] *Prose Works*, vol. i, p. 171.   [2] Ibid., p. 116.
[3] Ibid., p. 156.   [4] Ibid., p. 116.

like all emotions it is at its best and purest in these high moments of stress, can also exist in times of peace—nay, must exist if the state is to have a healthy life. Nationality, then, must coincide with the state, and form the basis of political organization. Germany and Italy, for Europe's good as well as their own, should unite their scattered fragments into a true state. The nation, an organic union of independent beings, a true expression of the general will, a natural projection outward from the individual, is the highest political entity. Its guide in its dealing with other nations is no other than the code which regulates the dealings of men, honour, understood in its highest ethical sense. It is national honour that drives England to oppose the aggressions of France, national honour that drives Spain and Portugal to resist the attack on their independence. If the standard of honour among all nations can be raised high enough— and it can be raised if sufficient scope is given to the purest and best feelings from which patriotism springs— nations can live in amity and peace. It is through the operations of ethical principles on the national conscience, and the consequent control exercised by national opinion over governmental action, that satisfactory international relations will be brought about.[1]

Thus, in 1809 Wordsworth had sketched as completely as Mazzini ever did a theory of nationalism that was to become the political faith of the century. The lineage of this theory is no less interesting than its content ; for it is quite clear that in this nineteenth-century nationalism the doctrine of the natural goodness of man has at last found a settled lodging. That Wordsworth still held to what he considered the essentially good part of his Jacobin faith is clear from his reference to the Napoleonic system as ' a child of noble parents—Liberty and Philanthropic Love '. ' Perverted as the creature is ', he continues, ' from no inferior stock could it have issued. It is the Fallen Spirit, triumphant in misdeeds, which

[1] *Prose Works*, vol. i, p. 78.

was formerly a blessed Angel.'[1] Now if the Revolution
in ideas meant the natural goodness of man, the Revolution in fact meant the supremacy of an ill-educated
middle class. Great numbers of men, hitherto not
directly sharing in political action, were made conscious
of the fact that they were by way of acquiring political
power. They had to find some embodiment of this new
power. There lay at hand the crude and obvious fact
of national differences, so much more evident than real.
In the consciousness of the new man nationality played
a far greater part than it had in the culturally richer
consciousness of the old aristocrat. It is not surprising
that, when the revolutionary movement had at last
triumphed over the old aristocratic society, it should
build up a society of its own on a principle within the
intelligence of its members. Thus came into being the
democratic nationalism of the nineteenth century, so
different from the aristocratic and dynastic nationalism
of the previous century ; as different, indeed, as Waterloo
and Fontenoy.

Wordsworth, in common with many a less articulate
contemporary, had evolved from his original desire for
self-expansion this faith in a nation-state mystically produced by the union of popular virtues. He is in this at
one with his fellows. But we are constantly reminded
that he was a political renegade, a ' lost leader ', and
that he became a carping and usual Tory. We are not
writing his biography, and need not defend him against
all implication of having changed sides in politics. But
we must at least try to discover in the politics of his
declining years some trace of his youthful hopes, or
abandon him to the harsh judgement of radical opponents
like Hazlitt and Byron.

Assuming then that Wordsworth remains true to his
ideal of a society where man's purest and most natural
instincts find at once free play and control, it remains
to consider whether he honestly and intelligently sought

[1] Ibid., p. 128.

out specific political measures to realize that ideal.
What was the real England of government and law that
Wordsworth tried to put beside this England of his
devotions ?

Popular education, the corner-stone of modern democratic practice, still seemed desirable to the author of
The Excursion :

> O for the coming of that glorious time
> When, prizing knowledge as her noblest wealth
> And best protection, this imperial Realm,
> While she exacts allegiance, shall admit
> An obligation on her part to *teach*
> Them who are born to serve her and obey.[1]

But by the time of the Reform Bill he has come to
doubt the value of popular education. ' Mechanics
Institutes ', he complains, ' make discontented spirits
and insubordinate and presumptuous workmen.' [2]   He
has expressed what is surely the most conservative of
attitudes toward life : ' Can it, in a *general* view, be
good that an infant should learn much which its *parents
do not know* ? ' [3]   Let us hope that future historians of
the nineteenth century will read their Wordsworth
before they declare a faith in progress to have been
the universal characteristic of the age.

In parliamentary politics Wordsworth opposed Catholic
Emancipation, the Reform Bill, the ballot, and in general
all innovations.   He wrote poems against these, and
a sonnet sequence against any remission of capital
punishment.   Too many people have laughed or mourned
over these and other poems of his old age.   The only
justice to Wordsworth is to note their existence and
their intention, but to forbear quoting them.   The trend
of English politics, he thinks, is inevitably towards the
rule of an ignorant and lawless proletariat ;   he foresees
the end of English greatness, and wishes himself safe ' in

[1] *Poems : Excursion*, Bk. IX, 293–8.
[2] *Prose Works*, vol. i, p. 347.
[3] Ibid., p. 345.

the quietest nook I can find in the centre of Austria '.
After the Reform Bill he writes :

' The predominance given in Parliament to the dissenting
interest, and to towns which have grown up recently, without
a possibility of their being trained in habits of attachment either
to the Constitution in Church and State, or what remained of
the feudal frame of society in this country, will inevitably bring
on a political and social revolution.' [1]

Indeed, he is convinced that this revolution is already
half achieved. He always retained his faith in the simple
goodness of those Cumberland ' statesmen ' of whom he
wrote so much and knew so little ; [2] and after 1832 he
told the young Gladstone that he wished to enfranchise
the rural labourer to balance the corrupt townsmen
granted the vote by Lord Grey's Bill.[3] These townsmen
seemed to him unfit for civilized life. The fault, it is
true, he admitted to be with the men whose greed had
built the towns, and whose materialism had filtered
down through all ranks of society. Against these men
and their work, the industrial revolution, Wordsworth
declared war to the utmost. Except in moments of
petulance he never refers to the victims of industrial
tyranny but with deepest sympathy ; and he wished to
relieve the manufacturing poor by extending the Poor
Laws, by permitting free combination of workmen, and
by government regulation and inspection of industrial
undertakings.[4] This is the explanation of his often
quoted remark that he was never a Whig, but always
something of a Chartist—a remark strangely at variance
with his fulminations against the ballot.

Freedom for self-expansion had not resulted for the
business man and the manufacturer in the peaceful and
orderly life that seemed to Wordsworth natural and

---

[1] *Letters of the Wordsworth Family*, ed. Knight (1907), vol. ii, p. 495.
[2] *Reminiscences of Wordsworth among the peasantry of Westmorland*, in
Transactions of the Wordsworth Society, No. 6 (1884).
[3] Morley's *Life of Gladstone* (1905), Bk. II, Chap. III.
[4] *Prose Works*, vol. i, pp. 273–94.

desirable. Nor had patriotism since the end of the
Napoleonic war brought to unruly passionate men the
quiet agreement of those who share an equal and restraining faith. The energies of the nation were directed to
an unbounded material expansion. The official philosophy of this expansion was precisely that man's desires
are good, and impel him to act in the way most necessary
to social good. Every man knows his own interest to be
the acquisition of as much wealth as possible by his
labour ; therefore if every man were free to follow his
own interest, everybody would have as much wealth and
happiness as possible. The natural goodness of man
translates itself into the doctrine of economic freedom.
Utilitarianism, like an apparition from the Age of Reason,
came to demand absolute freedom for individual initiative.
Wordsworth began to believe that some purely external
restraint must be placed on men, even though that
restraint be not the product of a mystic loyalty willed
by themselves. He had begun to doubt the natural
goodness of man ; which, indeed, as a good anglican, he
could hardly find consistent with original sin. 'Good
men turn instinctively from inferences unfavourable to
human nature ', he writes, with a lingering fondness for
his old way of thought, ' but there are facts not to be
resisted, where the understanding is sound.' [1]

Since this is so we must encourage whatever experience
has shown to be useful in controlling men. And now
Wordsworth goes back to the eighteenth century, takes
up the stiff frame of that old society, and tries to impose
it on the new. In poetry he harks back instinctively to
the diction he once thought worthy of demolition in his
prefaces. Milton is no doubt in these lines, but so is
the eighteenth century :

> ' Where Mortals call thee ENTERPRISE,
>   Daughter of Hope ! her favourite Child
>   Whom she to Young Ambition bore—— ' [2]

---

[1] *Prose Works : Address to the Freeholders of Westmorland*, vol. i,
p. 254.   [2] *Poems*, vol. i, p. 364 (*To Enterprise*).

' Forth rushed from Envy sprung and Self-Conceit,
  A power misnamed the SPIRIT OF REFORM.' [1]

' Tempt the vague will tried standards to disown.' [2]

This last line, detached though it be, has surely the mark of the didactic heroic couplet upon it. Wordsworth uses it in a sonnet. So in politics he returns to the prescriptive rights of the landed aristocracy with the firm conviction that such rights are the necessary social consequence of men's passions. Through property alone, he writes, ' can be had exemptions from temptation to low habits of mind, leisure for solid education, and dislike to innovation, from a sense in the several classes how much they have to lose ; for circumstances often make men wiser, or at least more discreet, when their individual levity or presumption would dispose them to be much otherwise '.[3]

Wordsworth's political thought has then to the very end this tenuous thread of unity ; he seeks to make ' the sentient, the animal, the vital ' in human life the guide to a social and political state where these most natural elements can find the satisfaction they demand. In youth he sees this state in the democratic republic suggested by French experience. But the French seemed to reject all authority and to throw the individual back on himself to find a standard of conduct, without affording him external aid in forming it. Wordsworth could foresee the mad course of materialistic expansion which was to result in England from the emancipation of the individual and the stimulus given to the acquisitive instincts. He had to grope about for a means of disciplining the energies of natural man. In middle age, he searched, and rightly, for a discipline that would have its source in those energies themselves. The way to this discipline was pointed to him by his early conception of

[1] Ibid., vol. iii, p. 443 (*Sonnet on the Ballot*).
[2] Ibid., vol. ii, p. 392 (*Sonnet on Capital Punishment*).
[3] *Letters of the Wordsworth Family*, vol. iii, p. 411.

the General Will. Man's desires are for ever attaching themselves to an abstraction, and becoming faiths. There is a sound mysticism by which we pool our desires with the desires of our fellows, and draw satisfaction from the common stock. If we are loyal to something inside ourselves, then we willingly submit to restraint outside ourselves ; and the problem of government is to reconcile external restraint and the inner man. Wordsworth had then to find some common thing, some abstraction, for which men could feel a mystical attachment, and from which they could obtain at once satisfaction and discipline of their desires. He saw that the idea of nationality provided this meeting-place for men's minds ; and that the modern nation, which imposes a vague but real similarity of thought and habit upon its members, and conceives itself to be a product of the general will, might afford the social restraint upon the individual which had been lost in the decay of the old régime.

Unfortunately, Wordsworth stopped here, and never sought to elaborate by patient intellectual effort a political system in consonance with this conception of nationality. He was too easily discouraged by the failure of the England of George IV to measure up to his standard of a patriot state. Therefore the world is right in its common judgement that Wordsworth in his old age was a reactionary. His mind was in the past. He saw only too clearly the need of authority in his age ; but he erred in choosing the obvious, ready-made system of authority which lay at hand in the eighteenth-century tradition of government. He did not see that the very completeness and fixity of this aristocratic system was in itself a weakness, that it was an authority which had outlived the loyalty that produced it. He shirked the real problem, which was and is, how to bring reason and social experience to bear on the creation of democratic forms which will encourage loyalty and enforce discipline ; and tried to solve the problem by neglecting its conditions.

Perhaps there was always something wrong with his methods; and certainly his ideal of a life of rural ignorance and simplicity could have no permanent hold on human beings whom Aristotle once defined as animals dwelling in city-states. There are times when Wordsworth seems curiously inhuman. Long after his Nature worship had softened from the absurdities of the ' impulse from the vernal wood ', he was discoursing in a London company on the necessity of defending the Anglican Church and its sacred mission. He would, he said, gladly give his life in its defence. Some one asked him a question about his parish church in Westmorland. He was forced to admit that he had not been inside it for years ! [1] Religion, politics, ethics—everything was within his own soul and Nature's ; his opinions are the opinions of a recluse never quite at home in society. He himself wrote

> a Traveller I am
> Whose tale is only of himself.[2]

2

It is most unfortunate that we are not able to separate the ideas of Samuel Taylor Coleridge from the intricacies of his personality. For much is gained in the way of simplicity—and Truth is surely simpler than psychologists will have it—if a man's ideas be granted a degree of objectivity, a certain independence of the petty twistings and turnings of his inner self. With Wordsworth, for instance, many biographical details, such as the recently unearthed *amour* in France, can be neglected by the student of ideas ; for Wordsworth's philosophy, individualist and introspective though it be, is bound definitely to the concrete outer world, to the simple Nature of the eighteenth century, not as yet fallen victim to Science. It is quite otherwise with Coleridge. It is not merely

[1] *Diary of H. C. Robinson* (ed. Sadler), vol. i, p. 389.
[2] *Poems : Prelude*, Bk. III, lines 195-6.

that, as his correspondence shows, he had an obliging way of adapting himself to the views of the person with whom he was dealing, so that it is difficult to decide what are his own opinions. The difficulty goes deeper, and lies in the extraordinary detachment of his views. Matthew Arnold held this detachment to be the first approximation in England to the critical method. But it is difficult not to feel that Coleridge's detachment is often mere irresponsibility. Like all the romantics, he searched in himself for wisdom ; but since he possessed, unlike most of them, a subtle, reasoning intellect, he found, not a few simple desires, but a whole world of jarring impulses, of dreams, sensation, and thought. Above all, he found in himself a desire to understand. Coleridge ought to have been a Schoolman. He had, however, the misfortune to be born in an age when old forms of thought were losing credit everywhere, and he was forced to construct new ones for himself. The story of his opium-broken life is now too well known to all. In view of the quality of his experience, it is surprising not that so much of his speculation should be wayward and inconsistent and speciously detached from life, but that so much of it should be sound and genuinely critical.

Coleridge wrote a great deal ; and a large part of what he wrote is directly or indirectly concerned with politics. Profoundly influenced by the Germans though he was, he is not often convincingly metaphysical. He is never very far from the ethical problem ; and, in common with the great tradition of English thought, he refuses to consider politics save as a branch of ethics. Most of his political thought is to be found in his prose, which for very good reasons is little read, and not in his poetry, which is read a great deal. Much of the less known poetry of his earlier Della Cruscan period is on subjects political, such as the inescapable topic of the Fall of the Bastille. Some of the poetry of his maturity, like that *France : an Ode* which Shelley admired, is concerned with politics. But when he felt the poetic impulse

weaken and the didactic impulse grow stronger, he gave
up the poetic form entirely, and with it the chance that
a posterity of Coleridgians might fuse his poetry and his
preachings in an uncritical enthusiasm and worship the
poet as a prophet. We thus find no Coleridgians in the
later nineteenth century, but Wordsworthians a plenty.
Coleridge's tortured prose, though not great prose, has
a substantial content of its own, and is still undeservedly
neglected. Our fathers hardly dared to neglect Wordsworth's later poetry, which was long undeservedly read
for its philosophical content.

In his later years Coleridge was accustomed to maintain that he had never been a democrat, a ' Jacobin ' in
the accepted sense of the term. Now, although we have
no interest in affirming or denying Coleridge's claim to
personal consistency, we cannot be indifferent to the
question of the exact nature of his youthful political
views. For hitherto all our literary Jacobins have been
found to share certain fundamental doctrines : the
natural goodness of man, the corruptness of governments
and laws, and the consequent right of the individual to
obey his inner voice against all external dictates. If
Coleridge, who was certainly from the first one of the
romantic school, fails to share these beliefs, we must
modify our conclusions as to the place of romanticism in
politics.

There is no doubt that he moved in very Jacobinical
circles. Even at school, he confesses, he was attracted
by ' the levities of Voltaire ' and ' the reasonings of
Helvetius '.[1] At Jesus College, Cambridge, he threw
himself into politics. His old friend, Le Grice, testifies
that his rooms were a centre of political agitation and
what we should now call ' advanced thinking '.[2] He
was, of course, an ardent supporter of Frend, a don who
had turned Unitarian, and seems to have made himself
conspicuous at the trial of that dangerous heretic. He

[1] *Letters* (ed. E. H. Coleridge, 1895), p. 69.
[2] *Gentleman's Magazine*, December 1834.

won a prize for a very topical Greek ode on the slave trade, and at about this time he addressed a letter to a newly-made friend at Balliol, ' S. T. Coleridge to R. Southey, Health and Republicanism to be ! '[1] As experience has not proved democracy and republicanism synonymous, this is perhaps not damaging evidence against Coleridge. Soon after leaving the university he wrote for the *Morning Chronicle* a series of sonnets which are filled with the idiom of sentimental radicalism. In them Erskine, Priestly, Koskiusko, La Fayette, Sheridan, Stanhope, Godwin, Southey, Mrs. Siddons, and the Rev. W. L. Bowles are praised with an enthusiasm at least catholic enough ; Burke's apostasy is mourned ; and Pitt,

> Who with proud words of dear-loved Freedom came
> More blasting than the mildew from the South !
> And kissed his country with Iscariot mouth.[2]

is doomed to die by ' Mercy's Thunderbolts '.

For a time he thinks himself destined for the Unitarian ministry. He is next to be found in Bristol, delivering his *Conciones ad Populum*, and editing the *Watchman*, a journal that seemed to the sober citizens of Bristol dangerously revolutionary. Here was concocted between Coleridge and Southey the great scheme of pantisocracy. In spite of its pedantic name, this was simply a project for forming a small communist society in America, and in conception hardly differs from the many Utopian experiments, like Brook Farm in Massachusetts, that help to make American social history something more than a dull record of expansion. Pantisocracy was never established on the flowery banks of the Susquehanna ; but the project could hardly have taken hold on an imagination untouched by the possibilities of the return to Nature.

Coleridge's activities during this last decade of the century had nearly been such as to give some justifica-

---

[1] *Letters*, p. 72.
[2] *Poetical Works* (ed. J. D. Campbell, 1898), p. 40.

tion to his friend, Thomas Poole, who writes of him :
' In religion, he is a Unitarian, if not a deist; in politics,
a Democrat, to the utmost extent of the word.' [1]   Let
us see whether his opinions, recorded in the Bristol
pamphlets, his correspondence, and his poetry of these
years bear out this judgement.   The drift of his *Conciones
ad Populum* is plain enough.   ' That vice is the effect
of error and the offspring of surrounding circumstances,
the object therefore of condolence, not of anger, is
a proposition easily understood, and as easily demon-
strated.' [2]   But among the circumstances that produce
evil must be numbered monarchy and ' that leprous
stain, nobility '.[3]   Priests and judges do but serve to
bolster up the iniquitous fabric of government.   A better
time is coming, however, a time heralded by events in
France.

' France ! whose crimes and miseries posterity will impute to
us.   France ! to whom posterity will impute their virtues and
happiness.' [4]

Now indeed we can say :

' The age of priesthood will soon be no more—that of philosophers and christians will succeed, and the torch of superstition
be extinguished for ever.' [5]

No longer will men brutally mock such natural benevolence as that of the lines *To a Young Ass :*

Innocent foal !   Thou poor despised forlorn !
I hail thee brother.[6]

To achieve this better state, Englishmen need only to
follow the genius of their constitution.   For it is the
glory of the English constitution that it is progressive ; it
is founded on the belief that civil government is capable
of steady improvement ; ' its whole endurableness consists

[1] Sandford, Mrs. H., *Thomas Poole and his Friends* (1888), Chap. VI.
[2] Coleridge, *Essays on his own Times* (1850), vol. i, p. 28.
[3] *Poetical Works*, p. 43.
[4] *Essays on his own Times*, vol. i, p. 82.
[5] Ibid., p. 47 *n.*   [6] *Poetical Works*, p. 86.

in motion '. The motive force for this change cannot come from a corrupt government which is doing its best to prevent the proper working of the constitution. It must come from private citizens inspired with a high sense of duty and a lofty benevolence, working by means of painstaking illumination of all classes. These true leaders of men will guide the state towards its goal of government by the people; that is, by the people *morally* present in a representative body whose members act according to instructions from their constituents. England, with her unrepresentative parliament would still be a mere despotism, were it not for the freedom of the press. This is therefore the only real English freedom, and must be cherished inviolate. Through it Englishmen can achieve democracy without violent revolution.[1]

It must be evident from all this that Coleridge has a definite revolutionary belief. Although he has not committed himself to a formal organization of democracy, he has indicated that his political ideal is a representative government chosen by universal suffrage, and governing not by free discussion but by mandate from the electors. He had been influenced by Helvetius and Hartley, and the groundwork of his politics at this period is a conviction that society is a vast machine that goes wrong solely by reason of the neglect of the men in charge of it. Coleridge held at one period a form of that simple and deadly rationalism which made the way easy for revolutionary ecstasy.

Nor did he fail to attain some share of this ecstasy. Indeed, few men have put warmer feelings into a philosophy so cold as to find its best representatives in the chilly Bentham and the clammy Godwin. Reason does but provide him with a starting-point for a voyage into infinity; unitarianism becomes a gateway to a mystic world of faith. He wraps his naked philosophy in the warmest cloak he can command. The *Religious Musings*,

[1] *Essays on his own Times*, vol. i, p. 68 ; pp. 82–98.

published in 1796, which he himself bravely calls a
'desultory poem', sums up the more transcendental
features of his philosophy, and furnishes the final con-
secration of his early political activity. He begins with
eternity. It is by merging ourselves with the infinite,
by surrendering all to love, that we most exalt ourselves.
By an effort of love we can

make

> The whole one Self! Self, that no alien knows!
> Self, far diffused as Fancy's wing can travel!
> Self, spreading still! Oblivious of its own
> Yet all of all possessing!

It is the task of 'philosophers and bards' to communicate
this gospel to mankind, sorely in need of its healing
power. Everywhere the wretched *Many* bow to foul
Oppression. 'Blessed Society' is best 'depictured by
some sun-scorched waste' inhabited by beggars, pros-
titutes, soldiers and their widows, paupers, and all the
'children of wretchedness'. But there is hope. Events
have given warning to

> the Great, the Rich, the Mighty Men,
> The Kings and the *Chief Captains* of the World.

Coleridge assures us in a foot-note that he is 'alluding to
the French Revolution'. He, at least, did not foresee
Napoleon. The poet does not, however, despair at the
picture of horror he has evoked. He has visions of
a better world here below :

> Return pure Faith! return meek Piety!
> The kingdoms of the world are yours ; each heart
> Self governed, the vast family of Love
> Raised from the common earth by common toil
> Enjoy the equal produce.[1]

Shelley himself is not more prophetic.

What then did Coleridge mean in after-life in denying
that he had ever been a thorough and convinced democrat ? It is obvious from this brief sketch of his early

[1] *Poetical Works*, pp. 53–60.

opinions that he worked with democratic associates, and shared many of their ideas. But he seems always to have made reservations. He never loved the crowd, never had even the missionary pity of the settlement-worker for the poor and down-trodden. At the height of his ' republicanism ' in 1794 he can write :

' At the Inn I was sore afraid that I had caught the itch from a Welsh democrat who was charmed with my sentiments ; he grasped my hand with flesh-bruising ardour, and I trembled lest some disappointed citizen of the *animalicular republic* should have emigrated.[1]

The jesting of a youth of twenty-two ; but most irreverent jesting in a philanthropist. Coleridge was not, as a matter of fact, a lover of the people like Thelwall or Holcroft. Nor could he even persuade himself, as did Wordsworth, into a distantly avuncular relation to them. Men have indeed found it possible to combine a contempt for the lower orders with radically democratic politics ; but they rarely grow old in that belief. It is not a satisfying state of mind ; and Coleridge was, above all, seeking for mental peace.

This instinctive distrust of flesh and blood democrats comes out in one of Coleridge's Bristol addresses, which he reprinted in 1818 to prove his assertion that he had never been a convert to Jacobinism. He sets out to describe more accurately the ' oppositionists to things as they are ' whom public opinion has roughly classed as ' democrats '. They are to be divided, he finds, into four groups. The first is composed of men of small education and little disposition to arduous thought, who yet feel vaguely that something is wrong, and will give an indolent vote for reform if they are not too much frightened by news from France. The second class, also ignorant of philosophy, and in addition unrestrained by religion or by indolence, are completely carried away by their bitter feeling of exclusion from the good things of life. These are the men who make violent revolutions ;

[1] *Letters*, p. 79.

but they are rarely moved in dangerous numbers unless by sheer physical deprivation. There are many signs that the state of the English poor is approaching this danger-point. The third class of friends of change are those who pursue freedom because it means profit to them. They wish the abolition of privileged orders, the destruction of the taboos of the old society, the pulling down of whatever is above them, in order that they may pursue wealth and power. But they will not listen to plans for the amelioration of the lot of the poor ; these are the dreams of idle visionaries. Equality of rights is all that men can claim. But, Coleridge points out, equality of rights becomes an empty phrase when used to justify a blind struggle for economic power, and ' it is a mockery of our fellow creatures' wrongs to call them equal in rights, when by the bitter compulsion of their wants we make them inferior to us in all that can soften the heart, or dignify the understanding '. There is, of course, a fourth class of reformers, the small but glorious band of true guardians of the republic. These men are not the slaves of jealousy or lust, but calm, pure-minded followers of a rational idea of the good life for all. They alone can lead a successful revolution.[1]

Coleridge's democracy was then really a sort of ' Tory democracy '. Wisdom and ability to govern are the possessions of few ; but the few must exercise their powers to mitigate the sufferings of the many. He was a zealous propagandist of Jacobinical ideas ; but he had little faith in their mainstay, the doctrine of the natural goodness of man. That we have been able to cull from his work so much that indicates a half-belief in this doctrine merely shows how great a part it played in English thought. The early career of Wordsworth is scarcely a tribute to the influence of Rousseau in England ; for Wordsworth was born to return to Nature. But that Coleridge, city-bred, book-loving, system-seeking, should

---

[1] *Essays on his own Times*, vol. i, pp. 6–29 ; *Friend* (1837), vol. ii, Essay XII.

have been led into a seeming belief in the purity of man's
instincts is a valuable indication of the extent to which
Rousseau's ideas had filled the spirit of the age. It is
tempting, and perhaps not wholly unjust, to remark that
Coleridge could hardly find in his own cravings a support
for the theory that instinctive desire is the best guide in
ethics and politics ; and that a consciousness of his own
weakness impelled him to seek support in the discipline
of authority and institutions. Certainly his Jacobinism
is inspired by the mystic feeling that seeks a guide and
an ally in institutions. He had not only to satisfy a longing for something to feel for and in and with, but he had
also to find place for his system-building intellect.
A crude belief in natural benevolence could not satisfy
his intelligence : and the cold, empty rationalism of the
revolutionists gave no hold for his affections. His
youthful philosophy failed him on both sides. Everywhere, in French wars and in English industries, a vast
store of human energy had been unlocked, and was
making use of the revolutionary doctrines of individual
freedom to justify its unlimited expansion, an expansion
incomprehensible to a reasonable man, immoral to a just
one. When the nineteenth century began Coleridge
had come to the conclusion that the problem of politics
was not to free men, but to discipline them. He therefore abandoned democracy and its machinery of frequent
elections, popular assemblies, universal education, and
the rest.

It seemed to him that in this revolutionary democracy
rights had been claimed on behalf of unreal good men
by very real bad, or at least undisciplined men. This
emphasis on rights Coleridge came to consider the chief
error of Jacobinism. The true political wisdom is to
demand something in the way of works in return for
rights granted ; in other words, to insist that rights and
duties can never be separated. Now, in one form or
another, this problem of rights and duties has always
troubled political thinkers, and several thousand years

have not discouraged men from writing about it. A real individualist, however he may dismiss rights in one shape, is bound to call them back in another. Both Godwin and Bentham pooh-poohed the Rights of Man : and then proceeded to erect systems based on the indefeasible right of the individual to follow his own enlightened self-interest against the necessarily stupid decrees of the state. An emphasis on duties is, however, almost inevitably an emphasis on authority or restraint, on the power of institutions and laws. Therefore Coleridge founded his new philosophy of the state on the conception of social responsibility. He wrote in 1818 :

' The principle of all constitutional law is to make the claims of each as much as possible compatible with the claims of all, as individuals, and with those of the common-weal as a whole ; and out of this adjustment, the claims of the individual first become *Rights*. Every Canal Bill proves that there is no species of property which the legislature does not possess and exercise the right of controlling and limiting, as soon as the right of the individuals is shown to be disproportionately injurious to the community.' [1]

There still remains the problem which neither libertarian nor authoritarian can dodge : What power is to arbitrate between the individual and the community and fix the proper limits of each ? This arbitrator Coleridge readily finds in reason. A startling statement, one thinks, from a man who so hated the eighteenth century and its Right Reason. But one of Coleridge's favourite whims was to call eighteenth-century reason ' understanding ', and reserve for ' reason ' a definition more romantically his own. Besides, he had read the Germans, and had accepted the distinction between *Vernunft* and *Verstand*. As he filled pages of the *Friend* with such scholasticisms as ' Unity + Omneity = Totality ' in an attempt to explain this ' reason ', he frightened his good Georgian readers, and acquired a disastrous reputation for abstruseness.

[1] *Two Addresses on Sir R. Peel's Bill* (privately printed by T. J. Wise, 1919), p. 20.

We must try, however, to get at his meaning, since on it is built his *Idea of the Constitution in Church and State*. Men live in two planes of higher consciousness. The lower is that of the ' understanding ', miscalled reason by Voltaire and his crew. This is a purely mechanical faculty by which we calculate means. It is incapable of arriving at moral judgements. The higher plane is that of ' reason '. This faculty alone can arrive at ends, and guide our moral judgements. It does not follow the petty logical road of the ' understanding ', but has a logic of its own, by which it perceives ideas. Now ideas, as Plato described them before pedantry and affectation had cheapened the word, are eternal forms which exist before the objects of the ' understanding ', and of which therefore these latter are but imperfect copies. In the simplest terms Coleridge is affirming that there are experiences open to human beings which cannot come within the activity of the perceptive or the logical faculty, but which are evident to a superior faculty which he calls reason and others have called imagination or even faith.[1]

Reason, then, marks out the duties of the good citizen. It discovers these duties implicit in the idea of a constitution of the state. A constitution is not simply a written or unwritten fundamental law ; it is an antecedent reality which has produced all the historical forms a given state has assumed. It is not merely the material accumulation of historical experience ; it is a standard by which we can try past and present achievements. It is, in short, an idea, and cannot be arrived at by an empirical process. Here Coleridge becomes frightened at such a complete throwing over of good English common sense in politics, and hastens to remark that since the idea realizes itself, makes itself intelligible, in contingent forms, we must allow for material imperfections, ' meditate on the law of compensation and the principle of compromise ', and, in short,

[1] *A Lay Sermon* (1816), Appendix B.

make room in politics for some empirical standards of usefulness.

Coleridge is now faced with the problem of the specific content of this ideal constitution. It may be said of the constitution of any civilized state that it is an attempted equilibrium between two antagonistic powers, those of permanence and progression. Like the positive and negative poles of a magnet, neither of these powers can exist without the other. Both are essential to the well-being of the state. In the English constitution permanence is represented by the landed interest, progression by the commercial interest. The possession of land binds a man to the past, gives him a firm hold on the present, and makes him reluctant to run risks in the future. The possessors of the land can be divided into two classes, the Major Barons and the Minor Barons, or Franklins. The former class, small in number and strong in privilege, is the most completely conservative force in the state. The Franklins are much more numerous, and more willing to run the risks of expansion, but, on the whole, they are on the side of permanence. Commerce and industry, however, have everything to gain by change. The most sober business is a speculation in its way. The merchant must always act upon uncertainties ; he comes to believe all things human as unstable as prices. Thus arises in the state the commercial, or personal, interest. It is through this personal activity that are made the advances in material civilization indispensable to society. For the alternative to progress is not stability, but death.

The parliament of the realm provides a meeting-place for these interests of permanence and progress. The Major Barons have a house themselves ; the Franklins and the personal interest combine to elect another house, where the burgesses, or representatives of the personal interest, have a majority. Parliament represents not the people in the sense of an aggregate of individuals, but the interests, the group-loyalties, into which the people are really divided, and in which alone they have a political life. Through parliamentary institutions these interests are so balanced that none can tyrannize over the others. This, Coleridge reminds us, is the idea of the British Constitution, and not its actual form at any time. It is the *lex legum* to which men have appealed when seeking to justify political change. If at present any interest is inadequately represented, it must of course take all measures to get itself represented. Owing to the breakdown of the borough system, the commercial or personal interest is at present incompletely represented in parliament. But Coleridge thinks that it possesses a compensating influence through newspapers and the mechanical improvements it has itself created. He decides, in 1830, that a reform of parliament would be superfluous.

The constitution then, in the narrowest sense, balances these powers of permanence and progression derived from two kinds of property. But, in a wider sense, it must include a power which is not that of property. The English state includes a National Church. Coleridge has, of course, a definition of his own for these words. The National Church is an endowment for the perpetuation of the spirit of civilization, without which the well-being of the property-side of the state is vain, and indeed impossible. This National Church is not the Church of Christ. The latter is not of this world ; it is indeed opposed to this world and to the state. The National Church is simply a trust fund for the support of certain men. These men have no personal interest in the property, which is used merely to keep them above the struggle for material acquisitions. They are the teachers who keep alive art, letters, and all things spiritual. They are the clerisy, or clergy in the old sense in which any educated man was a clerk. It is only in modern times, when lawyers, physicians, and artists have forsaken this body and entered the commercial struggle, that it is composed solely of clergymen. Actually, clergymen of the Church of England are the only ones who benefit from this national fund. This is unfortunate, as in the idea of the Constitution it is destined to a wider use. It has in the past, even when administered by the Roman Church, enabled merit and intelligence to rise from humble circumstances, and has furnished a career open to talents without the temptations to crude aggression so often found in commerce. At present, it is urgently necessary to devote this Nationality, or National Church, to three purposes : (1) the support of the great universities and schools of liberal learning ; (2) the maintenance of a pastor, presbyter, or parson in every parish ; (3) the maintenance of a schoolmaster in every parish, who should be the natural successor to the pastorate.

Thus, the landed and commercial interests, or the Proprietage, and the spiritual and intellectual interest, or the Nationality, are trusts, bodies of men who find their duties marked out by their position in life. Through the operation of these trusts by the trustees, men of property and men of education, life is made tolerable for the dispossessed masses, and society enjoys good health. Such is the idea of the English Constitution. What is the England of 1830 ?

In the name of a ' mechanico-corpuscular theory raised to the title of a mechanic philosophy ' men are denying that the English Constitution ought to exercise this restraining influence over Englishmen. They refuse to see anything in society but the atomic individuals of which it is composed. Learning has become mere science, and its aim control over matter. Education is like everything else, an unorganized private activity, an uncontrolled competition, guided by the morals of grab. Meanwhile the great masses, instead of being objects of care to the propertied classes, become objects of exploitation.

' Then we have game laws, corn laws, cotton factories, spital fields, the tillers of the land paid by poor rates, and the remainder

of the population mechanized into engines for the manufactory of
new rich men ; yea, the machinery of the wealth of the nation
made up of the wretchedness, disease, and depravity of those who
should constitute the strength of the nation ! ' [1]

Labour is declared free, although ' if labour were indeed
free the employer would purchase and the labourer sell,
what the former had no right to buy, and the latter no
right to dispose of, namely, the labourer's health, life,
and well-being. These belong not to himself *alone*, but
to his friends, his parents, to his King, to his country,
and to God.' [2]   Coleridge continues this description of
his age in several pages of brief, pithy phrases, dictated
by an indignation that clears his style wonderfully and
makes one wish he had oftener lost his temper and his
metaphysics. 'A state of Nature, or Orang outang
theology of the origin of the human race, substituted
for the first ten chapters of the Book of Genesis ; rights
of nature for the duties of citizens ; . . . Talent without
genius ; a swarm of clever, well-informed men ; an
anarchy of minds, a despotism of maxims. Hence
despotism of finance in government and legislation, of
vanity and sciolism in the intercourse of life, of presumption, temerity, and hardness of heart in political
economy.' [3]

Coleridge progresses as far as this in his *Constitution
of the Church and State* with extraordinary coherence
and unity. But he soon trails off woefully into a dialogue
between Demosius of Toutoscosmos and Mystes the
Allocosmite, where οἵ τούτου κόσμου φιλόσοφοι dis-
cuss the *reine Anschauung* and the *mundus immundus*.
We may decline to follow him into this polyglot twilight,
and turn instead to an important part of his political
philosophy neglected in the *Constitution of the Church
and State*. His daughter says that, like Goethe, he
never had the real patriotic impulse ; but that unlike

---

[1] *On the Constitution of the Church and State* (1830), p. 67.
[2] *Two Addresses on Sir R. Peel's Bill*, p. 21.
[3] *On the Constitution of the Church and State*, pp. 69–70.

Goethe, he acted and wrote as if he did, because he felt
it to be a necessary part of morality. One is tempted
to ask whether this explains his religion, too. At any
rate, he insists in *The Friend* that ' in order to be men
we must be patriots '.[1] The nation is at least an object
of loyalty that can take men out of their petty selves.
It is a natural corporate entity. But there are limits
to the demands a nation can justifiably make. First,
towards her own citizens, she cannot so far pursue
a unifying policy as to ' blend men into a state by the
dissolution of all those virtues which make them happy
and estimable as individuals '.[2] The economists who are
willing to sacrifice men to the creation of a national
wealth (which is *national* only in statistical tables) are
forgetting that even for patriotic purposes no person
should be treated as a thing. Secondly, in its relation
with other states, a nation is limited by the ordinary
laws of morality.

' It were absurd to suppose that individuals should be under
a law of moral obligation, and yet that a million of the same
individuals acting collectively or through representatives, should
be exempt from all law : for morality is no accident of human
nature, but its essential characteristic.' [3]

Since there can be no superior power to enforce a code
of laws between independent nations, this rule of morality
must subsist in the consciences of statesmen and guide
their relations with statesmen of other countries. Ask
for no letter of the law, for there is none, but ask if the
spirit of morality prevails. Coleridge's nationalism, like
Wordsworth's, is from the very goodness of its intentions
impotent before the difficulty of relations between
sovereign national states.

This is the most systematic political philosophy we
have yet encountered among the romanticists. Its failings are evident. The Major and Minor Barons, the

[1] *Friend*, vol. ii, p. 134.   [2] Ibid., p. 138.
[3] Ibid., p. 124.

Clerisy and the Proprietage, are names that suggest
outworn trappings, and do but serve to conceal the life
beneath them.　Nor is the much ado about ' reason '
and ' understanding ' very helpful.　Whatever one may
think of the matter, it is clear that the *Constitution of
the Church and State* suffers from the introduction of an
unsolved problem in epistemology.　Moreover, Coleridge
is unduly severe with scientists and economists.　Science
and economics are not necessarily harmful in themselves.
It is when they treat man as if he were a thing, as Coleridge
saw, that they are harmful.　Scientists and economists in
this day hardly need defence, however ; we shall do
better to remark the modicum of truth in Coleridge's
attitude.

A more serious weakness in this philosophy is its failure
to accept the aid of corporations within the state.　' If
I met a man who should deny that an *imperium in
imperio* was in itself an evil ', Coleridge writes, ' I would
not attempt to reason with him ; he is too ignorant.' [1]
But corporate bodies within the state may help to achieve
the equilibrium between liberty and authority, progress
and permanence, that he desired.　These groups stand
between the individual and the state ; they take him
out of himself ; they command his loyalty and impose
on him their discipline.　They are really the ' interests '
of Coleridge, but more numerous than he would allow.
They can be defended on his own principles.　A man
who is merely a member of a nation is almost rootless,
lost in an abstraction and driven to selfishness.　A, who
is but a man and a Frenchman, may well have a tendency
to unbridled political action in both capacities ; B, who
is a man, an old Blankonian, a cricketer, a clubman,
a Justice of the Peace, a Liberal, an Anglican, and an
Englishman, will be a better citizen from the very variety
of his interests.　The political problem is perhaps not
simplified by the frank admission of these group-loyalties

---

[1] *Constitution of the Church and State*, p. 159; also *Biographia Literaria*
(1847), vol. i, p. 189.

within the state, but is at last put on a more realistic basis.

When all these criticisms have been made, however, and even when the usual reproach of incompleteness, so universally levelled at all his work, has been added, there remains much sound political wisdom in the later work of Coleridge. His Toryism is never mere hankering after primitive simplicity, like Wordsworth's, and consequently he never becomes an advocate of blind resistance to change. With a temperamental dislike for the commercial classes, he yet admits the necessity, and indeed the goodness, of commercial expansion. He cannot welcome the industrial revolution, but he does not wish it away, nor deny the courage, the enterprise, the eager life that produced it. He faces hopefully the possibility of educating, by an intelligent use of the fund of the Nationalty, the new ruling class of stockholders. Where Wordsworth refused to see anything in this class, Coleridge at least saw its pitiful need of education. His proposal to convert the joint-stockholders to a feeling for their responsibilities to society by a national system of education under the ' clerisy ', is perhaps not even now wholly old-fashioned and useless. It is possible that the new upper classes can still justify their promotion. But they must first learn from Coleridge the lesson that ' the possession of a property, not connected with especial duties, a property not fiduciary or official, but arbitrary and unconditional . . . is not the distinction, nor the right, nor the honour of an English baron or gentleman '.[1]

From this firm ground of ideas, Coleridge was able to support many ' liberal ' measures, such as Catholic Emancipation, free trade, repeal of game laws, universal education, factory Acts ; and thus he incurred the distrust of his new friends the Tories as he had already incurred that of his former Jacobin comrades. It is sometimes doubtful whether a man who stands outside

---

[1] *Constitution of the Church and State*, p. 44.

party is above or below it ; it must be admitted that Coleridge's was not the skulking independence of the fanatic, but, when he was at his best, the generous impartiality of the critic. He never ceased to point out the real meaning of the truism that man is a political animal : first, that man is not at all a mere animal ; and second that he is bound by his humanity to corporations which possess a reality above abstraction. It is in his relations to such corporations, of which church and state are the most important, that man is dignified above his animal self, and becomes human. For Coleridge saw clearly enough that the ' natural ' man is on the whole selfish, rebellious, unrestrained. To give this man nothing bigger than himself to cling to is to invite him to self-destruction. Individualism is the ruin of the individual. Only in a voluntary surrender of himself to a corporate society can man find that mystic repayment of desire that is at once an expansion and a limitation. Only in state and church can the anarchy of nature and the order of civilization be reconciled. It is certainly possible for this surrender to be too complete ; we may accept laws that stifle our animal instincts instead of disciplining them. Coleridge thinks, however, that the danger in his time lies the other way, in an excess of disorderly striving after material gratification, justified by an appeal to nature and freedom. After all, the *Constitution of the Church and State* is a contemporary of Macaulay's famous dictum that the cure for the evils of freedom is more freedom. Were it but a partial antidote to that extravagance Coleridge's work was not written in vain.

3

Posterity has paid Robert Southey the doubtful compliment of preferring the man to the author. No one has read his epics, though any one who has seen their titles in a manual of English literature may be clever at the expense of *Thalaba* and *Kehama* and *Madoc*. Every

one is agreed that his lyrics fail in depth, intensity, and
dignity, that his histories are not only dull, but unscien-
tific, that his controversial writings have no life-giving
connexion with eternal truths to raise them above their
subjects. He was not a great poet, because his easy
facility in verse led him to circumvent, rather than
surmount, obstacles in the conquest of which the poet
is proved. He was not a great philosopher, because his
powers of ratiocination were but the feeble servants of
his lusty prejudices. This last was the opinion of
Macaulay, who is surely qualified to judge of such matters.
But if criticism is admirably unanimous in justifying the
popular neglect of *Thalaba* and the *Colloquies on Society*,
it is almost equally unanimous in praising the character
of their author. Thackeray and Leslie Stephen have
singled him out among the eccentric and irritable tribe
of authors as a rare example of sound, homely virtues,
of high honour, courage, and Christian fortitude. Now,
although the *Life of Nelson* is still more popular than
any other prose work of the Lake School, no one would
be so rash as to quarrel with the critical verdict of
a century upon Southey's work. It is just these facts
about him, his freedom from the qualities of genius, his
nearness to ordinary human beings, his respectability,
that make his political thought valuable to us. He is
not that abstraction, an ' average man ' ; but he is very
much of a man. His frank acceptance of life, his dislike
of systems, his common sense, always at the mercy of
his enthusiasms but never the dupe of introspection,
happily complement the other-worldliness of Coleridge
and the self-searching intensity of Wordsworth. Without
Southey, our study of the political ideas of the Lakists
would risk reproach for the eccentricity of its subjects ;
with Southey, it returns to common things.

The Revolution could hardly fail to hold the young
Southey. His early learning was intrusted to a maiden
aunt, who prepared herself for the task by reading the
Emile. So thoroughly did the boy learn the lessons

derived from that work that he got himself expelled from Westminster for an article in the school paper condemning flogging as an invention of the devil. With this stain upon his character he was refused admission at Christ Church. He was received at Balliol, however, and, like most of her articulate sons in the eighteenth century, found the university a miserable nursery of idle and dissipated youths and masters. Here he met Coleridge, and devised the great scheme of pantisocracy to be realized in some American Arcady. He soon returned to his aunt in Bristol, unfolded the plan of pantisocracy and another of marriage to a penniless young lady, and was promptly turned out of the house by his outraged aunt, who had apparently forgotten or misunderstood her *Emile*. After lecturing a while with Coleridge to aid the revolutionary cause, he settled down to read for the bar, and began to drift away from his earlier Jacobin faith. A pension from his friend Wynn enabled him to give up the uncongenial profession of the law, and devote himself to letters. Just as with Wordsworth and Coleridge, the new century finds him about to take up a Conservative position in politics. In 1809 he helped to found the Tory *Quarterly Review*, and in 1813 he succeeded Henry Pye as Poet Laureate. He was thus rather more in the public eye as a politician than his brothers of the Lakes, and was chiefly blamed for their common apostasy from the revolutionary faith. This position was made worse in 1817 by the pirating of a lost republican rant of his Balliol days, *Wat Tyler*, a play in blank verse. Southey was then Laureate, and the appearance of this violent attack on kings created no small sensation. The affair was actually brought up in Parliament, and for a moment the political ideas of a man of letters became a concern of professional politicians. From this time on, the *Morning Chronicle* and *The Examiner* gave ' turncoat Southey ' little rest. Convinced, doubtless, that a man so heartily abused by Whig and Radical alike must be a powerful pillar of

society, Lord Radnor had him returned to Parliament
from Downton in 1826. Southey, who knew his own
limitations in some respects, at least, insisted that his
pen was his best weapon in the cause of right politics,
and wisely declined to take his seat. Thus, throughout
the greater part of an active life, Southey was in the
public eye as a political figure, and he does at any rate
serve to bring the Lake poets into the field of public
opinion.

We must begin the study of Southey's ideas with his
Jacobin days. He had, of course, a supply of suitable
revolutionary principles. We have already heard so
much of benevolence and nature and the rights of man
that we can afford to run very hastily over Southey's
stock to assure ourselves that it is of the right sort.

There is first the dogma of natural goodness. Joan of
Arc pleads before her judges :

> Ye have told me, Sires,
> That Nature only teaches man to sin !
> If it be sin to seek the wounded Lamb,
> To bind its wounds and bathe them with my tears,
> This is what Nature taught ! No, REVERENDS ! No,
> It is not Nature that can teach to sin :
> Nature is all Benevolence, all Love,
> All Beauty ! [1]

Then there is the corruption of civilized society :

> The train of courtiers, summer flies that sport
> In the sunbeam of favour, insects sprung
> From the court dunghill, greedy blood suckers,
> The foul corruption gendered swarm of state.[2]

Therefore must the uncorrupted, the common people,
rebel. The trumpet of rebellion is sounded in *Wat
Tyler*.

> What matters me who wears the crown of France,
> Whether a Richard or a Charles possess it ?
> They reap the glory—they enjoy the spoil—

[1] *Joan of Arc* (1796), Bk. III, lines 431-8.
[2] Ibid., Bk. IV, lines 89-92.

We pay—we bleed—The sun would shine as clearly,
The rains of heaven as seasonably fall,
Tho' neither of these royal pests existed.[1]

For is it not true, as John Ball tells the multitude,

My brethren, these are truths, and mighty ones :
Ye are all equal ; nature made ye so.
Equality is your birthright.[2]

But there is always hope, and never a brighter one than
now. France is pointing the way, through freedom and
equality to

. . . ONE BROTHERHOOD
ONE UNIVERSAL FAMILY OF LOVE.[3]

This is Wordsworth, Coleridge, and the Jacobins once
more. Yet there is a quality in Southey's early political
faith that is his own. Perhaps it is boyishness, although
it never forsook him in maturity. It is in some ways
akin to that ' gusto ' that Hazlitt found and that the
eighteenth century had lost. It is a bright directness of
purpose, an energy, not yet dammed up into a reservoir
of sentimentality but flowing harmlessly on to no goal.
In this spirit he can welcome Holcroft's *Anna St. Ives*
as ' a book of consummate wisdom ' ;[4] can write
impatiently at Oxford of his feeling that it is ' rather
disgraceful, at the moment when Europe is on fire with
freedom—when man and monarch are contending—to
sit and study Euclid or Hugo Grotius ' ;[5] or can hail
with delightful inconsequence two recruits to pantisocracy, ' Favell and Le Grice. . . . They possess great
genius and energy. I have seen neither of them, yet
correspond with both. . . .'[6] This immediacy of purpose
in Southey softens his Jacobin faith. He never sees far
enough ahead to be a good revolutionary. The true
revolutionary is a very patient man, and one who rarely

[1] *Wat Tyler* (1817), Act I.   [2] Ibid., Act II.
[3] *Joan of Arc*, Bk. IX, lines 743–4.
[4] *Life and Correspondence* (ed. C. C. Southey, 1849–50), vol. i, p. 283.
[5] Ibid., p. 169.   [6] Ibid., p. 224.

acts at the spur of present impulse; for he looks so far
ahead into a future of his own, guides himself so by this
future, that his actions acquire a deliberate consistency
unattainable by most of us who live in a present that is
not wholly our own. The youthful Southey lived very
much in the present. He believed in the natural goodness of man because he wanted men to be good. It never
occurred to him to believe in it merely as a dogma; and
he could not believe in it as a means of unchaining men's
energies without regard for consequences. He soon discovered that revolutionary doctrines had not made men
good; he characteristically jumped to the conclusion
that they had made men bad.

His disillusion, too, was a vivid personal experience,
and for a while the world was very black indeed. 'Man
is a beast, and an ugly beast, and Monboddo libels the
orang-outang by suspecting them to be of the same
family.'[1] But this does not last long. If rationalists,
revolutionists, and Frenchmen are bad, if faith in liberty,
equality, and fraternity results in licentious misdeeds,
some things are good, some faiths result in virtuous
actions. As ever, Southey finds the test of this in his
own relations with specific things. He will cling to what
has given him comfort. He will be unashamedly pre-
judiced, for prejudice gives men something fixed in
immediate experience. He will have no more of systems
or dogmas, for their fixity is a delusion, a fixity outside
experience. Let the world call him Tory, renegade,
apostate, so that he gain inner peace, a consciousness of
doing good.

This is, of course, itself a philosophy. Southey, like
Burke, has a systematic dislike for system. But to a proposal that carefully avoided clothing itself with generalizations he could be singularly open-minded. Had he
known Robert Owen as a socialist he would have damned
him in the *Quarterly*; but since he knew him simply
as the mill-owner who had built the unabstract town of

[1] *Life and Correspondence*, vol. iii, p. 5.

New Lanark, he welcomed him as an actual producer of political good. In this way his politics kept gathering new accretions of projects, although his political philosophy, once he had renounced Jacobinism, remained unaltered. A list of his enthusiasms would be long ; but some of them are too instructive to be omitted.

He hates France not merely because she is fighting England, but because hers is the spirit of Boileau, Racine, and Voltaire. For the same reason he likes the Germans, blood-brothers in romance. From Portugal he writes home : ' Cintra is too good a place for the Portuguese. It is only fit for us Goths—for Germans or English.' [1] He detested the utilitarians as the heirs of eighteenth-century rationalism, and, still incurably boyish, refers to Bentham as ' the metaphysico-critico-politico-patriotico-phoolo-philosopher '.[2] Indeed, he was never able to consider the English reform movement apart from the utilitarian philosophy. For the ' papists ' he had no mercy. His last word is that if Roman Catholics want to sit in the British Parliament they should be willing to change their faith. Parliamentary Reform he is sure will open the flood-gates to all sorts of evils, revolution, anarchy, *bellum servile*, *Jacquerie*.[3] He has, however, his own little plan of a decent reform to quiet the people. This involves three concessions : first, seats actually sold *sub rosa* for private profit should be put on the market and sold *openly*, like commissions in the army, and the proceeds used for public purposes ; second, certain large sinecures should be given up ; third, a number of new seats should be given to large manufacturing towns hitherto unrepresented, but with a franchise carefully restricted to prevent the mob from influencing elections.[4] In 1832 he fully expected immediate civil war, and was apparently a bit disappointed

[1] *Life and Correspondence*, vol. ii, p. 89.
[2] Ibid., vol. i, p. 24.
[3] *Essays, Moral and Political* (1832), vol. ii, p. 368.
[4] *Life and Correspondence*, vol. iv, p. 220.

at Lord Grey's escape from this natural consequence of his action.[1]

Toward that palladium of English liberty, freedom of the press, Southey expressed himself in terms most un-English. He would let the decent press be free, but not the press of the ' Yahoos '—that is, the Radicals. At Perceval's assassination he wrote :

' This I am certain of, that nothing but an immediate suspension of the liberty of debate and the liberty of the press can preserve us. Were I minister, I would instantly suspend the Habeas Corpus and have every Jacobin journalist confined, so that it would be impossible for them to continue their treasonable vocation. There they should stay till it would be safe to let them out, which it might in some seven years.' [2]

His most amazing scheme, however, is that of a Royal Academy of Literature. This was to be modelled after the French Academy, but it was destined not so much to preserve literary standards as to provide a way of satisfying the vanity of men of letters, who are always too prone to strive for notoriety by flattering the mob and attacking the natural leaders of society. Make your rebellious man of letters an R.A., says Southey, and he will become a bulwark of the state. The Academy thus created will add the pen to the bayonet as a force for the preservation of order. The scheme, unfortunately, never got beyond printer's ink ; its effect on Cobbett and Hazlitt might have been a permanent addition to literature.[3]

Southey's connexion with the *Quarterly*, and his position in the public eye, enabled him to gain no small audience for his political suggestions. They were not all so absurd as his proposed Royal Academy. He advocated a national grant for education ; the diffusion of cheap literature of a wholesome kind, such as the English classics and the Bible ; an extensive and well-ordered

---

[1] Ibid., vol. vi, p. 145.
[2] Ibid., vol. iii, p. 342.
[3] Ibid., vol. vi, pp. 132–6.

scheme of emigration to the colonies; a better order of
hospital nurses; the establishment of government-aided
savings banks in market towns; alteration of the game
laws; alteration of the factory system for the benefit
of the operative; child labour restrictions; commuta-
tion of tithes; allotments of land to labourers.[1] And
on still more unorthodox ground he dared to welcome
the beginnings of the co-operative movement, and to
approve the activity of Robert Owen. Indeed, he gave
a very convenient indication of the direction in which
his best thoughts flowed when he said that the three
men of his day who had done most to give an impulse
to the moral world were Clarkson, Bell, and Owen.[2]

If Southey seems an inconsistent politician he is
always a consistent humanitarian. It is a shame to use
so dull a word for the rare feeling that touches his
absurdities with life, and even with wisdom. Southey
felt in himself the sufferings of others. The sight of
cruelty always impelled him to be cruel to the doer of
the cruel thing—an impulse which the bad man would
not have and the reasonable man would not indulge.
' I have read of the Slave Trade and of the Inquisition ',
he writes to Caroline Bowles,

' but nothing ever thrilled my heart like the Evidences [on factory
conditions] which you have been reading. It distracted my sleep
and I laid the book aside in horror. . . . After such an experience
I wonder (as far as I can wonder at anything in these times) that
none of those cotton and worsted and flax kings have yet hanged
themselves; that none of them have been pulled to pieces; that
none of their factories have been destroyed; that the very pave-
ment of the streets has not risen and stoned them.' [3]

This sympathy for the oppressed, this horror of the
oppressor, is shared with none of his contemporaries so
much as with Shelley. Both were altruists of the senses.
Their bodies quivered at blows struck at others; and

[1] *Life and Correspondence*, vol. v, pp. 5–6.
[2] *Colloquies on the Progress and Prospects of Society* (1829), vol. i, p. 132.
[3] *Correspondence of Southey with Caroline Bowles*, ed. Dowden (1881),
p. 266.

this by no cheating, imaginative transference to themselves of the blows, but by a direct, physical sensation.
That they should have differed so totally in their political
allegiance is a warning to the psychologist in his excur-
sions into political theory. For it does matter very
much with what ideas men clothe their feelings, be the
garment ever so thin.

This feeling for human suffering led Southey, as it led
Shelley, to seek some immediate remedy. Having failed
to find it in the system of the Jacobins he turned more
and more to his books, until he could write in one of the
few lyrics of his that survive : ' My days among the
dead are passed.' Living among old books he came to
believe the world of their pages as real as this of ours,
and as attainable. But books are better than men, and
the past of their pages is greater than the past of life.
To look forward to Utopia or to look backward to the
Golden Age is in either case to escape the present by
an effort of the imagination. The two are very far from
having the same practical results in all cases, but both
are opposed to the contented acceptance of things as
they are. If Southey found in his books ' old honours,
old generosity, old heroism ', it was but a re-discovery
of old hopes. Pantisocracy, lost on the banks of the
Susquehanna, he found again in the library at Keswick.

For Southey was an incurable meliorist. From whatever source, past or present, he drew his ideals he always
thought of them as attainable. To the end he retained
a subdued and corrected faith in the goodness of human
nature, and in the possibility of lessening human vice by
improving political institutions. He wrote in 1829 :

' The sum both of moral and physical evil may be greatly
diminished by good laws, good institutions, and good governments. Moral evil cannot indeed be removed, unless the nature
of man were changed ; and that renovation is only to be effected
in individuals, and in them only by the special grace of God.
Physical evil must always, to a certain degree, be inseparable
from mortality. But both are so much within the reach of
human institutions that a state of society is conceivable almost as

superior to that of England in these days, as that itself is superior
to the condition of the tattooed Britons or of the northern pirates
from whom we are descended.' [1]

All this is simple enough, deep with the depth of all
good commonplace, and no bad summary of a position
which is probably that of the great majority of human
beings in this century of progress.

Thus softened into a belief in progress the doctrine
of the natural goodness of man persists in Southey's Conservatism. The Revolution has established itself, and
ceased to be revolutionary. Southey is a nineteenth-
century Conservative. Burke had believed the problem
of poverty insoluble ; Southey was sure that the English
industrial worker could be raised from degradation.
Burke had never really believed in freedom because he
had never believed in growth ; Southey to the end was
an innovator in spirit, and steadily refused to limit the
freedom of the artist. *The Doctor*, as far as literary form
is concerned, is as revolutionary as his youthful *Sapphics*.
It is true that he did not believe that practising innovation in metre implied countenancing innovation in
business, or that to revolt against Pope was to justify
an attack on the unreformed House of Commons. But
the literary freedom he indulged was his own, and he
could hardly judge its results ; the political freedom was
that of others—manufacturers, merchants, and statesmen—and the results of this he could not fail to understand. The very evident failure of the freedom of the
industrial revolution to produce the sort of satisfactions
he found in the freedom of the literary revolution made
him seek an authority, a discipline, in politics. He did
not see, as Coleridge did, that the real problem was to
control, but not to suppress the new energies of the
Revolution. Nor did he ever attain the momentary flash
of insight that permitted Wordsworth to comprehend
the part nationality must play in the new world. He
felt the need of discipline as he had felt the need of

[1] *Colloquies on the Progress and Prospects of Society*, vol. i, p. 30.

freedom. He could never reconcile them, because they are reconcilable only in the intellect; and Southey never used his intellect for purposes of reconciliation. Instead, he used it to defend a haphazard collection of political expedients designed to curb specific instances of human cruelty. But he had the impatience of the man of action, and brought to the defence of all sorts of institutions the crusading zeal, the contempt for the other side, the conviction of righteousness that is more often seen in attack than in defence of social institutions. Hazlitt said bitterly of him that he had lost his way in Utopia and found it in Old Sarum. It was the same road.

But one cannot thus bitterly take leave of Southey. His faults are buried in his books. That remarkable farrago *The Doctor* is a work not unworthy of its author, a helter-skelter assembly of odds and ends, of bad puns and worse pedantry, of childish jokes and grown-up sentiment. And yet one cannot study the man sincerely without feeling that he preserves through it all a very high quality which is best denoted as soundness. Perhaps it is because he frankly admits that he has not a philosophic mind; perhaps because he is not vain enough to be modest about his work. But chiefly it is because of that quality of human goodness in him which has allowed the man to survive the poet. It is a quality that can hardly be illustrated by extracts. But something of it appears in a letter which he wrote in reply to a request that he write an article on the Spanish situation for the first number of the *Quarterly* :

' I have not the sort of talent requisite for writing a political pamphlet upon the state of Spain ; these things require a kind of wire-drawing which I have never learnt to perform, and a method of logical reasoning to which my mind has never been habituated, and for which I feel no natural aptitude. What I feel about Spain you know ; what I think about it is this—the country has much to suffer, in all probability there will be many and dreadful defeats of the patriots. . . . Joseph will very likely be crowned at Madrid, and many of us may give up the cause of

Spanish independence as lost. But so surely as God liveth, and
as the spirit of God liveth and moveth in the hearts of men, so
surely will that country eventually work out its own redemp-
tion.' [1]

This is not clever ; it has not proved quite true in the
event. But it could have been written by no shallow
man, no unsound man, no bad man, but only by a good,
and perhaps a wise man.

4

If the Lake poets are to be taken at their own estimate
they are not safe guides for the historian seeking to learn
what common men thought and felt in their day. Wordsworth is responsible for a theory of literary martyrdom,
whereby no poet could possibly be great unless he were
at once reviled and neglected by his fellow-men. As
Wordsworth was a great poet he happily found a suitable
persecutor in Jeffrey. Coleridge and Southey, too,
thought of themselves as bold speculators far ahead of
their contemporaries, and gloried in being misunderstood.
Leslie Stephen in his essay on Landor has lightly put an
end to Wordsworth's general theory. Yet even now
poets are not uncommonly held to gain poetic power
from contempt and neglect. The Lake poets retain the
credit of martyrdom. But even if Wordsworth, Coleridge,
and Southey were neglected by their contemporaries
their ideas are none the less representative of their age.
For in less than a generation from the deaths of most of
them, and while one of them was still physically, if not
poetically alive, they were all admitted to the public's
Parnassus ; and it is incontestable that the ideas and
even the tastes of one generation originate in the most
active elements in the generation preceding. But Wordsworth and his friends were certainly not neglected as
Chatterton, for instance, was neglected. Like all innovators they were abused by some critics with a bitterness

---

[1] *Life and Correspondence*, vol. iii, pp. 182–3.

in proportion to their success; and again, like all innovators, they readily acquired a following whose flattery
knew no such proportion, and who were well aware that
the friend of the misunderstood is indeed a friend. It would
be easy to show from the journals of the day how seriously
the Lake poets were taken as men of letters. But our
immediate concern is with their credit as political writers.

To their fellow-men of letters, at least, they seemed
to possess sober political wisdom. Lockhart thought
Coleridge's *Constitution of Church and State* ' a store-
house of grand and immovable principles ' ;[1] and of
Southey he wrote in 1842 :

> ' What a wonderful political writer Southey was ! On looking
> back now to his articles of thirty or twenty years ago, how few
> are there of the questions now pressing that he had not foreseen
> the progress of ! His views were always for the paternal manage-
> ment of the poor people. He knew how easily they might be
> kept right if their hearts were appealed to by those above him.'[2]

De Quincey writes eloquently of the ability that has
wasted itself on newspapers, and concludes :

> ' Worlds of fine thinking lie buried in that vast abyss . . . but
> nowhere, throughout its shoreless magazines of wealth, does
> there lie such a bed of pearls, confounded with the rubbish and
> *purgamenta* of ages as in the political papers of Coleridge.'[3]

Nor do their enemies withhold their tribute of dislike.
Byron referred to Wordsworth as ' this new Jacob
Behmen, this . . . whose pride might have kept him true,
even had his principles turned as perverted as his soi-
disant poetry '.[4] *Don Juan* was sardonically dedicated
to Southey in lines that Murray refused to print. The
dedication was, however, struck off as a broadside, and,
Southey complains, circulated at large among the people
for political purposes.[5] Hazlitt seems obsessed with the

---

[1] *Quarterly Review*, January 1834, p. 37.
[2] *Croker Papers* (1884), vol. ii, p. 412.
[3] De Quincey, *Works* (ed. Masson, 1889), vol. ii, p. 187.
[4] Byron, *Letters* (ed. Prothero, 1898–1904), vol. iv, p. 238.
[5] *Correspondence of Southey with Caroline Bowles*, p. 270.

idea that the Lake poets were the chief prop of the Liverpool administration. If every passage against the politics of that ' whiffling turncoat ', Wordsworth, that ' whining monk ', Southey, and that ' maudlin, Methodistical lay-preacher ', Coleridge, were reprinted from his works, a fair-sized volume would doubtless result.[1]

So much for the opinions of men of letters. But they may well exaggerate the influence of their kind. If, indeed, the test of the political value of their work is to lie in their relations with statesmen they do not come off very well. Wordsworth met Fox on several occasions. But we have Rogers's word for it that all the statesman said to the poet on their first meeting was, ' I am very glad to see you, Mr. Wordsworth, though I am not of your faction '.[2] Fox also tried, courageously but unsuccessfully, to read *Madoc*. Coleridge played a larger part in the life of the Whig leader, for Fox paid him the compliment of believing that his articles in the *Morning Post* in 1802, urging a renewal of the war, were by Mackintosh, and referred to them in the House of Commons as one of the causes of the rupture of the Peace of Amiens. Coleridge, himself, thought still more of the importance of these articles, and imagined that agents of Napoleon were seeking his life in revenge for them.[3] At Holland House the poets were known ; and Lord Holland threw off an epigram on the new laureate :

> Our Laureate Bob defrauds the king.
> He takes his cash and does not sing ;
> Yet on he goes, I know not why,
> Singing for us who do not buy.[4]

Lady Holland notes in her *Journal* : ' I hear nothing but of Coleridge, which makes me regret not being acquainted with him.'[5] In their Jacobin days, at least,

---

[1] Hazlitt, *Works* (ed. Waller and Glover, 1902–4), vol. iii, pp. 311–12 written in 1818, in a review of Moore's *Fudge Family in Paris*.

[2] Rogers, *Table Talk* (1903), p. 55.

[3] Coleridge, *Biographia Literaria* (1847), vol. i, p. 222 *n*.

[4] Moore, Thomas, *Journal* (1853–6), 8 September 1825 (vol. ii).

[5] Lady Holland, *Journal* (1908), vol. ii, p. 238.

the poets were objects of interest to another Whig statesman, for Lord Grey wrote to a friend to ask him to send
' Southey's and Coleridge's poems; those gentlemen being
interesting young enthusiasts in the Democratic cause '.[1]

On the Tory side we learn that Canning said of the
Tract on the Convention of Cintra that ' he could not
deny that Wordsworth had spoken with the bone of
truth '.[2] The poet himself is our authority for this,
and also for the astonishing statement that the *Idiot Boy*
was an especial favourite of Canning's.[3] Neither Wordsworth nor Coleridge, however, was ever admitted to
the ranks of those who made Tory policy. Southey was
on the outer edges of this inner circle. He was apparently respected by his fellow reviewer, John Wilson
Croker, a humdrum politician, but nevertheless a politician and concerned with affairs as well as with books.
Among the very important class that found its political
leader in Wilberforce, Southey was held in honour.
Indeed, Wilberforce himself found in him a ' moral
sublimity ' lacking in other poets.[4] Southey worked
quietly and helpfully with a man whose labours, less
striking than those of the men who impose themselves
on political history, are perhaps more useful to a world
which has to live as well as to write its history. Lord
Ashley admired the *Colloquies on the Progress and Prospects of Society*, and asked the assistance of their author
in his efforts to improve English factory legislation.[5] It
must altogether be admitted that Southey gave valuable
aid in the work of rescuing the Tory party from the
Eldonian tradition. But he was not liked by those in the
tradition. To Wellington is given the *mot* which destroys
him: ' I do not think much of Southey,' said the
Duke.[6]

[1] Trevelyan, *Lord Grey of the Reform Bill* (1920), p. 103.
[2] Knight, *Life of Wordsworth* (1889), vol. iii, p. 229.
[3] Ibid., vol. i, p. 499.
[4] *Correspondence of William Wilberforce* (1840), vol. ii, p. 230.
[5] Southey, *Life and Correspondence*, vol. v, pp. 5–6.
[6] Rogers, *Recollections* (1859), p. 205.

If we turn from politicians, always too much interested
in themselves to be quite trustworthy witnesses as to how
the world is running, to the newspapers and periodicals,
we find abundant evidence of the existence of a public
to whom the political thought of Lake poets is known.
Not even the stillborn *Tract on the Convention of Cintra*
entirely escaped notice. It was reviewed in the *British
Critic*, which remarks on the ' generous spirit which this
pamphlet breathes and the knowledge of human nature
it evinces '.[1] Long before the Laureateship Wordsworth
was quoted. A passage from the *Cintra* is in the *Quarterly*
for 1815 ;[2] a political sonnet is brought forward in
a leader in the *Morning Chronicle* in 1821 ;[3] and another
sonnet, as a climax of glory, was quoted in the House in
the debates on the Reform Bill.[4] *Blackwood's* had found
that Wordsworth ' shows how virtue, religion, independence, and freedom are the ministers of morality, and
that the science of politics is simple to the wise and
good '.[5]

Coleridge was a journalist of reputation. His *Sonnets
on Eminent Men* appeared in the *Morning Chronicle* for
December 1794, and roused one friend of liberty to
compose some admiring verses beginning :

To S. T. C.

How the warm soul with indignation glows :—
    How VIRTUE mingles horror with delight,
When thy nerv'd lines seize on thy Country's Foes,
    And drag the lurking felons into light ![6]

Cobbett, still the patriotic and respectable Peter
Porcupine, writes of him to Windham as ' Poet Coleridge,
a not uncelebrated Jacobin '.[7] Nor was he less cele-

---

[1] *British Critic*, September 1809.
[2] *Quarterly Review*, 1815, p. 234.
[3] *Morning Chronicle*, 8 February 1821.
[4] *Parliamentary History*, Series III, vol. iii, p. 293.
[5] *Blackwood's Edinburgh Magazine*, August 1822.
[6] *Morning Chronicle*, 27 December 1794.
[7] Melville, *Life of Cobbett* (1913), vol. i, p. 171.

brated in after years as a Tory. Wilson, in *Blackwood's*, attests his popularity while he doubts his sincerity. ' The truth is ', he wrote, ' that Mr. Coleridge has lived, as much as any man of his time, in literary and political society, and that he has sought every opportunity of keeping himself in the eye of the public as restlessly as any charlatan who ever exhibited on the stage.' [1] By 1830 he had so far succeeded in impressing himself on the thought of the time that, in a leader in the *Morning Chronicle* on education, the ' mystical writers of the Coleridge school ' are contrasted with clear-thinking men like Jefferson, and it is admitted that the strength of the former school must be respected.[2]

But it is Southey who figures most largely in the pages of English journals. It was his fate, in spite of his academic tastes and tranquil life at Keswick, to be as much attacked for his politics as if he had been a cabinet minister. His Jacobin years were quiet enough, and he appears as an obscure ' Bristol poet ' and contributor to the *Morning Post*, in whose pages [3] many unreprinted poems of his, translations from the Spanish and Portuguese, simple democratic ballads, and inscriptions for historic spots, lie buried, awaiting the new life modern pedantry can bring to ancient dullness. But Southey's conversion to a new political faith was so complete, and Southey himself such an excellent butt, that he became the favourite mark for Whig satirists. After the publication of *Wat Tyler* no shaft could possibly miss him. Hone reprinted *Wat Tyler* in a cheap edition, with an introduction calling attention to the fact that Southey had written other pieces, like the *Battle of Blenheim*, well calculated to spread the spirit of radicalism in 1817. Joseph Hume said in Parliament that 30,000 copies of this edition were sold at once, chiefly among the

---

[1] *Blackwood's Edinburgh Magazine*, October 1817.
[2] *Morning Chronicle*, 1 January 1830.
[3] *Morning Post*, 28 May, 10 July, 25 July, 12 October 1798 ; 23 April, 1 May, 1799, etc.

discontented poor.[1]   Byron saw fit to remark that *Wat Tyler* was the best thing Southey ever wrote.[2]   Most of the jibes at the unfortunate laureate, however, are verbose, in bad taste, and not worth quoting.   For honesty's sake, let us have one :

> When the Court and Land has differ'd
> Call in S[outhe]y, call in G[iffor]d,
> S[outhe]y will explain the evil,
> G[iffor]d will whitewash the devil.
> Scribbling colleagues, do not slacken,
> G[iffor]d bite, and S[outhe]y blacken.
> Do not spare John Bull, but bang him,
> If he tries to reason, hang him ;
> And if hanging will not do,
> Try the *Quartering Review*.[3]

Cobbett's contempt for Southey and his colleague Gifford is more downright—' bloody guillotiners of reformers ',[4] he calls them.   Even across the Channel Southey contrived to make political enemies, and a French pamphleteer concludes a tirade : ' Ce n'est pas moi qui prétends mal parler de M. Southey ; sa vie et ses œuvres sont la satire la plus sanglante de lui-même.' [5]   It was left for Hazlitt, whose fine critical intelligence so often and so successfully overcame even his taste for invective, to discern the love of humanity, the hatred of poverty and oppression that made up Southey's Toryism. Southey's articles, he writes, leaven the *Quarterly*, and go to show that ' once a philanthropist, always a philanthropist '.[6]

The Lake Poets are now a part of our education ; as abstractions, they go to make up our abstract view of

---

[1] *Hansard*, New Series, vol. ix, p. 1379.

[2] Parry, *Last Days of Lord Byron* (1826), p. 221.

[3] *Morning Chronicle*, 9 June 1817 ; also 13 February 1819 ; 10 January 1823 ; 14 August 1823 ; 1 January 1824 ; 17 December 1824.   *Examiner*, 26 September 1813.

[4] Cobbett's *Political Register*, 29 March 1817.

[5] A. R., *Essai sur la constitution pratique et le parlement d'Angleterre* (Paris, 1821), pp. vii–viii.

[6] Hazlitt, *Spirit of the Age*, Essay on Southey.

life. The *Life of Nelson* has joined with Livy to teach
English schoolboys civic virtue. Coleridge and Wordsworth have helped to make that posthumous son of the
Age of Reason, John Stuart Mill, a feeling Victorian like
his contemporaries. Coleridge dead has entered into an
Oxford movement he could hardly have approved alive.
He has influenced many men—Sterling, Maurice, New-
man, Dr. Arnold—though he has not achieved the
difficult task his daughter hopefully marked out for him
when she wrote : 'I have often heard that the more
intellectual among the Americans have begun to study
my father's writings—every condition of society has its
besetting sins, and for those which attend upon the state
of things in America, it is thought that these metaphysical productions [of Coleridge]'s will afford a powerful
remedy.'[1] Wordsworth resumed his Tyrtaean role in
the last war.[2] But this final fame and influence need
concern us only in so far as it enables us to fix the position
of Wordsworth, Coleridge, and Southey in the Revolution which came over England in their lifetime. A passage
from a modern historian gives a clue to this position.
Mr. Trevelyan writes : 'Even if we regard the war
against Republican France as having been forced on us
by the French Jacobins, we must at least feel that it
has indeed proved the tragedy that Fox, Grey, and
Wordsworth then believed it to be.'[3] It is not difficult
to imagine the laughter such an association of names
would have caused during the Regency. Wordsworth
was then only a poet to most men, and not a great one.
We can now see his true position, and that of his fellows
of the Lakes : morally, politically, artistically, he was
not a member of the group or groups that directed
English life ; but he was a member of a group that had
already half won over the floating indecisive spirits that

[1] Sara Coleridge to Thomas Poole, 5 September 1834, B. M. Adds.
35344, f. 104.
[2] Dicey, *Statesmanship of Wordsworth* (1917).
[3] Trevelyan, *Lord Grey of the Reform Bill* (1920), p. 72.

at any moment form the bulk of a people, a group that was destined to a rapid and decisive victory. The Wordsworth who wrote the *Convention of Cintra* was after all a prophet : but he did not sing in a wilderness.

5

Wordsworth, Coleridge, and Southey were throughout their lives in close agreement as to politics ; and it is this agreement among men so different in character and so alike in social origin that gives their political thought importance. What they may differ over in politics can perhaps be dismissed as the result of the artistic temperament ; the far more fundamental things on which they agree are undoubtedly common to their class. As Jacobins and as Tories these poets are, after all, educated Englishmen of the middle class. If it is ever safe to come to any merely logical conclusion about as vague and unincorporate a society as that which writers still apologetically call the middle class, then the political careers of the Lake poets may be said to provide material for such conclusions.

On the eve of the French Revolution the English middle class was prosperous, and free to use the opportunities of the industrial revolution to become still more prosperous. From De Foe to Johnson it had steadily developed a civilization of its own, in which common sense ever approached nearer to the systematic restraint and mechanical rigidity we like to see in the Age of Reason. So at least it seemed to our young poets. All three young men went up to the Universities, where the inadequacies of eighteenth-century England were apparently rather caricatured than exhibited. There they were impelled to proclaim aloud a belief doubtless born of the contrast between their natural youth and their unnatural university education, that the facts and ideals of English life, the government, the society, the literature of Georgian England, demanded reformation. They

would not, like Johnson, rest content with a *bourgeois*
adaptation of aristocratic reasonableness. They and
their comrades in youth sought aesthetic and philosophic expression for the aspirations, the gropings, the
blind desires of thousands of their fellows who knew
nothing of the official philosophy of the day but its
constraint.

The French Revolution drove much of this activity
into political channels. In the hasty codification of the
new demands much was inserted that frightened sober
spirits, and it would seem that the English middle class
has repudiated its prophets. But those who held to the
doctrines of the Revolution until the advent of Bonaparte
were the real representatives of their class. Now that
that class and its philosophy have come to dominate,
who are the heroes of the State Trials of 1794 ? Hardy,
the cobbler founder of the London Corresponding
Society, accused of treason for his efforts to raise the
standards of his class, or Reeves of the ' Association for
preserving liberty and property against republicans and
levellers ? ' Erskine, the advocate for the accused
Radicals, or Scott (later Lord Eldon) their prosecutor ?
The general sympathy now prevailing for the more
moderate English Jacobins surely arises from a conviction that they held fast to principles justified by their
ultimate success.

That success was achieved in politics with surprising
ease in 1832 ; and it was achieved because in economic life
there had never been any serious checks to the expansive
spirit that made the Revolution all through the Western
world. In terms no doubt falsely simple, what happened
was this : men everywhere sought to do something, or
make something, or find something, new ; but newness
is unlawful in a society that has erected past experience
into logic, and logic into law ; men were therefore
forced into revolt, and freedom became worth a struggle.
But in England a certain kind of freedom could be had
without fighting. The inhabitant of Manchester was

not free to vote ; but he was free to build a factory and a fortune, and if he possessed to a great degree this nameless energy that has made the modern world, he need not despair of success though his birth be of the humblest.   Now, the anarchical consequences of this expansive movement were perhaps less obvious in England, where it was purely economic at first, than in France, where it was also political, but once distinguished, these consequences were so shocking as to cast doubt on the goodness of the force that had produced them. Freedom seemed to mean in France and in England that the strong man, or perhaps the lucky man, was to be free to force weaker men to give him new delights, new luxury, new strength.   This was not the novelty the Lake poets had intended.   They recognized that new things must also be good things, and that the test of goodness is unfortunately but unavoidably in human experience.   They became Conservatives.

If, indeed, their conservative politics differed in no way from the conservatism of the *Essay on Man*, there would be little use in studying the political thought of the English romanticists.   But, on the whole, it is a new conservative faith, the faith of men who wish to preserve something more in literature than the standards of Pope, and something more in politics than the aspirations of *The Patriot King*.   It is a new faith first of all because, born of unrest, it would keep its birthright.   Coleridge, lecturing on the Gothic mind, describes first the cold, formal limits within which the Greek mind was imprisoned, and continues to a sympathetic audience of Northmen.   ' But no statue, no artificial emblem, could satisfy the Northman's mind ; the dark, wild imagery of nature which surrounded him, and the freedom of his life, gave his mind a tendency to the infinite, so that he found rest in that which presented no end, and derived satisfaction from that which was indistinct.'

Whether this is a paradox in fact as it is a paradox in form time alone will tell.   At any rate Coleridge and

his fellows sought to live up to it, and, under the name
of Progress, the modern world has held the same faith
for over a century. They believed that although this
unchecked pouring out of oneself in feeling may degene-
rate into anarchy, and the abolition of moral distinctions,
it may also be guided into unselfishness and into genuine
conformity with morality. But it must itself produce
that guide; the old forms of discipline, the old aristocratic reason, are of little avail in restraining this new
force. In this belief they sought for objects to which
men could become attached, objects stable in themselves but capable of slow growth through the devoted
efforts of men. This attachment must be mystic; that
is, men by a mystic surrender of their freedom to the
service of the loved object must feel that this surrender
has really added to their freedom by adding to their
importance. The nation, the Church of England, the
romantic traditions of the Middle Ages, the family, all
seemed to these poets objects worthy of loyalty; and
around them they cast an atmosphere of what in Germany
is called ' Gemütlichkeit ', and in England ' middle-class
morality '. Men brought up in this atmosphere were
distinguished by a love of social and political order,
a pride in England, a devotion to the Church, a strong
domesticity, a distrust for any logic but that of common
sense, a strain of humanitarianism, a certainty in human
progress. In business they still believed in disorder,
competition, and themselves; there they had not found
rest in unrest by any loyalty to something more than
the individual. But their love of ethical and political
order helped to balance their trust in economic disorder,
and England was the stabler for it.

III

TORY AND RADICAL

SCOTT was born a Tory, and died a Tory; Hazlitt was born a Radical, and died a Radical. The two writers have at least consistency in common. This quality is a useful standard of measurement in a period so full of change as that from the outbreak of the French Revolution to the Reform Bill of 1832. Scott was born into Jacobite traditions, and bred to the conservative profession of the Law. He was of a distinguished family—he preferred, indeed, to refer to it as a clan—and professed the episcopalian faith. Everything thus conspired to make him an unfailing supporter of tradition, of permanence, of things as they are. Hazlitt, however, grew up amid dissent from dissent. His father was a Unitarian minister, and an Irishman to boot. The boy spent part of his youth in the United States, whither the elder Hazlitt had gone at the end of the successful American revolution. But Channing had not yet made New England a paradise for Unitarian ministers, and Hazlitt was obliged to return to England for lack of a flock. So the younger Hazlitt grew up in a lonely Shropshire town a rebellious subject of his king, filled with republican zeal for the betterment of mankind.

Here, then, are two men who enter active life with their political beliefs firmly fixed. They hold these beliefs, and the outward allegiances that express them, throughout their lives. But what is fixed in them is perhaps peculiar to their age. Is there not a common quality in their ethical and political thought, something that distinguishes them from the politician of Queen Anne's day as surely as there is something common to

their art that distinguishes them from Addison and
Pope? This is the problem. Scott and Hazlitt, in their
consistency, serve as excellent gauges of the force of the
Revolution in ideas.

I

Mark Twain used to attribute much of the unpro-
gressiveness, aristocratic pretensions, and false chivalry
of the southern states of America to the universal habit
of reading and acting upon the Scotch novels. Be that
as it may the world has certainly not failed to discern
a political gospel in the tales of Scott. 'The political
bearing of the Scotch novels has been a considerable
recommendation to them', wrote Hazlitt in 1825;[1] and
in the next generation, Ruskin could say: 'From my
own masters, then, Scott and Homer, I learned the
Toryism which my best afterthought has only served to
confirm.'[2] It is not, of course, that the novels are at
all what we have lately become so well acquainted with
as the novel of propaganda. They have as little resem-
blance in content as in form with the *New Machiavelli*
or *Joan and Peter*. They set forth a Tory view of life,
not a Tory programme. It is a view evident in the
choice of subjects for the novels and in their settings.
Whether the scene be laid in the court of Prince Charlie,
or in the England of Richard Cœur de Lion, or in the
struggles of the Crusaders, the same glory is cast about
the heads of princes, the same tribute paid to those who
serve loyally and without question, the same attempt is
made to show man at his best when most conforming to
the usages and institutions of society. 'I am no politician', says the Major in *Old Mortality*, 'and I do not
understand nice distinctions. My sword is the king's,
and when he commands, I draw it in his cause.'[3]

[1] Hazlitt, *Works*, vol. iv, pp. 248–9.
[2] Ruskin, *Works* (ed. Cook and Wedderburn, 1907), vol. xxvii, p. 168.
[3] *Old Mortality*, vol. ii, Chap. IV (references to the Waverley Novels
are to the Border Edition, 1893–4).

Without tainting his art with anything so false to it and to life as systematic defence of a set of abstract political principles, Scott does, then, manage to leave the impression that one way of life is better than another, that a society based on the old idea of personal submission to an external authority is better than one based on the modern idea of personal freedom, as far as possible, from all authority. How he produces this impression must be evident in a dozen passages in any of the novels. No insistent partisanship is intruded into the sweeping description of the Porteous Riot in *The Heart of Midlothian.* But how differently would a Whig like Macaulay have treated them! What a lesson of civic virtue he would have taught us, of British love of liberty and hatred of oppression! There is none of this in Scott. The mob is a set of unruly rebels and dour Cameronians, not unmixed with still more unpleasant elements, and by no means inspired with high ideals of civic virtue.

There was room within the capacious limits of the Waverley Novels, however, for even more direct communication of political wisdom to the reader. Scott would hardly have been so popular with his public had he not inserted a few brief sermons and moral aphorisms from time to time. These, unlike their fellows in modern programme novels, are so far from being inextricable from the body of the work that collections of them have actually been published under such attractive titles as *Diamonds from the Waverley Mines.* It is commonly supposed by the youth who now form the greater part of Scott's audience that these passages were designed to be skipped. But it is not unlikely that many of his Georgian readers found as much profit as pleasure in bits like ' Even an admitted nuisance of ancient standing should not be abated without some caution ',[1] or ' Nature has her laws which seem to apply to the social as well as to the vegetable system. It appears to be a general rule, that what is to last long should be slowly

[1] *Guy Mannering*, vol. i, p. 53.

matured and gradually improved, while every sudden
effort, however gigantic, to bring about the speedy
execution of a plan calculated to endure for ages is
doomed to exhibit symptoms of premature decay from
its very commencement.'[1]

It is no easy task to arrange systematically these
political opinions, scattered as they are through so many
novels, journals, essays, and letters. Scott himself would
never have taken so revolutionary a step as the organization
of his ideas in any field. He hates ' philosophers ' as
Burke had hated ' metaphysicians ', and insists that the
pursuit of abstract knowledge in politics is foreign to the
British race. He cannot be consistently dogmatic even
about party. At one moment he talks about ' Whig
dogs ', and asserts the impossibility of living under their
rule[2]; at another he refers to Whig and Tory as the
two stays which, by straining in opposite directions, keep
the mast of state upright;[3] and when thoroughly
frightened at the progress of the Radicals, he insists
that there is no difference at all between Whig and
Tory.[4] He does indeed hold views on the dangers of
government without party by the mere exercise of royal
prerogative that would have shocked Swift and Johnson,
his predecessors as leaders of literary Tories ; but this is
no more than an indication of the debt owed by the
Toryism of 1820 to Wilkes and the Whiggism of 1765.
Scott was of course an opponent of Reform, humanitarian
as well as political. Prison reform he could not approve
except it imitate the ways of a captain reforming a
mutinous ship by discipline of the strictest sort. Although
he was willing to countenance well-governed attempts to
teach the people to read the Bible, he thought Joseph
Lancaster ' a mountebank '.[5] He was always quite
willing to grant Catholic Emancipation. For, he argued,
since we tolerate the Roman Catholics at all, there is

[1] *Count Robert of Paris*, Chap. I.
[2] *Familiar Letters* (1894), vol. i, p. 170.   [3] *Visionary* (1819), p. 5.
[4] *Journal* (1890), vol. ii, p. 91.   [5] Ibid., pp. 126–7.

no need to bother about such little pin-pricks as deprivation of political rights. The great mistake was in not
rooting the Roman Church out completely; but that
mistake is now irretrievable.[1] It must be added that he
showed himself occasionally capable of being what many
another British Tory has been, a good Liberal in the
politics of foreign countries. He points out in his *Life
of Napoleon* the impetus that had been given to the
unification of Italy and Germany by the rule of Napoleon,
and warmly expresses his hope that these two countries
may before long achieve national unity.[2]

Scott never embodied his political ideas in the form
of a treatise; but he was once persuaded to join the
' paper war on anarchy ', and in 1819 published anony-
mously a little pamphlet, the *Visionary*, directed against
the Radical heresies of the time. It is very slight, and
in its gentle condescension to a misguided but essentially
loyal people it reminds one of its author reproving
a mischievous collie, or Mrs. Hannah More reforming
a Somersetshire miner. But it is as good a piece of
Scott's political mind as can be found, and will prepare
us for the ungrateful task of judging as a whole a body
of political thought never conceived by its author to be
more than fragmentary.

In his first vision Scott sees an old castle on a com-
manding site. Vitruvius Whigham, an architect, is
inspecting the building. He has just decided that a few
old garrets which now serve no real purpose, and are
not in the style of the rest of the building, must be
pulled down, when up comes an angry mob of villeins
bent on pulling down the whole castle for the sake of
plunder. The garrison of the castle prepare for defence.
Whigham, however, tries to mediate, and urges the
crowd to help him pull down the garrets, and then go

[1] Lockhart, *Life of Sir Walter Scott* (ed. Macmillan, 1900), vol. iv,
pp. 203–4.
    [2] *Life of Napoleon*, in *Miscellaneous Prose Works* (1834–71), vol. xvi,
p. 342.

home, leaving the rest of the castle untouched. The leaders of the mob pretend to fall in with this plan, and suggest that Whigham join his friends in the castle and let down the drawbridge. This he prepares to do, not with treacherous intent towards his good friends in the castle, but obsessed with his desire to pull down the garrets. At this horrible juncture Scott awakes and is spared for the moment from witnessing the destruction of society through Whig treason.

He soon falls again into a troubled sleep. He seems to wake in a barren but not unfamiliar land ; it is Scotland, now the prey of the victorious Radicals. He learns this unhappy truth from a brutish scoundrel with matted hair and ragged clothes who offers to be his guide. He walks along with this creature through a most desolate landscape of waste fields and ruined cottages. He learns that after the successful revolution the victors had quarrelled among themselves, and that three-quarters of the population of the British Isles had perished in the resulting disturbances. He comes to a seaport, but sees not a ship in the harbour. No hammer is heard in the deserted shipyards. Capital once destroyed is never replaced. 'We do not so much care for the want of capital', says one of the citizens of this Radical state, 'for it is our maxim that a man had better starve as a master than live in plenty as a domestic.' Wealth, now mostly reduced to land, has been equally divided ; but it has been found necessary to redistribute it every quarter in order to get rid of the difference between rich and poor.

Arriving at the capital city, which has been largely reduced to ruins, Scott finds a crowd gathered to elect the executive head of the state. He learns from the confidences of a popular orator that the people continue to show themselves gullible fools. The ballot had been tried, but the ballot-box was invariably found stuffed with many more votes than there had been voters. The extension of the franchise had meant merely an extension of bribery. He witnesses a brawling election amidst open corruption and all sorts of drunken disorder. Suddenly a column of soldiers appears, takes possession of the hustings, and declares its Colonel elected head of the republic. The people remonstrate, but the Colonel threatens force and is accepted. The land of the Radicals is under military dictatorship.

Now, this conviction that democracy must inevitably end in disorder to be quelled only by military dictatorship has been a part of the stock-in-trade of Conservatives since Western civilization began. It suggests what is after all the chief interest of Sir Walter's politics for us. Are they normal Conservative politics, timeless and changeless because the expression of an eternal type of human being, as true for Aristophanes as for Professor Saintsbury? Or do they show the mark of the great Revolution which was building machines, overturning thrones, founding faiths, creating nations? To both questions a qualified affirmative must be given. Scott was a Conservative by instinct, as no doubt was Aristophanes ; but the Revolution had so far sway over his instincts that he differed greatly in his politics from the Conservatives of the preceding generations. He cannot claim exemption from the lot which makes us all resultants of the forces of time and eternity.

As for what is eternal in this matter there is surely other authority for the division of mankind into Liberals and Conservatives than that of the guardsman in *Iolanthe*. The division is not perhaps as between black and white ; but even in the neutral greys the line can be drawn. In any society Scott must have been rather for what is accepted than for what is trying to get itself accepted. But he had the good fortune to be born into a very honourable position in a comfortable provincial society, and to attain by his literary skill a still more honourable position. He was a satisfied man, and not of the stuff of rebels. He ' had, as it were, no message whatever to deliver to the world, wished not the world to elevate

itself, to amend itself, to do this or to do that, except
simply pay him for the books he kept writing '.[1] Carlyle
himself was much too fond of bullying the world into
amending itself, and this judgement of his fellow countrymen is not quite fair. But it does bring out the fact
that Scott was no reformer, that his was the real conservatism of content.

To go no further into Scott than the well-fed country
gentleman, however, is to repeat Carlyle's injustice, and
to make the too easy assumption that all prosperous
Conservatives are callous men, indifferent to the world's
sufferings. Scott was honestly, and not superficially, a
disciple of Burke. He was not blind, as too many
a Liberal has been blind, to the part played in men's
lives by desire, by prejudice, by love and hate, and other
illiberal motives. His own mind was too obviously a
part of this disorder for him to deny its existence ; yet
he instinctively sought for some principle of order. The
more deeply he felt about the men and women of the
border balladry, the more whole-heartedly he became
absorbed in ' old, unhappy, far-off things ', the more all
human life seemed, like these, chaotic and unresting.
When he turned to the observation of civil society, its
ordered institutions seemed little short of miraculous,
growing up out of the disorder of human passions, and
yet somehow immune from their unhappy flux. It is
the imagination, and not the intellect, that resists change,
for only to the imagination is it given to see the odds
against which the intellect must struggle. To Scott,
as to his master Burke, society was law divinely imposed
on the anarchy of Nature. He was most sincerely convinced that the British Constitution was a dispensation
of Providence. With the Christian religion it is all that
stands between man and the passions that must ever
consume him. It is the product of ages of human
experience directed in accordance with the divine will ;
and that will works in man through these very passions

[1] Carlyle, *Works* (Centenary edition, 1896–9), vol. xxix, p. 54.

that are in themselves so destructive. Any society is
a holy thing because men believe in it ; and belief
soothes, where knowledge irritates, the passions. A social
order is not, therefore, rashly to be amended simply
because so untrustworthy a faculty as abstract reason
can find fault with it. You destroy it by seeking to
repair it with such a tool ; what you have destroyed is
your anchor, and there is always a storm.

This desperate clinging of the imagination to institutions that are fixed in racial experience is evident through
all the formal rhetoric of Burke. It is a poignant under-
tone in his rather stilted correspondence. And in Scott
it is evident through all the cheerfulness he wore so
naturally. It is seen in his fear of the English manufacturing poor, in his dislike of mobs, in his distrust of
the utilitarian spirit that seeks to make all men alike
because it judges all men alike. Here is a passage of
his on a proposed reform of the Scottish judicial
system :

'Even on a general view, the innovations it sanctioned were
much too rapid and extensive : too little attention was given to
the genius and character of the law of Scotland, and too little
deference paid to the unalterable habits of the people. An
established system is not to be tried by those tests which may,
with perfect correctness, be applied to a new theory. . . . A
philosopher is not entitled to investigate such a system [Scottish
law] by those ideas which he has fixed in his own mind as the
standard of possible excellence. The only unerring test of every
old establishment is the *effect* it has actually produced ; for that
must be held to be good from whence good is derived. The
people have, by degrees, moulded their habits to the law they
are compelled to obey : for some of its imperfections, remedies
have been found ; to others they have reconciled themselves, till,
at last, they have from various causes, attained the objects which
the most sanguine visionary could promise himself from his own
perfect *unembodied* system.' [1]

This is commonplace, and now very far away—farther
from us than anything in Burke. But it is the work of

[1] *Edinburgh Annual Register*, 1808, Part II, pp. 351–7.

a sincere man, to whom Conservatism is a faith. And
faith is more than contentment.

Sir Walter Scott, then, is the eternal Conservative.
But what he wished to conserve was in spite of him
determined by the conditions of his time. We are now
at the heart of our problem. The whole romantic movement has often enough, and not unjustly, been called
the romantic revolt. Scott clearly belongs to the movement ; but equally clearly he never considered himself
as being in revolt against anything. Revolt of any sort
was, indeed, temperamentally distasteful to him. Now
it is possible for a man to wish to change art and leave
society untouched. But such men, it can be said in
general, are able to assume this attitude only because
they are willing to shut themselves up in an ivory tower
and let society go its way. A man who has a lively
interest in his fellows as political beings, however, can
hardly keep his politics and his aesthetics in separate
compartments. If such a man is satisfied with existing
social conditions it can only be because he believes they
fulfil the ideals of his art. This is precisely the case with
Sir Walter. He is a romantic, but he is not in revolt,
because he finds that his contemporaries in the main
sympathize with his view of life.

That is not to say that he is entirely contented with
all that goes on in the England of his day. No man is
ever a complete conformist, except he be a solipsist.
But Scott found that he could live happily in Georgian
society. Now life was to him worth living chiefly because
of its richness and variety. Just as he secured content
from the happy order of society for that inner part of
him that demanded stability, so he drew nourishment
from the disorder of the world for that very large part
of him that craved adventure. He opposed reform not
only because as a gentleman he was satisfied with a society
in which he held so enviable a position, but because as
a romantic he could not be happy in a society without
picturesque gradations and interesting prejudices. Of

one thing we may be sure ; the edifice of Scott's politics is in the Gothic style. It may, indeed, be bad Gothic, like Abbotsford ; but it is no dull Palladian building planned under the influence of that unfeeling political architect, Jeremy Bentham.

For Scott shared the sound English instinct of the time against the simplicity of the Radical plan in politics. Utilitarianism, he felt, was not natural. It did violence to all the old ties, religion, patriotism, family loyalty, that make men a part of something bigger than man. ' Scotland ', he writes to an English friend, ' completely liberalized, as she is in a fair way of being, will be the most dangerous neighbour to England that she has been since 1639. . . . If you *unscotch* us you will find us damn mischievous Englishmen.' [1] Patriotism, narrow and selfish though it seem, is a *natural* feeling, and hence one that makes a good man. Cosmopolitanism is unnatural and makes a bad man, one isolated from his fellows and from their common restraint. Nature is diversity :

' Let us remain as nature made us—Englishmen, Irishmen, Scotchmen—with something like the impress of our several countries upon each ! We would not become better subjects if we all resembled each other like so many smooth shillings. Let us love and cherish each other's virtues—bear with each other's failings—be tender to each other's prejudices, be scrupulously regardful of each other's rights. Lastly, let us borrow each other's improvements, but never before they are needed or demanded. The degree of national diversity between different countries is but an instance of that general variety which Nature seems to have adopted as a principle through all her works, as anxious to avoid, as modern statesmen to enforce, anything like an approach to absolute uniformity.' [2]

Is it necessary to point out how different this Nature is from the rational norm of Pope ? But it is not a Nature that leads men on to revolt. The new Nature—feeling, diversity, unreason, romance—is from the first with Scott, as it came to be with the Lake poets, a bulwark

---

[1] Lockhart, vol. iv, pp. 182–3.
[2] *Miscellaneous Prose Works*, vol. xxi, pp. 373–4.

of defence against the revolt of the unnatural reason that persists in assimilating politics to mathematics and logic, men to machines.

Just as Scott feared the individualism of utilitarian political theory, so he feared the industrial revolution which had been the fruit of utilitarian economic practice. But the advantages of the latter movement were too obvious for him to wish it away. It is true that he writes indignantly of the state of Lancashire in 1820 :

'God's justice is requiting and will yet further requite those who have blown up this country into a state of unnatural opulence at the expense of the health and morals of the lower classes.' [1]

But this is an opinion common to most men of letters, always a trifle jealous of the world of business. Scott never showed any sympathy for the workmen who revolted against their employers. Lockhart has told how large a part his master played in the suppression of labour troubles in Galashiels ; and the preface to the *Visionary* is a sermon to the workpeople on the virtues of the capitalist employer and the rewards of proper submission to his benevolent rule.

In this matter, as in so many others, Scott was content with a characteristic compromise ; he accepted the institution, even though it were an innovation, but he brought himself to *feel* about it as he had felt about older things. Critics and others have wondered at his being at once a Jacobite and a Hanoverian, at the impressive devotion he spent upon the memory of Prince Charles and on the actuality of King George IV. Since the former was as worthy of romantic attachment as the latter was unworthy it has been assumed that Scott knew well how to separate romance and profit. That, of course, is not so. Scott really thought of George IV as a feudal prince, and his loyalty was of the same quality as his loyalty to the Stuarts. The fact that the illusion was profitable made it perhaps the more completely an illusion.

[1] *Journal*, vol. i, p. 313.

So it was with his attitude toward the restless days of the contemporary revolution. He never thought of the feudal age of his ideals as on another plane of reality from the age in which he lived. The good life, the natural life of man, never really changed, because it depended not on things, but on the way men felt about things. Our kings have not ceased to be Richards and Saladins, our women to be Rowenas, our youths to be Quentin Durwards. Nor will they if we keep our minds fresh, and filled with the past. Scott saw this past not crudely as an antidote to the present, but rather as an undistinguishable part of it. The past cannot be known to the senses, but only to the imagination. Yet it is not an illusion. It is only through the life where the past and present are one that man can be free and happy. If man is reduced to the present he can never be happy, because he can never find compensation for the inevitable disappointments of daily life in an imaginative possession of the past achievements of the race. To Scott the adventurous careers of his border ancestors and the quiet existence of the novelist lord of Abbotsford were one. Again an illusion ; but one very close to that illusion by which men are made more than ' the flies of a summer ', and which so many of them have held to be highest truth.

This good life had, of course, to be partly vicarious. Its adventures were undergone in a library chair. But much of any life is vicarious, even of the bad life of the utilitarian philosophers. The point is that these vicarious enjoyments should complement rather than merely continue our ordinary pursuits. If these ordinary pursuits consist in the acquisition of material wealth at expense of our neighbours, then our ideal pursuits must at least be generous and unselfish, or we shall indeed be sorry fellows. Nor is this analysis meant to be cheaply cynical at Scott's expense. It is perfectly clear that Scott's generation—and Scott himself—were occupied in turning their activity to individual profit. This undoubtedly

made every one richer ; but it was a sad scramble, and
some became so much richer than others that it is clear
that they benefited out of all proportion to their labour.
Scott lost in the scramble the money he had made in it.
He bore the loss in a way that was not to be learned
from the struggle itself ; and indeed his whole career
was from the standpoint of contemporary success the
better from the mere fact that he held these impossible
ideals, that he lived vicariously in the Middle Ages. He
was consistently romantic, investing his loyalties to
family, clan, class, and church and country with the
cheating, consoling, steadying support of sentiment. He
was also very successful ; and Abbotsford remains to-day
as much a monument to him as the Waverley Novels.

This compromise of Scott's was not his own. If we
must avoid calling it Victorian, we may at least be permitted to call it that of the English middle class. He
himself would have been deeply hurt by inclusion in any
social group short of the gentry ; but in early nineteenth
century the gentry were well on their way to total
absorption in the growing middle class, following sadly
on the meaningless extension of their title of ' esquire '.
The distinguishing mark of Scott's Conservatism is just
this : it is the Conservatism of a new dominating class ;
it is the Conservatism of the triumphant Revolution.
His Toryism is a mixture of common sense and sentiment,
not like Johnson's a mixture of common sense and reasoning. And this sentiment is that which has come to
pervade English literature since the romantic revolt.
There is even a trace of Rousseau in him. When Jeanie
Deans gets to Lincolnshire on her journey to London,
she is warned of dangers on the road. These, when her
simple Scotch virtue does not comprehend them, are
thus explained to her : ' Ay, but highwaymen, lassie !
for ye are come to a more civilized, that is to say, a more
roguish country than the north.' [1] A little of this belief
in primitive rural simplicity is always present in Scott

[1] *Heart of Midlothian*, Chap. XXVIII.

and in Victorian city-dwellers. So, too, his ethics are those of his class. 'For the poorest man's house has a glory, when there are true hands, a divine heart, and an honest fame.'[1] We should expect the author of these words to be a firm believer in the family and to disapprove of sexual irregularity—though not to the point of being silent on the subject. Now it is hardly necessary to point out that history shows that extreme domesticity and stern disapproval of sexual irregularity are not characteristic of aristocracies. They are part of moral standards spread by religion and literature in the nineteenth century to balance the extreme licence of economic life. They are the standards of the *Waverley Novels*.

But it is useless now to multiply examples. Even Scott's medievalism has the obvious purpose of making men more contented, partly by giving them vicarious outlets for their emotions, partly by inculcating age-old virtues. The lesson of romance —for it had a lesson to Scott and his contemporaries—was conformity. The author of *Waverley* had rescued romance from Monk Lewis and Mrs. Radcliffe and made it comfortable and respectable. It may be worth while as a matter for serious meditation to make the rather facile remark that it thereby ceased to be romantic. The Revolution was not going to be content with Scott's compromise with the past.

2

Almost everything that Hazlitt ever wrote—and being a journalist, he wrote a great deal—is coloured with politics. So active were his political prejudices that they pushed over into all his work, into descriptions of paintings and criticisms of the stage, into notes of travel and memories of youth. Yet it is not easy to describe them, largely because they are so widely dispersed through all his writings. Moreover, Hazlitt's reputa-

[1] *Heart of Midlothian*, Chap. XXVI.

tion has always been that of a dog in the manger, and it is often assumed that his politics are mere snarling. He was simply against every one, we are told ; Castlereagh he hated for a reactionary, Canning for an adventurer, Jeffrey for a trimmer, Bentham for a materialist, Cobbett for a vulgarian and a schismatic, Southey for a turncoat, Leigh Hunt for a butterfly that had got itself broken on the wheel, and was very proud of it. Yet Hazlitt was by no means the surly misanthrope that he appears to be in the literary traditions of a circle so full of sweetness, if not of light, as that of Lamb and Leigh Hunt. His character has had a recent rehabilitator ; and even were he as much of a bear as he has been painted, his political ideas would not be meaningless for us. Had he been the outlawed libertine he seemed to the urbane writers of *Blackwood's* to be, he would yet be significant as an example of the degeneration of the romantic ideal into antinomianism. But it is impossible to study Hazlitt's writings without coming to the conclusion that he had a real desire for conformity, that he wished to work with other men, and that he was by no means lacking in common sense. His writings have at least the objectivity of the printed page. We need not assume them to be abnormal and eccentric because their author was awkward in drawing-rooms, had the misfortune to be fond of housemaids, and could content himself entirely with no man or no party. After all he was an Englishman, and played fives.

Hazlitt's politics have at least the temperamental consistency of the rest of his work. He was always what the French call *frondeur*—a word which is not in the English language, no doubt because it is not in the English Constitution. For him the presumption was always against what was established. He was thus, as we have already observed, at the opposite pole from Scott. But since, like Scott, he made no outward changes in his political allegiance, we must try to follow the subtler differences by which the age set its mark

upon his philosophy. For the whole significance of the
period we are studying is that in it everything grows,
develops, produces something new. Hazlitt may have
been the eternal *frondeur* ; but unless he was also something more common and earthly we have no use for
him now. It is the Hazlitt who expressed his rebellion
by adhering to the ideas of the French Revolution and
who remained faithful to these ideas when the Lake
poets had deserted them, that must interest us. Was
he simply of constant temper, or did the French Revolution have a different meaning for him than for the Lake
poets ?

He was much too young during the great days of the
revolutionary struggle to come to any written conclusion
about the matter. We must content ourselves with his
later rhetoric. ' At this time the light of the French
Revolution circled my head like a glory, though dabbled
with drops of crimson gore ; I walked comfortable and
cheerful by its side

> And by the vision splendid
> Was on my way attended.' [1]

From these memories, and from such fragments as the
following, written at the age of thirteen, we may assume
that he was an enthusiast like any other English Jacobin.

' The man who is a well-wisher to slavery, is always a slave
himself. The King, who wishes to enslave all mankind, is a slave
to ambition. . . . The man who is a well-wisher to liberty wishes
to have men good, and himself to be one of them, and knows
that men are not good unless they are so willingly, and does not
attempt to force them to it, but tries to put them in such a situation as will induce them to be good.' [2]

Godwin, Holcroft, Thelwall, Horne Tooke, and many
others, were known to him, a young and timid disciple.
But his most beloved master was the Reverend Joseph

[1] *Works*, ed. Waller and Glover (1902–4), vol. xii, p. 236.
[2] Hazlitt, W. C., *Four Generations of a Literary Family* (1897), vol. i,
p. 68.

Fawcet, an upright and intelligent man, a humanitarian by instinct and position—he was a dissenter—and the author of a poem, *The Art of War*, which is quite in the orthodox vein of mild literary Jacobinism.

The best approach to Hazlitt's politics, however, is an essay on a *Project for a New Theory of Civil and Criminal Legislation*, begun when he was a fourteen-year-old student at the Unitarian College at Hackney and published long after, no doubt in a much refurbished form, when its author had become well known. Both for the kernel of its thought, which is clearly that of the young enthusiast, and for its modifications, which are clearly those of the old enthusiast, this essay is valuable. It is at any rate our best means of reconstituting the stock of political ideas with which Hazlitt faced the world.[1]

Hazlitt begins with a definition of *a right*. All men have rights in common. Now, since their notions of beauty, goodness, and usefulness all differ, these cannot be the source of rights. *Will* alone is common to all men, and will alone makes a right. That is, a man has theoretically a right to whatever he wants; and for a man alone on a tropical island, this is true in practice. But in society his desires come into conflict with those of other men. Moral justice is the true arbiter between these conflicting desires, and it is through this arbitration that desires become rights. But as men now are, this arbitration is not enough, and political justice must be brought into play. Political justice is cruder than moral justice, and uses force to carry out its decrees.

But we must be careful lest by this introduction of force to decide between warring desires we destroy the rights we are trying to set up with the engine we have devised for erecting them. Political justice implies a police, a government and objective laws—the state, in fact. But the individuals who compose the state exist before the state, since whatever exists in combination

[1] *Works*, vol. xii.

exists beforehand in an elementary condition. Hazlitt
compares the state to a mosaic in which the separate
tiles are persons. Each tile fits tightly into its place,
cannot encroach upon its neighbours, nor be encroached
upon by them. The individual in society has a right to
do as he likes within the bounds of his personality and to
preserve this personality as intact as the tile in the mosaic.
There are thus certain *natural* rights to which all men
must lay claim by the mere fact of their being men.
Political theorists may attack natural rights as much as
they like, the fact of their existence remains ; and they
will only cease to exist when men shall cease to have
wills. Natural rights are simply the materials of the
little fortress within which every man guards the precious
consciousness that he is not as other men. From the
point of view of political justice they are those rights
the infringement of which cannot on any supposition go
unpunished.

Now, the individual in society has these natural rights
to the exercise of his own will ; within them he is as
firmly fixed and independent as the tile in the mosaic.
But unfortunately, men are mobile creatures, and their
relation to society is by no means so simple as this illustration. Granted that a rock-bottomed conviction of
inalienable rights to his animal being, to certain conditions of bare existence, is present to every man, even
to the slave, and that he will prove the existence of those
rights by revolting if deprived of them, there remains
a vast and shadowy domain of conflicting desires seeking
to make themselves rights. The problem of what the
individual can do of his own free will and what the
state can force him to do, the old problem of liberty
and authority, must be faced. To Hazlitt the state was
a mere police power to prevent men of overweening
desires from encroaching on the citadels of other men.
But even he was forced to recognize the fact that the
police power of the state was in itself a right, or at least
a will striving to get itself accepted, and that the very

existence of the state meant that some sort of tribute
must be yielded by the individual in his castle.   He
feared indeed that the payment of the tribute would
wipe out the castle ; and he is always seeking for some
means of strengthening the individual to resist the
state.   An awareness among citizens of the extent of
their personal rights seemed to him the best guarantee
that the state would be kept within the bounds that any
will must have.   The personality of each member of
a state is like a little plot of ground, and his rights are
the walls which guard it ; and so long as those walls
stand, he is a man and a citizen.   For he has the will of
a free man, and the self-respect without which he must
be a slave.   What are the limits of this little plot ?

To comprehend these, says Hazlitt, it is necessary to
see how far a man is complete master of the four things
that he may especially call his own ; his person, his
actions, his property, and his opinions.   As for the right
to his person, that is marked out by its purpose to
' secure to each individual the determination and pro-
tection of that portion of sensation in which he has the
greatest, if not a sole interest, and, as it were, identity
with it '.   This means that he has a right to preserve his
person from bodily harm, and even from nuisances.
The test as to the nuisance is the interest of the person
committing it.   I have a right to preserve my person
from the annoyance of having a drum beaten outside my
window, because such an action is obviously malicious ;
but I have not a similar right to object to a man's playing
on the horn in the next apartment, because he is pre-
sumably doing it for his own benefit, and I would wish
to reserve the same privilege for myself.   Assault, battery,
and nuisance are thus infringements on the rights of the
person, and punishable by law.   But injury to a person
by expression of opinion, slander, and libel ought not to
be punishable by law.   Opinion is free, and no one is
bound to respect me unless he wants to.   My person is
not injured by slander, and my reputation cannot be

defended by physical force. Secondly, as to rights of
action. These have no limits, except the rights of
persons just described, or those of property to be described. Every one has a right to use his own natural
powers as his will impels him as long as he does not
trespass on the equal right of others to do the same.
This principle will operate to curtail existing law. There
will be, for instance, no laws for the enforcement of
morals ; drunkenness, gambling, incontinence are no
concern of the law's, save as they produce actual violence
against individuals. Most decidedly there should be no
laws regulating a man's religion. Thirdly, as to rights of
property. These are necessary because no man can be
secure unless he can appropriate the means of existence
and be sure they will not fail him. Labour is the most
fundamental sort of property, and a man has always a
right to receive a living wage in recompense for his
labour. As for other kinds of property, inheritance or
fair purchase obviously give a right to its possession.
But no one has a right to property taken at the expense
of another. Now the upper classes in the last two
generations have been growing richer, and the poor have
been growing poorer. The individuals comprising the
capitalist class have been infringing on the property
rights of the poor. Hazlitt virtually comes to the conclusion that they should be deprived of their illegitimate
wealth. Finally, as to rights of opinion. These are
unlimited, and no government should attempt to inter-
fere with them.

In Hazlitt's opinion, then, a system of laws can be
constructed ' on the principle of the right of self-defence,
or the security for person, liberty, and property '. This
means a very great diminution in the power of the state
and in the amount of necessary legislation. But it does
not imply anarchy. The individual rights on which the
state is founded are clear enough in respect to their
fundamentals, but there are many marginal rights that
require interpretation ; it is the function of the whole

people, acting under universal suffrage, to decide on the ultimate boundaries of these rights.

This is the work of a true disciple of the Revolution. It is evident that most of the familiar vocabulary of our English Jacobins recurs here. There is no need now to repeat it. Hazlitt has shown himself on the side of revolt because he believes that man is better than society, and that freedom from outer law must mean freedom to follow a better inner law. If one must use the word, the essay is that of a defiant individualist. Moreover, Hazlitt believes rightly that natural rights mean merely that all men make certain demands on society and that in the worst case, if those demands are refused, they will revolt. The first purpose, however, both of practical and theoretical politics, is to locate this *point of revolt*, which differs vastly in different classes and countries. Now Hazlitt, who did not go at things empirically, places these natural rights, this point of revolt, at an absurdly high level. For men sell all but the innermost ward of their citadel and are often content with slavery. If the point of revolt of a given society is very low—that is, if its members will submit to a very great degradation of their manhood before protesting—it is of little use to maintain, as Hazlitt did, that it ought to be very high. It is far better to seek means for improving the conditions of life and in other ways to attempt to increase men's self respect ; for surely a man's natural rights are determined by his nature. Hazlitt—the misanthrope of literary tradition—thinks too well of his fellows. It is the old doctrine of the natural goodness of man.

Yet this is not quite Godwin, nor even Thelwall. Even in this highly theoretical work it is possible to find signs of the intrusion of an outer world that has undergone thirty years of change. One can imagine readily the circumstances of the composition of this ' novel ' theory. Hazlitt in his youth, steeped in the thought of his London Jacobinical circle, set himself to work out for his own use a political creed. The mere fact that he sat down before a sheet of paper to clarify his thoughts and record them, doubtless gave him the illusion of originality. Then, long after, he took up this youthful sketch and sought to revise it in the light of his experience. What he actually did was to attempt to salvage what he could from the destruction time had effected in the essay. The glory of his youth he would preserve at all costs—the thrilling conviction that he had that within him which was above all accident of time and rank and wealth. To the boy the dignity, and hence the happiness, of every one was the first purpose of that revolutionary doctrine which elevated the common man's pride into right. And, stripped of verbiage, what form is left to this doctrine in Hazlitt's mature essay? Simply the conviction dear to the hearts of Englishmen for ages, but never so dear as in the last century, that an Englishman's home is his castle.

For that is really what Hazlitt means with his insistence on the place of the tile in the mosaic. His anarchical defiance of society has been infinitely pared down, and is no longer the vague revolt of the revolutionary enthusiast. Most of the *Project for a New Theory of Civil and Criminal Legislation* had the currency of true folk-wisdom by 1850. And in other respects Hazlitt's later writings give evidence of this almost instinctive modification of the revolutionary gospel of the rights of man into the Victorian gospel of the rights of Englishmen.

In the first place there was the problem of finding some new loyalty to take the place of the old social subordination—a problem all the more serious because there was nothing to bind men together in the mere worship of political freedom. Now for the makers of the revolutionary movement benevolence had been this binding force. To balance the disruptive Rights of Man was this uniting love of man, whereby every one's right was every one's burden. But benevolence—in the revolutionary sense—was no longer accepted as an active force in nineteenth-century England. Bentham and Malthus and other hard-hearted theorists were not to be touched by appeals to PHILANTHROPY; neither capitals nor personification could move a practical generation. Yet Hazlitt, in whom anti-social impulses were so strong, felt the need of saving something of benevolence as a balance to these impulses. In his *Essay on the Human Understanding* he attacks the Benthamite notion of man as a calculating animal, and tries to prove that men are not inevitably actuated by self-interest alone. The Benthamites, he says,

' proceed by rule and compass, by logical diagrams, and with none but demonstrable conclusions, and leave all the taste, fancy, and sentiment of the thing to the admirers of Mr. Burke's *Reflections on the French Revolution.* That work is to them a very flimsy and superficial performance, because it is rhetorical and figurative, and they judge of solidity by barrenness, of depth by dryness. Till they see a little farther into it, they will not be able to answer it or counteract its influence; and yet that were a task of some importance to achieve.' [1]

The utilitarians by banishing art and emotion are leaving their cause—the cause of the Revolution—without the only allies that can bring it to triumph. For even though all men be actuated by self-interest, they are certainly not actuated as the Benthamites maintain by *intelligent* self-interest. They are guided by habit, emotion, instinct, by anything except a prolonged-process of calculation. ' Our moral sentiments are made up of sympathies and antipathies, of sense and imagination, of understanding and prejudice. The soul, by reason of its weakness, is an aggregating and exclusive principle; it clings obstinately to some things, and violently rejects others.' [2] And hence, men in the mass, as subjects of government, must be moved by passion—that is, by an appeal to their *irrational* self-interest.

Yet Hazlitt would still believe in altruistic emotions. He thought that he had made a great metaphysical discovery, which was this: I can only be conscious of my

[1] *Works*, vol. vii, p. 247.   [2] Ibid., vol. iv, pp. 192–3.

identity through memory of past sensations and through experience of present ones. I cannot be sure of my future identity. Hence, I cannot will a future action from self-interest since I do not even know my future self. I can, indeed, construct an idea of my future self through my imaginative power. But my imagination can be as vividly turned on the future sensations, and hence the future being, of others. My programme for the future may be selfish, but it is not necessarily so. The future is equally uncertain to all men, and it can be partially penetrated only by a faculty, the imagination, which is as readily applied to others as to self.[1]

The world was not astonished at the discovery announced in this essay; perhaps because its really valuable truth was no discovery at all. What is actually in Hazlitt's mind is something like this : Man is not the sport of sensations evoked by a mechanically associated set of external objects, but can exercise a control over his life by an imaginative projection of his being into the future. The faculty of imagination is not purely intellectual, and is therefore genuinely social, in that it enables one man to put himself in the place of another and share at least the essentials of his experience. Benevolence is not indeed as universal as Hazlitt liked to think he believed; but he was right in asserting that the imagination can make many lives one life and can keep these lives together when calculation would keep them apart. The imagination deals kindly with absurdities like benevolence, recognizing their humanity.

This same preoccupation of Hazlitt's with the problem of bringing down the revolutionary philosophy to the level of human nature is evident in his relations with Malthus. The ideas of Malthus are to him a perversion of ideas inherited from the French Revolution, and hence essentially good. But they have been separated by Malthus and his adherents from their sources and

---

[1] *Works*, vol. i (*Essay on the Human Understanding*) ; vol. xii (*Self-Love and Benevolence*).

used to further reactionary measures. Tories have made
of the principle of population a defence for all sorts of
abuses ; they have used it to consecrate for ever the
present order, to make effort on the part of the poor
man useless, and to put the privileged classes in a position
of disastrous irresponsibility. Hazlitt loses his temper in
his *Reply to Malthus* and often overshoots his mark. He
pushes much of Malthus to a *reductio ad absurdum* which
that author himself would not have recognized ; and he
is not even willing to admit the bottom of truth in the
Essay on Population, that large families in the lower
classes do glut the market for unskilled labour and are
a factor in low wages and poverty. But he does expose
the great Malthusian fallacy that an improved standard
of living among the poor must in itself cause an increased
birth rate and a relapse into misery.

' If improving the condition of the lower classes of the people ',
he writes, ' is generally found, instead of leading to an unrestrained
increase of population, and thus adding to their misery, to give
them a greater attachment to the decencies and comforts of life,
and to make them more cautious how they part with them, to open
their ideas and prospects, to strengthen the principles of moral
restraint, and so confine population within reasonable limits, this
will be an additional motive for improving their condition.' [1]

Again, Hazlitt writes soundly on the wage-fund theory
of Malthus. Like Southey, he was not a scientific
economist ; but, again like Southey, he manages to bring
out truths that were outside the closed system of the
schools. He definitely admits the relative strength of
the workman at bargaining as an important factor in
determining wages. There is no iron law of wages, he
insists.

' The case is not that of a person both willing and able to
labour for himself, and imparting freely to another, who had
done nothing to deserve it, a part of the surplus produce of the
soil, but of a person bargaining with another to do all his work
for him ; and allowing him as a bribe part of the produce of his

[1] *Works*, vol. iv, pp. 67–8.

own labour in return. It is not therefore a question of right, any more than it is a question of expediency, but a question of power on one side and of necessity on the other. *On the degree of power, or on that of necessity, and on nothing else, will the price of labour depend.* . . . I contend that the mass of the labouring community have always the right to strike, to demand what wages they please.' [1]

This was not, and doubtless is not, orthodox economics; but it is nearer the lives of human beings than many a pretentious theory of wages, and perhaps nearer truth.

What Hazlitt is trying to do in politics is to reinforce his revolutionary aspirations by making sure that they are rooted in human nature. As a romanticist he knew how large a role unreason, prejudice, emotion, even mystery, must play in the lives of most men. As a man of common sense he knew that anything of value in politics must be communicable—capable of being made common. And so he criticized the abstract anarchy of Godwin, and tried to preserve the freedom and energy of the individual by expanding into a philosophy the surly English doctrine that an Englishman's home is his castle. He criticized the economic particularism of Bentham, and tried to correct it with an assertion of the herding instinct. He criticized the *laissez-faire* doctrine implicit in Malthus and explicit in most economists, and tried to prove that the individual is rightly bound in some respects by state, church, and trade union. This same desire to rescue the individual from the confused struggle into which the Revolution appeared to be degenerating is visible elsewhere in his work.

He is not, for instance, scornful of history after the fashion of the first Jacobins and Shelley. He values the Waverley Novels for their feeling for the continuity of life that separates the civilized man from the barbarian. Because there is more humanity he insists that there is more genuine liberalism in these works than in all the writings of the egocentric, pseudo-liberal Byron. Con-

[1] *Works*, vol. iv, p. 133. The italics are mine.

tempt for the past seems to him to argue more than mere ignorance. It is the sign of an envious and intolerant disposition.

' By despising all that has preceded us, we teach others to despise ourselves. When there is no established scale nor rooted faith in excellence, all superiority—our own as well as that of others—soon comes to the ground. . . . I would rather endure the most blind and bigoted respect for great and illustrious names, than that pitiful grovelling humour which has no pride in intellectual excellence, and no pleasure but in decrying those who have given proofs of it, and reducing them to its own level.' [1]

Again, Hazlitt has common sense, and uses it to preserve his political doctrines from the decay to which all doctrines and dogmas are liable. No one would now dare define common sense. But one of the results by which it is detected is the merging of extremes into something shockingly like the Aristotelian golden mean. Perhaps common sense achieves this by failing to see either extreme, and the true critical spirit, by seeing them both at once. At any rate, whether by common sense or by critical acumen, Hazlitt does bring his politics down to earth. The perversion of an abstract belief in the natural goodness of man into peasant-worship could not affect the author of the essay *On the Character of the Country People*. He knew the narrow, petty life of his own Wiltshire village too well to believe that the way to Utopia lay through the countryside. Again, the visionary character of Owen's schemes for the regeneration of humanity through the mills of New Lanark did not escape him, as it had escaped Southey, and he points out that from one point of view Owen is a survival from the hopeful days of the French Revolution.[2] So, too, he can reproach others at least with an excessive devotion to the spirit of contradiction, with a love of personal liberty so intense as to be a hatred of society. He calls Landor a ' Literary Jacobin ', and adds :

' We mean by this term that despotism of the mind which

[1] *Works*, vol. xii, p. 171.   [2] Ibid., vol. iii, p. 123.

only emancipates itself from authority and prejudice to grow impatient of everything like an appearance of opposition, and to domineer over and dictate its sudden, crude, violent, and varying opinions to the rest of the world. . . . Whatever is doubtful, remote, visionary, in philosophy, or wild and dangerous in politics, it fastens upon eagerly, recommending and insisting on nothing less.' [1]

Nor could his enemies of *Blackwood's* have been more outspoken in condemnation of envious hatred of superiority.

' Your true Cockney is your only true leveller. Let him be as low as he will, he is as good as any one else.' [2]

He could even write lightly about the natural goodness of man. The partisan, he says,

' lays the faults and vices of mankind to the account of sects and parties, creeds and classes. Man in himself is a good sort of animal. It is being a Tory or a Whig (as it may happen) that makes a man a knave or a fool. . . . Kings are not arbitrary, nor priests hypocritical, because they are men, but because they are kings and priests. We form certain nominal abstractions of these classes, which the more we dislike them, the less natural do they seem, and leave the general character of the species untouched, or act as a foil to it.' [3]

An ideal has lost most of its danger when it becomes possible to treat it humorously.

This unrevolutionary mildness is evident even in his direct journalistic writings. He is earnest and yet reasonable, as in the following alarmingly contemporaneous passage :

' If it is once laid down and acted upon as a maxim in national morality, that the best and most desirable security of a state is in the destruction of its neighbours, or that there is to be an unrelenting and ever watchful critical approximation to this object as far as possible, there is an end of civil society. A whole nation is no more justified in obtaining this best of all possible securities for itself, by the immediate subversion of other states, than the assassin is justified in taking the life of another to prevent

[1] *Works*, vol. x, pp. 233-4.   [2] Ibid., vol. i, p. 49.
[3] Ibid., vol. xi, p. 529.

the possibility of a future attempt on his own. For in proportion as a state is weak and incapable of subjugating us, is the manifest injustice of any such precaution ; and in proportion as a state is formidable and likely to excite serious apprehension for our own safety, is the danger and folly of setting an example which may be retaliated with so much greater effect, and like a devilish engine, recoil upon ourselves.' [1]

Comment on this passage would be ungrateful ; sceptic and believer alike will fit it into their private interpretation of history. If explanation still be necessary, let it be enough to say that Hazlitt is replying to a writer in the *New Times* in 1814, a certain ' Vetus ', who, in the name of the peace and security of the world and England, had demanded the complete destruction of France.

Nor is Hazlitt lacking in a power of aphorism not unworthy of Burke himself. Again, one can but quote :

' The moralist can no more do without the intermediate use of rules and principles, without the vantage ground of habit, without the levers of the understanding, than the mechanist can discard the use of wheels and pulleys, and perform everything by simple motion.' [2]

' True misanthropy consists not in pointing out the faults and follies of men, but in encouraging them in the pursuit.' [3]

' The world may altogether be set down as older and wiser than any single person in it.' [4]

One looks in vain in the pages of *Political Justice* for opinions like these.

It may be objected that in our endeavour to point out how Hazlitt differed from his revolutionary masters we have made him too mild and respectable—have tried to transform him in fact from a rough, distempered lion into a very commonplace sheep. There is no doubt much justice in the accusation. But so much has been written about Hazlitt the rebel that Hazlitt the conformist has been neglected. That there are ways in which Hazlitt is at one with his fellows ought to be evident. One final instance of the way in which he

[1] *Works*, vol. iii, p. 78.   [2] Ibid., vol. iv, p. 193.
[3] Ibid., vol. xii, p. 219.   [4] Ibid., vol. v, p. 130.

tries to find a common centre for radical politics in
sentiments that have ready currency among his fellows.
This is what becomes of the General Will in his hands :

'It is an absurdity to suppose that there can be any better
criterion of national grievances, or the proper remedies for them,
than the aggregate amount of the actual, dear-bought experiences, the honest feelings and heart-felt wishes of a whole people,
informed and directed by the greatest power of understanding in
the community, unbiassed by any sinister motive. . . .' [1]

The Hazlitt who hated upstarts, theorists, and tyrants,
loved the sturdy individual independence that is the
boast of the English family-man, and trusted for guidance
to a peculiarly subjective way of arriving at common
sense, was closer to the ways of Scott and the Lakists
than he would have cared to admit.

Yet he may have been right, and to see a real agreement beyond the superficial differences between his
Radicalism and their Toryism may well be one of the
characteristic errors of the temperament that believes
that history is simpler than men. Certainly there is in
Hazlitt much of that mysterious, unreasonable energy
that, escaping words, perhaps escapes the understanding
also. It naturally enough escaped Francis Place, who
refers to Hazlitt as a man not worth serious political
consideration, as a man ' wholly impelled by his feelings ' [2]. But Place believed that the repeal of the combination acts would end the trade union movement
and that the workmen would rest content with what
they had got. Perhaps after all even Place could have
picked up a crumb or so of political wisdom from Hazlitt ;
for the essayist shared too many of the feelings of the
workman, and was possessed—as Place was not—of too
much self-knowledge to believe that men will ever rest
content with what they have.

---

[1] *Works*, vol. iii, pp. 291–2.
[2] Letter of Place in *Broughton Correspondence*, B. M. Adds. 36457,
f. 340.

3

It would certainly never have occurred to their contemporaries to put Scott and Hazlitt under any common head. One was an oracle, if ever English writers can be said to attain a position so thoroughly French ; the other was merely a journalist. And so we find traces of one everywhere, at court as well as among London clerks, while the other had so little correspondence with the world that even his biographers must confine themselves to his works.

That Scott was something of an oracle in politics as well as in literature we are assured by Lockhart. Sir Walter's influence helped to lessen the ' Radical contagion ' among the Scotch weavers in the years after Waterloo ; and in general ' his services, direct and indirect, towards repressing the revolutionary propensities of his age were vast—far beyond the comprehension of vulgar politicians '.[1] Scott's circle of friends included many politicians, mostly on the Tory side, such as Canning, Melville, Croker, and Frere. Lockhart asserts that during his master's lifetime more people made the pilgrimage to Abbotsford than had ever gone to Ferney ;[2] and after his death, we are told on good authority that about eighteen hundred persons yearly came to visit the castle.[3] But Scott's prestige in the early nineteenth century is incontestable. Even Wordsworth, although obviously jealous, admits that Voltaire alone achieved so extensive a European reputation ; and Voltaire's influence, he notes, was unfortunately not ' pure '.[4] Samuel Rogers told Macaulay that ' when Sir Walter Scott dined at a gentleman's in London some time ago, all the servant-maids in the house

[1] Lockhart, *Life of Scott* (ed. Macmillan, 1900), vol. iii, p. 394 ; pp. 334 ff. p. 358.
[2] Ibid., vol. v, p. 445.
[3] Ticknor, G., *Journal* (1876), 22 April 1838.
[4] Knight, *Letters of the Wordsworth Family* (1907), vol. ii, p. 467.

asked leave to stand in the passage and see him pass '.[1]
The historian of opinion can hardly neglect such a man.

Scott's partisan views were noted and resented from
the first by the Whigs. Jeffrey in the *Edinburgh Review*
regrets that Scott has neglected to mention Sir John
Moore in his *Vision of Don Roderick*, and that he ' thinks
it a reason for defrauding a departed warrior of his
glory, that a political antagonist has been zealous in his
praise '.[2] In the diary of the poet Moore there is a note :

' Lord Auckland said that Mr. Scott did not seem to have left
any very favourable impression behind him in Ireland ; but there
is no trusting some of my Whig friends about Scott ; they have
such a horror of his politics.' [3]

And Macaulay went so far as to write of Scott that he
was ' in politics, a bitter and unscrupulous partisan . . . I
cannot think him a high-minded man, or a man of very
strict principles '.[4] But most Whigs, and even Radicals
like Hazlitt, admired the author of *Waverley* at least as
much as they disliked the Tory politician. Such was the
state of mind of ' A Reformer but no Revolutionist ', in
a letter to the *Morning Chronicle* during the struggle
over the Reform Bill.[5] The prestige of Scott as a literary
Tory must no doubt weigh against the Bill, says this
excellent Whig, who is forced to go back to Cowper to
find literary Whig opposition. But Scott's own violence
he thinks will undo him. Brandishing of claymores and
appeals to such a shadow of a faith as Jacobitism can be
of no avail in 1831. Scott's politics must always be
a blot on the fame of the author of *Waverley*.

Scott's friends were not silent, however. One journalist writes that Sir Walter Scott and the ' Great
Unknown ' are first ' among the benefactors of their

---

[1] Trevelyan, *Life and Letters of Lord Macaulay* (Popular edition, 1881),
p. 157.
[2] *Edinburgh Review*, August 1811, p. 290.
[3] Moore, T., *Journal* (1853–6), vol. v, 9 November 1827.
[4] Trevelyan, *Life and Letters of Lord Macaulay*, p. 344.
[5] *Morning Chronicle*, 1 April 1831.

country who in the present age have contributed to the
innocent amusement and moral improvement of mankind '.[1] The most remarkable testimony in favour of
Scott's political influence, however, is the case of ' a
young man who discarded Paine's *Rights of Man* for the
sake of indulging himself on a Sunday morning, by
reading the *Tales of My Landlord* in bed '.[2] A more
moderate appreciation of what Scott undoubtedly did
achieve is afforded by Leslie Stephen's remark that he
transferred to poetry and fiction the political doctrines
of Burke.[3] And there can be no doubt that all through
the last century he was a Burke for the multitude. This
in itself is no slight service.

Scott's contemporaries were not unaware of this deeper
foundation of his Toryism. Hazlitt again saw very
clearly, and we too can see, for all Hazlitt's rhetoric.
The Scotch Novels, he writes,

' carry us back to the feuds, the heart-burnings, the havoc, the
dismay, the wrongs, and the revenge of a barbarous age and
people. . . . As we read, we throw aside the trammels of civilization, the flimsy veil of humanity. . . . The wild beast resumes its
sway within us. We feel like hunting animals, and as the hound
starts in its sleep and rushes on the chase in fancy, the heart
rouses itself in its native lair, and utters a wild cry of joy, at
being restored once more to freedom and lawless, unrestrained
impulses. Every one has his full swing, or goes to the Devil his
own way. Here are no Jeremy Bentham's Panopticons, none of
Mr. Owen's impassable Parallelograms, no long calculations of
self-interest—the will takes its instant way to its object.' [4]

That is, Scott's novels satisfy the demands of the new
spirit of self-expansion, of wilful impulse, of primitive,
instinctive desire to sweep away restraint and ' let the
will take its instant way to its object ' that had grown

[1] *St. James's Chronicle*, quoted in *Gentleman's Magazine*, October 1822,
p. 351.
[2] ' Timothy Touchstone ', *Letter on the Moral Influence of the Waverley
Novels* (1820).
[3] Leslie Stephen, *The English Utilitarians* (1900), vol. ii, p. 367.
[4] Hazlitt, *Works*, vol. vii, p. 129.

so rapidly in England. Scott's politics achieve the same end. They achieve it by imposing, to a certain extent, suitable standards on this activity of the human spirit, and directing it to find satisfaction within those standards. They allow the blindly striving individual to merge his strivings with those of his fellows and yet not feel himself unduly limited or surpassed, and to satisfy his own self-importance by sharing the glamour of common deeds. For these standards are produced by emotional loyalty to old institutions tempered with a new consciousness of human dignity. Scott is in many essential respects a democrat. George Sand saw this, and wrote :

' S'il est le poète des lords et des monarques, il est aussi le poète du paysan, du soldat, du proscrit et de l'artisan . . . il faut lui savoir gré de nous avoir peint le peuple sous des couleurs poétiques, et d'en avoir tiré de grandes et sévères figures.' [1]

Jeffrey, too, called attention to Scott's feeling for the people, and his skill at painting peasants who were not clowns to be laughed at, nor idyllic shepherds, but ' human creatures, with as many pleasures and fewer cares than their superiors, with affections not only as strong, but often as delicate, as those whose language is smoother '.[2] Burke had this feeling for the dignity and mystery of human life, and held that political institutions must satisfy deep human cravings unknown to philosophers. In so far as English Conservatism shared this view, it identified itself with the Revolution. That is why in the nineteenth century Conservatism so often proved itself more Liberal than Liberalism.

Hazlitt has already spoken for himself. As a journalist he was ever in the thick of political debate ; but he has never formed a school, never had followers, never influenced the political thought of a Mill or a Disraeli. Beyond the little circle of Lamb and the Hunts he had scarcely any personal acquaintance ; and unlike Southey,

---

[1] George Sand, *Les Compagnons du Tour de France*, quoted in Maigron, *Le roman historique à l'époque romantique* (Paris, 1898).
[2] *Edinburgh Review*, March 1817.

he did not even have his Wilberforce among the great. Still he was undoubtedly one of the leading literary Radicals of his own day. Good Tories were taught by *Blackwood's* and the *Quarterly* to regard him as the ally of Cobbett, Burdett, and the rest of the forces of darkness. Scott, indeed, had held that ' to take notice of such men as Hazlitt and Hunt in the *Quarterly* would be to introduce them into a world which is scarce conscious of their existence '.[1] The *Quarterly*, however, could not long keep its readers in ignorance of this Radical danger ; [2] and when Gifford had finished, Lockhart in *Blackwood's* took up the task of putting down ' pimpled Hazlitt ' and the other ' vermin ' of the Cockney School of poetry and politics.[3] Hazlitt, however, continued to enjoy the patronage of such respectable publications as the *Edinburgh Review*, the *London Magazine*, and the *Morning Chronicle*.

There could, indeed, be no better indication of the transformation in English taste that had already been effected by the time of George IV than the acceptance given to Hazlitt's literary judgements by the very journals that so bitterly opposed his politics. After all, they felt as he did about Shakespeare, Claude Lorrain, old books, and the countryside. *Blackwood's* distinguished clearly between politics and aesthetics ; for after abusing Hazlitt on one page as a statesman of Cockaigne, a colleague of Orator Hunt, Cobbett and Burdett, it reported fully and respectfully his lectures on the English Poets at the Surrey Institute, and later referred to him as one of the ' most eminent speculators on literary topics of the day '. The *Gentleman's Magazine*, the last stronghold of the eighteenth century, said of him in 1825 :

' It must be confessed that Mr. Hazlitt is a man of no ordinary powers. . . . His style is peculiar to himself, it is deeply impregnated

---

[1] Scott, *Journal*, vol. i, p. 22.
[2] *Quarterly Review*, April 1817 ; January, December 1818.
[3] *Blackwood's Edinburgh Magazine*, February, March, June 1818 ; August 1824.

with the spirit of the masters of our language and strengthened by a rich infusion of golden ore, dug from the pure mine of classic antiquity.' [1]

Yet it must be insisted that the temper of Hazlitt as a man of letters and as a politician is one. It is passionate, and attains at times that form of mysticism which is a chewing of the cud of passion. At its best it is also critical and finely humane; but it is subject to lapses (as in the *Liber Amoris*) when it throws aside the restraints of experience, of taste and sense, and spends itself in revolt. Now, both in the peace that he attained and in the unrest that he never overcame, Hazlitt is a son of his age. By 1825 even the readers of the *Gentleman's Magazine* held a dominantly emotional aesthetic creed, and sought in art a requital of unending aspirations, of animal impulses, not an occasion for the exercise of reason in the recognition of form proportion and harmony. Some of these excellent people thought they could balance unrestraint in art by restraint in politics. They thought they could have Hazlitt without the Reform Bill. But they were inseparable, of one spirit; it was not wholly a spirit of rest.

4

It will not do to lessen the gap that divides the politics of Scott and Hazlitt. Sir Walter was the friend and supporter of Canning and Croker, loyal to king and country even to effusion, an opponent of the ideas of the French Revolution, of parliamentary reform, and indeed of all change. Hazlitt, so far as he could work with any one, worked with the editor of the *Examiner* for the cause of reform, hated monarchs and aristocrats like a good Republican, and actually believed in universal suffrage. Scott had in his disposition always something of the Jacobite; Hazlitt, of the Jacobin. Yet there is a point where the two come together. That this point

[1] *Gentleman's Magazine*, March 1825, p. 244.

is ethical rather than political is significant. In the morals of to-day are the politics of to-morrow. Scott and Hazlitt are fellows in the worship of Nature. They are convinced of the great importance of the natural appetitive life of man; and on the whole, and with many qualifications, they think that life is a good one. Both admit that it must somehow be disciplined; and both are agreed in at least one respect as to what that discipline must be. It must grow out of, and remain in consonance with, the appetites, instincts, and prejudices of the common man. It must be their master while seeming to be their servant. It must never set up, like the Reason of the last century, a contemptuous tyranny over these natural desires. Neither Scott nor Hazlitt is quite willing to dismiss the intellect from the ordering of the world; but it is obvious that they do not believe it should take the chief part in this task. Scott held that if youth were taught to admire the achievements of its heroic ancestors, its healthy desires would rest content with the maintenance of tradition. Hazlitt, too, would have the rising generation taught to revere whatever was good in the past and mould its personal idea of liberty on the great tradition of English liberty. They are both opposed to revolutionary methods, to attempts to achieve Utopia on earth, and to crude egalitarianism.

That is to say, they have transformed the natural goodness of man from an ideal of the Golden Age to one of the Victorian Age. It has lost its old aggressive simplicity, its clear-cut lines of social action, and has become vague, comfortable, a quieting assurance of progress. It is no longer a dogma, but rather what M. Georges Sorel calls a 'myth', a goal towards which society likes to believe it is marching. Scott and Hazlitt together have sketched that marvellous middle-class morality which seemed in the next age successfully to have found rest in unrest and to have reconciled material expansion with spiritual repose.

Was it all mere seeming? Hazlitt, at least, never seems quite certain of his peace. The last great poets of the age called romantic failed to evolve a discipline out of their rebellious beginnings. Their cry against reason is as loud as that of an earlier generation; but their cry of unrest and revolt is louder, and never stilled, not even with death. Hazlitt dying almost alone, almost friendless, could yet say, 'Well, I have had a happy life.' Neither Byron, nor Keats, nor Shelley could have said this. We must now ask whether the discontent of these poets has any social significance.

IV

THE SECOND GENERATION OF REVOLT

BYRON was born in 1788 and Shelley in 1792. When they began to write with something like maturity, the Lake Poets had sunk into middle age, conformity, and Toryism. They once more used poetry to further political revolt. Their activity coincides closely with the revival of political unrest and agitation for reform in the last years of the Napoleonic Wars. While Burdett, Cobbett, and 'Orator' Hunt were urging practical reform to working people, while Bentham and his disciples were gradually converting to their particular interpretation of eighteenth-century wisdom a large part of the most influential of the commercial classes, Hazlitt, Leigh Hunt, Byron, Shelley, and Moore were making use of polite literature for similar propaganda against the government in power. Just as in the days of the French Revolution, there is in England an active, noisy demand for political change. The reformers are not by any means united and do not even try to work together. The literary men hate the Benthamites as enemies of art ; Byron the aristocrat is filled with contempt for the plebeian Cobbett ; and all are agreed that Shelley is a fanatic. But they have one thing in common ; they are opposed to the system of Pitt and his successors, and demand as a minimum such a change in the structure of English government as will make that system impossible in the future.

There is then in English letters of the twenty years preceding the Reform Bill a revival of the spirit of revolt that had animated the Jacobin poets. But the situation has changed since 1794. There is no longer a solid little band, innovators alike in literature and in politics. The new school of romance, triumphant and secure (Jeffrey's review of *The Excursion* is the swan-song of their enemies), is now divided on the subject of politics, and the poets of the second generation stand sharply opposed to those of the first. Again, as we have been able to learn from Hazlitt, the rigour of orthodox French principles has been softened by long domestication in England. It remains to be seen whether the writings of Byron and Shelley will confirm the conclusions we have drawn from those of Hazlitt.

I

Those who explain everything about a man by heredity and the coarser accidents of environment have no difficulty in accounting for Lord Byron. His proud Norman ancestry, faulty upbringing, and lame leg explain it all— passion, revolt, gloom, despair, a life extreme in all things, good and bad. No doubt these are the influences that went to make him. But they do not tell us why he wrote poetry. Certainly he was born with the gift of metrical composition. It was not, however, a very high gift, not by any means a faultless sense of what was fitting in the construction of English verse. Nor was Byron driven to write by any divine impulsion, by any resistless demand of the poetic soul within him. Indeed, he always affected an indifference for his own poetic trifling and held in profound contempt such ink-submerged creatures as Southey. Byron was much more of an adventurer than a poet, and had circumstances favoured him, he would doubtless no more have made poetry his chief occupation than did Sir Walter Ralegh. But the adventurer, who is simply the romanticist in action, demands of life that it provide him with endless novelty, with danger and uncertainty, and that it give him occasion to strengthen his self-satisfaction by triumphing over difficulty. Just that sort of life was hardly open to Byron, even had he not been handicapped by lameness. Lion-hunting in Africa and mountain-climbing in Tibet had not yet become recognized outlets for the spirit of adventure in the upper classes ; and trade, the most romantic of pursuits at the time, was closed to him. As it was he did the best he could, and died like a soldier of fortune.

Byron's great adventure, after all, was his writing. That this should be so is surely due in part to the character of the age. Even though Byron had been destined by nature to be a literary lord, it is yet quite impossible to imagine him contenting himself with a career like that of the fourth Lord Orford. He could find in the romantic movement the opportunity for struggle and for triumph elsewhere denied him. After the dissolution of the ideals of the old régime, he could join in the search for new ones like some romantic explorer seeking undiscovered lands. It is a further indication of the almost universal preoccupation of men of that time with the task of fitting ethical and political standards to a rapidly expanding society that a man like Byron, not essentially a man of reflection, nor even, it will doubtless now be agreed, an artist, should devote himself to the solution of the problem of evil and to the emancipation of mankind.

For Byron's deeper interest is in the problem of man's conduct as an individual and as a citizen. This it was that caused Matthew Arnold, who was himself pre-occupied with much the same matters, to rank him above both Keats and Shelley, not because of the excellence of his poetry, but because of his sincere and courageous attempts to find a solution for the difficulties of man in society. And though much of what Byron wrote is as worthless as if it really had been written, as he proudly maintained of *Lara*, while dressing for balls and mas-querades, yet there is no doubt that he spent his high seriousness on ethics and politics. The results of his thinking on these matters were many and contradictory —a proof that, unlike most of his fellows, he did think about them. The easiest way to resolve them into an order as little unreal as possible is to begin where he began, and to follow, not so much in order of time as in order of ideas, his development.

He began with an inheritance. This was the doctrine of the natural goodness of man, handed down from the makers of the Revolution. There are times when he seems to have kept the inheritance singularly intact. It is the old strain : man is good in simple, rural societies, in repose on Nature's breast : cities, art, and restraint make him evil. Quite late in life he can write of Daniel Boone and the Kentucky pioneers :

> Motion was in their days, Rest in their slumbers,
>   And Cheerfulness the handmaid of their toil ;
> Nor yet too many nor too few their numbers ;
>   Corruption could not make their hearts her soil ;
> The lust which stings, the splendour which encumbers,
>   With the free foresters divide no spoil :
> Serene, not sullen, were the solitudes
>   Of this unsighing people of the woods.[1]

This idyllic Kentucky is the ' dark and bloody ground ' of American pioneer tradition.

As the corollary to this belief in Nature comes contempt for society and for its inevitable corruption. Juan and Haidée must have a fitting theatre for their exceptionally natural love, far from the

> black solitudes
> Called social, haunts of Hate and Vice and Care.

For, the poet reflects, the noblest of Nature's creatures are the most solitary, solitary most of all in the exercise of love.

> How lonely every free-born creature broods !
>   The sweetest song-birds nestle in a pair ;
> The eagle soars alone ; the gull and crow
>   Flock o'er their carrion, just like man below.[2]

For this reason Byron loves the ruder peoples, children of passion like the Italians, whom he misunderstands as

---

[1] *Works*, ed. Coleridge and Prothero (1898–1904), Poetry, vol. vi. p. 351.

[2] *Works*, Poetry, vol. vi, p. 191.

badly as his fellow Northerner, Stendhal. Greeks and South
Sea Islanders, too, he likes. The latter indeed had vices,

> But only the Barbarians—we have both
> The sordid civilization, mixed
> With all the savage, which Man's fall hath fixed.[1]

As for the Greeks, they are naturally as capable as their
ancestors, and once freed from foreign dominion will
astonish the world with their prowess.

Byron's heroes are creatures of this same unhappy
contrast between virtue and civilization. Conrad, Lara,
and the rest, says Nisard, are all a

> ' mélange du bien élevé jusqu'à l'héroisme et du mal poussé
> jusqu'au crime. Seulement, le bien est à l'honneur du per-
> sonnage et le mal à la charge de la société, qui n'a pas su lui faire
> assez de place ni lui donner assez d'air. C'est par sa volonté
> qu'il est grand ; c'est par les circonstances qu'il devient criminel.' [2]

Since this is so, one must change the circumstances to
preserve the greatness of man. But the circumstances
are social—state, church, the family : virtue is personal.
Again, like his predecessors in revolt, Byron demands
that the individual be free to assert his virtue against
the vicious restraints of society.

It is in defence of this idea of liberty that Byron wrote
lines that were long on the lips and in the hearts of
struggling Liberals on the Continent, and perhaps even
in England. Some are not yet forgotten.

> ' Yet Freedom ! yet thy banner torn but flying
> Streams like the thunder-storm *against* the wind.' [3]

> ' Eternal Spirit of the Chainless mind !
> Brightest in dungeons, Liberty ! thou art,
> For there thy habitation is the heart.' [4]

> '   They never fail who die
> In a great cause : the block may soak their gore :
> Their heads may sodden in the sun ; their limbs
> Be strung to city gates and castle walls—

[1] Ibid., vol. v, p. 602.
[2] *Revue des Deux Mondes*, November 1850, p. 423.
[3] *Works*, Poetry, vol. ii, p. 402.   [4] Ibid., vol. iv, p. 7.

> But still their spirit walks abroad. Though years
> Elapse, and others share as dark a doom,
> They but augment the deep and sweeping thoughts
> Which overpower all others, and conduct
> The world at last to Freedom.' [1]

Under the contagion of such poetry liberty ceases to be the negative thing it seems in many a philosophy : it becomes communicable, an emotion to draw men together, not a theory to keep them apart. Byron's eleutheria must have helped to turn abstract belief in liberty into Liberalism.

One of the ways in which the ideal of personal liberty transforms itself into a real, if vague, social faith like Liberalism, is by turning its attention upon those who are oppressed. Sympathy with those who lack liberty is the surest way to draw men together in her defence. Byron from the first was the friend of the poor and downtrodden. His maiden speech in the House of Lords was delivered in defence of the weavers who had taken part in the Luddite troubles over the installation of machinery. These men, whose lives the House is about to value ' at something less than the price of a stocking-frame ', are the people of England, and it is of no avail to dismiss them as a ' mob '. ' Are we aware of our obligations to a mob ? ' continues his lordship. ' It is the mob that labour in your fields and serve in your houses—that man your navy and recruit your army—that have enabled you to defy all the world and can also defy you when neglect and calamity have driven them to despair. You may call the people a mob ; but do not forget that a mob too often speaks the sentiments of the people.' [2]   This humanitarianism, the direct offspring of revolutionary ' benevolence ', is most important in modern politics. It is seen again in hatred of war and bloodshed :

> The drying up a single tear has more
> Of honest fame than shedding seas of gore. [3]

---

[1] *Works*, vol. iv, p. 386.   [2] Ibid., Letters, vol. ii, Appendix.
[3] Ibid., Poetry, vol. vi, p. 330.

This is from the misanthropic *Don Juan* ; and when Byron left for Greece he wrote :

' When I go there, I shall do my best to civilize their mode of treating their prisoners : and could I only save a single life, whether Turk or Greek, I should live " mihi carior ", and I trust not less so to my friends.' [1]

With this humanitarian feeling goes a little mild republicanism. Kings oppress ; therefore republics do not. Byron, in the midst of the wreck of Europe, can rejoice that

> Still one great clime, in full and free defiance
> Yet rears her crest, unconquered and sublime
> Above the far Atlantic.[2]

He is not at a loss, however, for a philosophical reason for his preference for the republican form of government :

' The greater the equality, the more impartially evil is distributed, and becomes light by the division among so many— therefore, a Republic.' [3]

Finally, this pervading sentiment of sympathy with all who are struggling against those in power finds its most congenial object in the cause of nationalism. The states of the old régime in Europe were largely constituted in defiance of the principle of nationality. The enemies of liberty were also the enemies of nationalism. To be a patriot in Italy, Germany, and Greece was to take the side of the undying human will, of energy, of nature, against the reactionaries who wished to cheat their fellow-men of life. Byron took up the cause of oppressed nationalities as he always took up the cause of the under dog. ' It is no great matter ', he wrote, ' supposing that Italy could be liberated, who or what is sacrificed. It is a grand object—the very *poetry* of politics.' [4] Italian politics were indeed worthy of the poet, and he found

[1] *Letters*, ed. Murray (1922), vol. ii, p. 258.
[2] *Works*, Poetry, vol. iv, p. 501.
[3] *Letters*, vol. ii, p. 284.   [4] *Works*, Letters, vol. v, p. 205.

some scope for his love of adventure in his activities as
a Carbonaro. The papal government had him carefully watched, and we have the word of the Countess
Guiccioli that he was considered ' il principale sostegno
del Liberalismo della Romagna '.¹   The world still
remembers his expedition to Greece and his death.
Perhaps no one now takes that event so much to heart
as the lady in the *Way of All Flesh*, who wept at the
mere mention of Missolonghi ; but the most prosaic of
us, even among historians, will do justice to the extraordinary effect of Byron's actions on the peoples of
Western Europe.   He was one of those who did most
to make nationalism the religion of the last century.

Byron is then a true heir of the literary Jacobins in
his faith in Nature, in his devotion to liberty, in his
sympathy for the oppressed, and in his hatred of the old
régime, now masked as Legitimacy.   From what we have
already seen of him, however, it is clear that his Liberal
leanings are not those of a violent, un-English rebel
against society.   But he was in many respects even more
orthodox than he has been painted.   He was rather
more conscious of his aristocratic position than it would
seem, to a plebeian mind, he should have been ; and it is
noticeable that, though he is as bitter against kings as
any Jacobin, he is not equally bitter against nobility.
He disliked popular agitators like Cobbett and Orator
Hunt and refused to have his name associated with
a movement in which they participated.²   When Hobhouse stood for Westminster, Byron was disgusted,
and wrote an unkind squib on the degradation of
his friend.

> Who are now the people's men,
>   My boy Hobby, O ?
> There 's I and Burdett—Gentlemen,
>   And blackguard Hunt and Cobby, O !³

¹ Moore, T., *Life of Byron* (1830), p. 518.
² *Letters* (ed. Murray), vol. ii, p. 116.
³ *Works*, Poetry, vol. iv, p. 424.

And although always in favour of a reform in representation, he wished it to be ' moderate '. The use of that hallowed word alone would largely redeem him from the charge of treating politics in an un-English spirit.

His love of liberty and his sympathy with the oppressed merges readily into the sentimental tone of the age. The Whig party, soon to become the Liberals, owe not a little to this satanist in his milder mood. No doubt it needed the traditions of a Grey, the ideas of a Bentham, the astonishingly sincere rhetoric of a Macaulay, as well as the plain business sense of its rank and file, to obtain its hold over the English people. But without something of Byron's comfortable enthusiasm for ideal liberty, it must have failed to hold together. So, too, Byron's written morals, at least, bear the common touch of respectability in many places. He, and not Mrs. Eliza Cook or Mr. Longfellow, wrote :

> to what gulfs
> A single deviation from the track
> Of human duties leads even those who claim
> The homage of mankind as their born due,
> And find it, till they forfeit it themselves.[1]

From such a position of undeniable respectability he calls Shelley ' a man of talent and honour, but crazy against religion and morality '.[2]

But the final evidence in his favour is his administration of affairs in Greece. For however accounts of what he did there may differ it is certain that he determined not to let theory or sentiment stand in the way of his objects to defeat the Turks and found a Greek state. Although he was careful to avoid any absolute alliance with any of the various Greek parties it is to be noted that he chose to favour the aristocrat Mavrogordato against the republican Odysseus. The crucial test, however, is in his relations with Colonel Stanhope. That gentleman, a disciple of Bentham, proposed to give emancipated Greece a state machinery of the latest

---

[1] *Works*, Poetry, vol. v, p. 88.   [2] *Letters*, vol. v, p. 75.

utilitarian type, including a republican constitution,
universal education, a free press, and complete religious
toleration. He quarrelled violently with Byron over the
suppression of a vernacular newspaper, in which German
Hellenists and other unworldly enthusiasts had been
making trouble for the provisional government. Byron
was rude and insulting about the practical value of
Bentham's ideas in a semi-barbarous land, and Stanhope
indignantly withdrew. Parry, one of Byron's lieutenants,
thus reports the poet's opinions of the matter. ' He
(Stanhope) is like all political jobbers, who mistake the
accessories of civilization for its cause ; they think if
they only hoist the colours of freedom, they will immediately transform a crazy, water-logged bark into a proud
man-of-war. Stanhope, I believe, wants discussion on
Greece—pure abstract discussion ; as if he were ignorant
that in a country where there are one hundred times as
many readers, proportionally, as in Greece, where the
people have been readers of newspapers for a century,
and read them every day, they care nothing about his
favourite discussion—will not listen either to Mr. Bentham's, or any other person's logic.' [1] Byron was after
all an Englishman and a peer. The arch-rebel, the
satanist, was reverting to type. The world lost more
than a poet at Missolonghi.

Yet this same Byron was held in abhorrence by a large
part of his countrymen. To all save a few rebellious
spirits he came to be a force for evil, for anarchy and
disruption. Part of this feeling was no doubt due to
superficial and accidental things—to his unhappy marriage, to his residence in Italy, to travellers' tales and
biographers' scandal. Part of it is due to his unsparing
use of an intelligence which, like all true intelligence,
was not content with compromise. Most of it, however,
is due to the fact that he carried to extremes doctrines
that were to a great extent common property. For

[1] Parry, *Last Days of Lord Byron* (1826), pp. 190–1 ; Stanhope, *Greece
in 1823 and 1824* (1824).

Byron stands to the rest of his countrymen, not as the
infidel to the true believers, but, what is much harder
for both to bear, as the heretic to his co-religionists. He
lived the life of sensation and emotion as thoroughly as
it could be lived, and he thought those men hypocrites
who, agreeing with him that it was a good life, stopped
short in their pursuit of it at a point dictated by common
sense or cowardice. With all this, he has flashes of
genuine critical intelligence, in which the whole ideal of
physical comfort soaked in sentiment, of ordered sen-
sualism glorified by mystical self-satisfaction, seemed to
him hateful. Thus there arises Byron the satirist—
perhaps the only Byron that is really great. He turns
against the middle classes the same arts by which he had
gained their admiration. His is no calm and disinterested
exposition of life as it appears to the believer in classical
reason ; his satire is as disordered as its object. It is
filled with sentiment and Nature, ardent and even hopeful, careless of form and decency, and yet in some ways
constant to a conception of life far more humane than
that of the respectable people who read *Don Juan* with
delight and disapproval. It is precisely this fitness for
its audience—another *Epistle to Dr. Arbuthnot* would
never have done—that gives Byron's satire its value as
a document in the history of the dissemination of revolutionary ideas.

The trouble with England, it seemed to the author of
Don Juan, was that it cared more for contentment than
for truth. ' In these days, the grand *primum mobile* of
England is *cant* : cant political, cant poetical, cant
religious, cant moral ; but always *cant*, multiplied
through all the varieties of life.' [1] Cant was simply
the common man's desire to expand combined with his
unwillingness to make the sacrifices necessary for expansion. The result was a way of life in which desire fed
on sentiment, not on action. English society was built
on cowardice. It was organized stupidity. Byron, it

[1] *Works*, Letters, vol. v, p. 542.

would seem, was almost aware that it was the organized natural goodness of man. At any rate he fixed upon this ' cant ' as the irrational self-satisfaction of a class that had come to be supreme in England. Matthew Arnold and ' philistinism ', Mr. Shaw and ' middle-class morality ', do but carry on the same *motif* through the century and into modern life.

It is one characteristic of the rule of cant that the truths discovered by disinterested investigation are ever regarded as unnecessary or unpleasant.

> But now I'm going to be immoral ; now
>   I mean to show things really as they are
> Not as they ought to be, for I avow
> That till we see what 's what in fact, we're far
> From much improvement with that virtuous plough
>   Which skims the surface, leaving scarce a scar
> Upon the black loam long manured by vice
> Only to keep its corn at the old price.[1]

English poets have helped establish this rule of cant over intelligence by perverting blunt English sense into sentimentality. Through them and their like the old gentry is being vulgarized, is losing its old sense of duty, and is adopting the selfish standards of the commercial classes. It is becoming dull and prudish, no longer daring in its leadership.

> For what were all these country patriots born ?
> To hunt, to vote, and raise the price of corn.[2]

Cant has found in domesticity its chief prop. And at the head of the nation is that pattern of domesticity, ' Farmer George '. The *Vision of Judgement* is aimed at the comfortable, muddled citizen at his fireside, rather than at Southey or at the king. Here, Byron seems to say, is the kind of king you will have if you set vulgar common feeling above knowledge in government.

> A better farmer ne'er brushed dew from lawn,
> A worse king never left a realm undone.[3]

[1] *Works*, Poetry, vol. vi, p. 466.   [2] Ibid., vol. v, p. 570.
[3] Ibid., vol. iv, p. 489.

This love of home and family easily degenerates into
petty contentment with inferior things, into a moral
and aesthetic slothfulness. Much of *Don Juan* is aimed
at the civilization of the domestic circle. 'That moral
centaur, man and wife ',[1] is Byron's feeling argument for
easier divorce. Now he ridicules the ugliness and smug
pretensions of suburban life. Don Juan approaches London

> Through Groves, so call'd as being void of trees,
> (Like *lucus* from *no* light) : through prospects named
> Mount Pleasant, as containing nought to please,
>   Nor much to climb ; through little boxes framed
> Of bricks, to let the dust in at your ease,
>   With ' To be Let ' upon their doors proclaim'd ;
> Through ' Rows ' most modestly called ' Paradise ',
> Which Eve might quit without much sacrifice.[2]

Now there is a passage meant to *épater le bourgeois*.
Don Juan drives up to his London hotel,

>   and around
> The mob stood, and as usual several score
>   Of those pedestrian Paphians who abound
> In decent London when the daylight 's oer.[3]

It is the little word, ' decent ', there that makes the
outrage. But to go at length into the social satire in
Don Juan would take much too long, and is somewhat
beside the point. The great enemy against whom Byron
is campaigning is Georgian England ; that is evident in
the choice of a virtuous, natural, unthinking Spaniard as
a hero.

The worst of this rule of cant is that it is discrediting
England abroad. Men like Wellington and ' that intellectual eunuch, Castlereagh ' have brought her down
in the world. She no longer appears to the oppressed
nations as a nurse of freedom.

> Alas ! could she but fully, truly know
>   How her great name is now throughout abhorred,
> How eager all the Earth is for the blow
>   Which shall lay bare her bosom to the sword,

---

[1] Ibid., vol. vi, p. 477.   [2] Ibid., p. 433.   [3] Ibid., p. 436.

How all the nations deem her their worst foe,
   That worse than *worst of foes*, the once adored
False friend, who held out Freedom to Mankind
And now would chain them—to the very mind.[1]

England, whose greatness was founded on rebellion, had come to be the most powerful support of legitimacy and reaction.

And so we return to Byron the rebel, to the Byron who could write :

I was born for opposition

.   .   .   .

But then, 'tis mostly on the weaker side ;
   So that I verily believe if they
Who now are basking in their full-blown pride
   Were shaken down, and ' dogs had had their day '
Though at the first I might perchance deride
   Their tumble, I should turn the other way,
And wax an ultra-royalist in Loyalty,
   Because I hate even democratic Royalty.[2]

Our sympathies must always be with the will that is beating against restraint, since our own wills would know no master. The early Byronic hero was just such a free agent, a man above the petty restraints of artificial society. Society did succeed, by weight of numbers, in achieving the ruin, usually catastrophic, of the hero ; that was the tragedy. But as Byron rose above the crude melodrama of his earlier romances, he began to question whether society was not a part of things, and injustice decreed from on high. In *Cain* he does not doubt the original assumption that man's will to follow his desires is good ; but he does come definitely to the conclusion that in this world to follow desire is to suffer evil.

For Cain revolts not so much against society as against life itself. He revolts because his mind conceives of a far better state, and because his desires reach out after this good life by the law of their being ; his revolt is unsuc-

---

[1] *Works*, Poetry, vol. vi, p. 420.   [2] Ibid., vol. vi, p. 550.

cessful because this world is inferior to the objects of desire, and reality must always cheat the aspirations of man. Spirit strives after the limitless and flesh must follow after. But flesh cannot go where spirit leads and the pursuit must end in failure. Cain cannot succeed ; his attempt must bring greater misery upon him and his innocent family. Yet pushed on by his uncontrollable desires for good, he must revolt against the littleness, the badness of worldly existence. *Cain* ends in a moral nihilism of the blackest kind. Between desire and gratification is an impassable gulf ; and the higher the desire the wider is the gulf. Yet no man can control desire. We all must suffer the fate of Tantalus. Worse, indeed, for if we turn to what seems the only possible gratification of desire, to sensual pleasure, we do but learn that though we secure the very food and drink dangled before our eyes it cannot nourish.

Wordsworth put very clearly this romantic contrast between the greatness of human desires and the little- ness of the material world in which they must try to realize themselves :

'The true sorrow of humanity consists in this : not that the mind of man fails ; but that the course and demands of action and of life so rarely correspond with the dignity and intensity of human desires.'

Wordsworth, however, ends in no Byronic despair, and this for a very important reason. Byron assumes that desire can neither be controlled nor requited. Words- worth actually does both control and requite his desires, by diverting them from the attempt to secure material gratification to a mystical attainment in religion, patrio- tism, and morality. As a Christian, an Englishman and a gentleman he feels that he is more than a man ; his desires have achieved the impossible, realized their dream, and are requited. Byron was at once too intelli- gent and too impassioned to rest content with an achieve- ment like Wordsworth's. He had in him as little of the mystic as possible, as may be proved from his superficial attempts to be Wordsworthian in the third canto of *Childe Harold*. In him that love of change, that desire for action, that striving of something within to thrust upward and outward and burst all barriers, that profound unreasoning longing for *more* of something—of life, perhaps—was far stronger than in ordinary men. With a life of adventure he might have satisfied this passion. But confined to the life of thought, he was constitutionally unable to divert sensual passion into mysticism, and render it respectable and contained by rendering it vicarious. Moreover, his active intellect seized the fact that this respectable, mystic sentiment of common things was slowly being erected into a formal system of taboos as capable of exercising a tyrannous control over the necessary spontaneous impulses of human life as ever had been the Right Reason of the last century. High, critical intelligence he saw had no place in this scheme—far less than it had had in the old régime. He could not be content with a civilization that excluded the highest elements of previous civilizations ; and so his championship of Pope is seen to be no hypocrisy, but the expression of a real, if unsteady, intellectual sympathy.

Byron is thus a rebel against society both as a champion of reason and as an advocate of the natural goodness of man. But as he was no theorist, he is never consistent, and often appears on the side of conformity. The truth is, he was in all things a son of the Revolution ; he was born in a tempest, and passed his life in one, and was contemptuous of anchors. It is only in the last respect that he differed from his fellows. He, as well as they, will admit the necessity of a ship to ride the storm. But he cannot believe that the anchor they have devised will hold ; and when it breaks, disaster is inescapable. This anchor is ' cant ', the standards of life which Wordsworth and the middle class had evolved from the revolt against reason. But since Byron himself revolted against reason, and since he accepted the doctrine of the natural goodness of man, he ends in despair. For if

neither reason nor faith is to control man's desires, the
fate of Cain is inevitable.

Faith in nature is perhaps not enough. If we have
learned anything from Byron and his writings, Nature is
not even justified by her works. The noble poet was
early disillusioned with Nature's children, the Italians
and the Greeks ; he ceased to be inspired by the ' poetry
of politics '. The reality was so far from his ideal, from
his desires. But weren't his desires *natural*? How could
he give them up? It was all very confusing, like *Cain*.
When he had gone to Greece, he ceased to ask himself
questions about ultimate things, and went to work like
an Englishman ; had he stayed behind, and continued
to ask himself whither Nature led in politics, he could
hardly have done more than write another *Cain*, or
a *Manfred*.

2

At twenty years of age Shelley, enriched in wisdom by
marriage and by expulsion from Oxford, set out to
reform mankind. He began with Ireland. He composed,
in a style so simple that his meaning must be clear to the
rudest intelligence, an ' Address to the Irish People '.
Standing with his wife on the balcony of their room in
Lower Sackville Street, in Dublin, he threw copies of
this pamphlet at passers-by who seemed to him likely
to profit by its message. Three measures, ran the
address, are necessary to the salvation of Ireland: Catholic
Emancipation, Universal Suffrage, and the Repeal of the
Union. Let Irishmen then bestir themselves, form
political associations, and press in every way these
demands. Once they are granted—and England will not
long oppose moderate and enlightened Irishmen—peace
and happiness will at last make Ireland their home.

This man was a fanatic. That he was also a great
poet is beside the point. This one action of his enrolls
him among the street orators, the ranters, the dispensers
of social salvation who haunt parks and street corners.

He is at first sight one of those political outcasts to whom not even martyrdom can bring honour and influence. Yet the world has chosen to accept him as one of its own children. Roosevelt, with his fine contempt for urbanity of speech, once called Tom Paine a ' dirty little atheist ' ; he would hardly have spoken thus of the author of *Queen Mab*, who was as open an atheist as Paine had ever been. Shelley, outlawed by his fellows, is now a reputable member of society. Is it that we forget the man and the politician in the poet ? One wishes that we could. But we have far too many biographies and studies to permit so desirable an achievement. And then, all three of the measures which seemed so visionary in the little pamphlet thrown from the balcony in Sackville Street have been realized in the Ireland of to-day. Was Shelley after all wiser than the politicians of his time ? Have his ideas become so much common property that we have forgotten their disreputable origin in revolt and eccentricity ? Before we can attempt to answer this important question, we must turn to Shelley's own stock of political ideas.

These ideas were taken over almost intact from Godwin, as all of Shelley's numerous commentators have pointed out. It is hardly necessary to add another to the list of these accounts of the indebtedness of the young man to his father-in-law ; and quotations from *Queen Mab* offer opportunities to be superior to Shelley much too frequent and too evident for the critic's good. Suffice it to say that if *Political Justice* were lost, it could be dug up again from *Queen Mab*, Necessity, Anarchy, Passive Resistance, Perfectibility, and all. For the rest *Queen Mab* might almost be the production of some Jacobin poet like Merry, so fresh and sweeping is its condemnation of kings, nobles, priests, and judges.

On one aspect of Shelley's inheritance from Godwin we must, however, dwell at some length, since it is a part of his moral and political essence. That is his

belief in Necessity. He longed above all things to find
on earth a state of complete happiness ; and to be completely happy meant to his sensitive body to be free from
all contact with suffering. He wanted to be free and
happy ; but he could not be unless every one around
him were free and happy also. He possessed to an extraordinary degree those aspirations toward unrestrained
personal expansion, toward infinite enjoyment, common
to all human beings ; but he could take no joy in expansion at the cost of a fellow human being, because his
fellow's sufferings would mar his victory, disturb the
peace he was seeking. But from the checks of common
sense, habit, inertia, cowardice, and perhaps intelligence,
which normally restrain men in this world from taking
their desires as measures of their deeds, Shelley was
strangely free. He saw nothing between himself and his
dream. He hungered after the golden age of his desires ;
and all his powers of intellect were at the service of this
hunger.

Now, he saw himself and his fellows perfectly free in
this dream-world, for freedom was essential if this
expansive energy within him was to have play ; but he
also saw himself and his fellows undergoing no changes,
no struggles, no suffering. He would be free, not only
in the positive sense of untrammeled self-expansion, but
in a negative sense free from the vicissitudes of outward
life. He would—and this is the most human thing
about the ethereal Shelley—both eat his cake and have
it. Like Rousseau, he would at once be free and sub-
missive to authority. But that authority must be
identical with his own will. Necessity, as Godwin and
his French teachers understood it, was such an authority.

> Spirit of Nature ! all sufficing Power,
> Necessity ! thou mother of the world !
> Unlike the God of human error, thou
> Requir'st no prayers or praises ;
> . . . all that the wide world contains
> Are but thy passive instruments, and thou

Regard'st them all with an impartial eye
Whose joy or pain thy nature cannot feel
Because thou hast not human sense
Because thou art not human mind.[1]

An alliance with Necessity presents all of the advantages, and demands none of the sacrifices, attendant upon submission to a supernatural power. Necessity leaves a man his essential freedom, since it binds him to no law but that of his own being. Shelley hated Christianity and its priests, not so much because the Church was actually in alliance with Legitimacy and every kind of reaction, but because it was a discipline, because it held back the flow of human sensation and prevented that complete projection of self into all things which was to him happiness. Society, too, he warred against, because it imposed on men the most unreasonable of disciplines, that of convention. Self alone can restrain self. And Necessity is the origin of self.

The Necessarian who is a political reformer, however, is obliged to avoid the fatalistic implications of his faith. For otherwise, princes and priests and lawyers might seem to rule by Necessity. But Shelley will not surrender to fatalism ; at the expense of logic, he will believe that man can direct his actions by his own choice. That is, there is the one choice of reason, and a host of other unreasonable choices. Reason, which is the voice of necessity, has not at present free access to men's minds ; custom, institutions, laws, all block its way. Necessity has apparently dictated something unnecessary. But it is hardly fair to poke fun at Shelley because he failed to solve the problem of determinism. It is more profitable to pass metaphysics humbly and decently by, and try to find out just how Shelley's mind worked. It was not an inferior mind, and the study of it ought not to be entirely vain.

Reason, then, the voice of Necessity, dictates actions that must result in perfect happiness. Once heard, no

---

[1] *Poetical Works*, ed. Forman (1876–7), vol. iv, p. 435.

man ever disobeys this voice. The sole problem of politics is to insure that every human being shall hear it. Every one would hear it were he free to do so. The institutions that suppress man's natural desire for expansion also suppress his natural ability to use the faculty of reason to guide that expansion. This dead weight of institutions cannot be overcome by any mere political struggle ; it is of no use to oppose institutions to institutions. It is revelation that is needed ; for in the cause of progress, to fight restraint with restraint, denial with denial, discipline with discipline, is to destroy the very thing for which we are fighting.

What is really needed is a prophet. Society suffers because truth and nature are shut out from the hearts of men. What more is necessary than to bring truth and nature back again into their hearts ? It is only to poets that men open their hearts :

' Poets are the hierophants of an unapprehended inspiration, the mirrors of the gigantic shadows which futurity casts upon the present ; the words which express what they understand not ; the trumpets which sing to battle, and feel not what they inspire ; the influence which is moved not, but moves. Poets are the unacknowledged legislators of the world.' [1]

It seemed to Shelley that the times were especially favourable for poet legislators. The French Revolution had shaken the old evil institutions. But just because it employed physical power in its work of destruction, that work had been incomplete. The hopes it had aroused were cheated, and a reaction of gloom and misanthropy—the day of Malthus and Byron—had followed. But Shelley was sure that a change was at hand. The revolution of violence had prepared the way for the true revolution of peace and love.

' I have made no attempt to recommend the motives which I would substitute for those at present governing mankind by methodical and systematic argument,' runs the introduction to the *Revolt of Islam*. ' I would only awaken the feelings so that

---

[1] *Prose Works*, ed. Forman (1880), vol. iii, p. 144.

the reader should see the beauty of true virtue, and be incited to those inquiries which have led to my moral and political creed, and that of some of the sublimest intellects in the world. . . . There is no quarter given to Revenge or Envy or Prejudice. Love is celebrated everywhere as the sole law which should govern the moral world.' [1]

' You talk Utopia,' Byron told him.   He did more than that, he lived Utopia.   Nearly all his longer poems end with a vision of a golden age, a vision somehow magically become a fact, heaven brought to earth by force of earth-born aspiration.   This is so in *Queen Mab*, in the lines beginning

> O happy Earth ! reality of Heaven. [2]

It is so in *Hellas*, though doubt and pain have crept into the famous lines, ' The world's great age begins anew.' [3]   And in *Prometheus Unbound* it finds its purest expression :

> The loathsome mask has fallen, the man remains
> Sceptreless, free, uncircumscribed, but man
> Equal, unclassed, tribeless, and nationless,
> Exempt from awe, worship, degree, the king
> Over himself : just, gentle, wise ; but man
> Passionless ?—no, yet free from guilt or pain,
> Which were, for his will made or suffered them,
> Nor yet exempt, though ruling them like slaves,
> From chance, and death, and mutability,
> The clogs of that which else might oversoar
> The loftiest star of unascended heaven,
> Pinnacled dim in the intense inane. [4]

Shelley never quite ceased to look forward to this effortless victory of light within the human spirit.   He is, as we shall see, willing enough to admit the necessity for a long and hard struggle to improve the physical surroundings and the education of the masses.   But whenever the mood of the vates comes upon him, he expects immediate perfection through a mysterious moral

[1] *Poetical Works*, vol. i, p. 85.   [2] Ibid., vol. iv, p. 454.
[3] Ibid., vol. iii, p. 93.   [4] Ibid., vol. ii, p. 236.

cataclysm. In the *Revolt of Islam*, Laon and Cythna achieve the regeneration of their decadent nation simply by showing themselves to the multitude. Demogorgon, the most powerful and unsubstantial of shades, conquers the vicious God of *Prometheus Unbound* with an ease that leads one to wonder why it was not done much earlier. In *Hellas*, the rebellion in Greece seems created and upheld by magic. Tyranny always falls without a struggle. Indeed, it has no chance. It exists only because men are wicked and foolish ; but men cease to be wicked and foolish, and return to their natural purity and intelligence, when they catch the spark flung off from the mind of their saviour. It is salvation by sentiment.

It is, however, unfair to Shelley to judge his political thought from these moments of unearthly inspiration. He did not limit himself to the abstract theories of Necessity and Revelation we have outlined ; nor was he always writing poetry and living poetry, as in the pages of Trelawney. He possessed in his later years rather more of that nameless quality that makes a civilized man —wisdom, sanity, common sense, all just fail to describe it—than his admirers will allow us to remember. And at all times he was willing to admit the necessity of making contingent reforms. The day of complete political regeneration may be far off and it is well to prepare the way for it by useful changes in political detail. And even the political saviour will need a programme. Shelley never lacked for concrete measures.

He would have annual parliaments because they serve to educate the electorate by keeping politics constantly before the minds of the people. But, both in the *Proposals for putting Reform to the Vote* of his youth, and the *Philosophic View of Reform* of his later years, he would not at first have universal suffrage. Only by gradual extensions of the suffrage can the great mass of the ignorant be properly prepared for it. The abolition of rotten boroughs should come first, and then the enfranchisement of the large unrepresented towns.

A small property qualification could be admitted.   In the early pamphlet he criticizes Major Cartwright for the impractical character of his propaganda.   He himself makes the proposal that the sense of the whole English people be taken in a rather complicated sort of plébiscite, to see whether the country really wants parliament to reform itself—a proceeding which in itself would mean the concession of just that principle of popular sovereignty the opponents of Reform were denying.   Of course, he would have universal education at public expense as a necessary adjunct to a wider suffrage.   And there would follow other changes :. disbanding of the standing army ; abolition of sinecures ; abolition of tithes ; disestablishment of the Church of England ;   complete religious toleration.[1]

Along with these Shelley advocated a radical reform in the English legal system.   It is unjust for a rule made in the past to apply to the present, for the circumstances of the present are different from those of the past.   Therefore, common law should be abolished, and judges should decide each case on its own merits, applying common sense instead of law.   By the time the *Philosophical View of Reform* was written, however, Shelley had so far yielded to the world as to demand merely that justice be made ' cheap, certain, and speedy ', and that the institution of juries be extended ' to every possible occasion of jurisprudence '.[2]

His policy on the public debt was equally definite. The emission of paper money and the extension of credit, he writes, have created a leisure class which must be supported by the labouring classes.   The bondholders and shareholders have done nothing to earn their incomes ;   they are a new aristocracy of commerce who have managed to secure a new set of serfs in English working men.   The national debt, which they hold, is

---

[1] *Prose Works*, vol. ii, *A proposal for putting Reform to the vote ; A Philosophical View of Reform* (1920), p. 72.

[2] *Prose Works*, vol. ii, p. 327 ;   *A Philosophical View of Reform*, p. 55.

as it were the charter of these wickedly acquired rights
over their fellows. Let us, says Shelley, simply repudiate
the debt, and we have destroyed this new feudalism.[1]
The capital levy is not entirely new.

For Shelley's economic proposals are not at the mercy
of any consistent economic theory. If orthodox economics
justify the conditions under which the English working
classes exist, then it is clear to him that orthodox economics are hopelessly wrong. He will have nothing to
do with them. Malthus he dismisses as immoral and
hard hearted, without even trying to disprove his
theories. That mere paper evidences like stocks and
bonds can be considered legitimate wealth he will not
admit. They clearly fail to represent any social good,
any contribution by the holder to the sum of human
enjoyments.[2] ' There is no real wealth ', he writes,
' but the labour of man.' [3] This alone is enough to make
him what later was called a Socialist. And although he
admits the rights of small property-holders, he considers
that large property, by the very fact that it is large, was
obtained by fraud, and ought to be confiscated, pre-
sumably by the state.

> What men gain fairly—that they should possess
> And children may inherit idleness,
> From him who earns it—This is understood ;
> Private injustice may be general good.
> But he who gains by base and armed wrong,
> Or guilty fraud, or base compliances,
> May be despoiled ; even as a stolen dress,
> Is stripped from a convicted thief and he
> Left in the nakedness of infamy.[4]

One could scarcely expect so difficult a bit of construction from him as even the least dogmatic of socialisms
must be ; but his sympathy with the poor, expressed in

[1] *A Philosophical View of Reform*, pp. 56–7.
[2] Ibid., pp. 63 ff.
[3] *Poetical Works*, vol. iv, p. 473 (Notes to *Queen Mab*).
[4] Ibid., vol. iv, p. 8.

a hundred passages, his contempt for the commercial classes, and his conviction that labour alone makes wealth, justify his later adoption by leaders of the Socialist movement.

Finally, the goal of all these changes must be a republic. Here again, Shelley does not insist on an immediate revolution ; he will tolerate kingship for a while. But there is no doubt as to his final purpose. Miserable Europe already has before her eyes a concrete refutation of the charge that republican governments are impractical in the modern world.

> There is a people mighty in its youth
> A land beyond the Oceans of the West
>
> .   .   .   .
>
> That land is like an Eagle, whose young gaze
> Feeds on the noontime beam, whose golden plume
> Floats moveless on the storm, and in the blaze
>   Of sunrise gleams when Earth is wrapped in gloom ;
>   An epitaph of glory for the tomb
> Of murdered Europe may thy fame be made,
>   Great People ! as the sands shalt thou become ;
> Thy growth is swift as morn, when night must fade,
> The multitudinous Earth shall sleep beneath thy shade.[1]

The United States of America are the fullest vindication of the dignity of man, the unanswerable reproach to kings and lords and priests. While they endure, no one need lack courage to believe in the ultimate salvation of mankind.

As to the methods of achieving these reforms, Shelley is not explicit. But in certain passages he has indicated methods of political action. There is first of all passive resistance, which he never ceased to believe a practical weapon in the hands of the people.

> Let a vast assembly be,
> And with great solemnity
> Declare with measured words that ye
> Are, as God made ye, free—

[1] *Poetical Works*, vol. i, pp. 283-4.

Let the tyrants pour around
With a quick and startling sound
Like the loosening of a sea
Troops of armed emblazonry.

And if then the tyrants dare
Let them ride among you there,
Slash, and stab, and maim, and hew—
What they like, that let them do.

With folded arms and steady eyes,
And little fear, and less surprise,
Look upon them as they slay
Till their rage had died away.[1]

This is, after all, what happened at Peterloo, plus a little Shelley. If you take away the poetical additions, you have left what is very sound and very practical tactics in the hands of good leaders. Passive resistance is hardly more than an extension of such useful political measures as the boycott.

Shelley expects a great deal from the aid of woman. Cythna is indispensable to Laon in his great work of reformation. And Cythna is the new woman, or rather, the natural woman, to whom the divine impulses of love necessary to the regeneration of the world have been given in a purer form than to man. Woman at present is a hindrance to man in his struggle for liberty, for she is bound by stronger chains of convention than he. But once she is free, she becomes the most precious of allies. Emancipated woman will help to rebuild the new world we have planned.[2] And then there is education, and prison reform, and vegetarianism. This last is especially needed, for the consumption of animal food renders us cruel and depraved. All of these methods will help to prepare society for political revolution.

In the *Philosophical View of Reform* Shelley has outlined a plan of action if parliament should refuse to reform itself. There must be a revolution, first through opinion ;

[1] *Poetical Works*, vol. iii, p. 172.
[2] Ibid., vol. i, pp. 143 ff.

failing that, through violence. The majority must be convinced that these measures are necessary. They will enforce these demands by the methods that led to Peterloo. Their leaders will agitate their grievances ceaselessly, defy the law of libel, and thus attract the persecution of the government, the surest way of furthering their own purposes. Taxes will be refused. Public meetings will be held everywhere. Petitions will load the tables of the House of Commons. Poets, philosophers, and artists will join in this petitioning. What weight, writes Shelley, would not be given wherever English is read, to memorials severally written by Godwin, Hazlitt, Bentham, and Hunt? If all this fails, Shelley is willing to countenance insurrection, though most reluctantly. 'I imagine, however, that before the English Nation shall arrive at that point of moral and political degradation now occupied by the Chinese, it will be necessary to appeal to an exertion of physical strength. If the madness of parties admits no other mode of determining the question at issue. . . .'[1] Here the manuscript breaks off. The *Philosophical View of Reform* was never finished.

Now, this is certainly a Radical programme, and one that hardly adjusts itself to a world as complex and unyielding as this one is to most of us. Yet there is much in Shelley that will not fit any pattern, not even that of the fanatic. In the first place, his prose, especially that of his later years, has far less of the youth who threw Utopian pamphlets from a Dublin balcony than has his poetry. The *Philosophical View of Reform*, if not profound speculation, is certainly not the work of a political miracle-monger. Of the political situation in England in 1819 he wrote :

'The great thing to do is to hold the balance between popular impatience and tyrannical obstinacy : to inculcate with fervour both the right of resistance and the duty of forbearance. You know my principles incite me to take all the good I can get in

[1] *Philosophical View of Reform*, p. 91.

politics, forever aspiring to something more. I am one of those whom nothing will fully satisfy, but who are ready to be partially satisfied in all that is practicable.' [1]

And again, he could write almost like a Burke that ' Nothing is more idle than to reject a limited benefit because we cannot without great sacrifices obtain an unlimited one '.[2]

Nor is his poetry utterly without this touch of earthly reservation. He gives a positive, if rather Utopian content to his notion of liberty which certainly is not to be found in Byron's vague eleutheria :

> What art thou, Freedom ? . . .
>
> .   .   .   .
>
> For the labourer thou art bread,
> And a comely table spread
> From his daily labour come
> To a neat and happy home.
> Thou art clothes, and fire, and food
> For the trampled multitude—
> No—in countries that are free
> Such starvation cannot be
> As in England now we see.[3]

This is wisdom that has been denied to many a worshipper of abstract political freedom since the first declaration of the Rights of Man. And then, in the midst of the bitter, distant, and almost unreal passion of *The Masque of Anarchy*, there comes the touching stanza, so much like the Sussex squire Shelley ought to have been, and was not :

> The old laws of England—they
> Whose reverend heads with age are gray
> Children of a wiser day ;
> And whose solemn voice must be
> Thine own echo—Liberty ! [4]

So much we owe to the Shelley whom no critic can reduce to a formula. Yet the Shelley with whom we

---

[1] *Letters*, ed. Ingpen (1909), vol. ii, p. 756.
[2] *Philosophical View of Reform*, p. 77.
[3] *Poetical Works*, vol. iii, p. 168.   [4] Ibid., p. 172.

are chiefly concerned is the hopeful young revolutionary. And he contrived to retain much of this young revolutionary throughout his thirty years of life. The very language of the *Philosophical View of Reform* is sometimes reminiscent of the intemperate youth who wrote *Queen Mab*. Malthus is ' a priest of course, for his doctrines are those of a eunuch and a tyrant '.[1] The indispensable framework of revolutionary ideas is there : individualism, insistence on the dignity of man as MAN, government as the cause of all political evil, the nation as sovereign, and the majority of people counted by heads as the nation. There is also that haunting sense of crisis, that mystic belief in a wonder-working catastrophe to follow on the generous contagion of his ideals, that fills so much of his poetry. And beckoning on to the weary toilers in the cause of humanity is the vision of perfect peace to be attained at last, of ' such absolute perfection as Plato and Rousseau and other reasoners have asserted, and as Godwin has with irresistible eloquence systematized and developed '.[2]

Furthermore, Shelley, far more than his brother rebel, Byron, is in full revolt against the middle class civilization that had already incorporated in institutional form the energies that in an earlier generation had gone into mechanical invention, industrial expansion, methodism, evangelism, political dissent, and literary innovation. A very great deal of Shelley's poetry can be made to appear not at all inimical to middle class standards ; indeed, it shares the naturalism common to the most respectable members of that civilization. In its infinite yearning, its contempt for limitation, its eternal cry for more, more, more, it is perfectly conformable to the spirit of the new master class. But Shelley's prose, the pamphlets, the notes to the poems, and the letters cannot be evaded. The spirit cannot here be taken for the letter. In the name of the very principles through which the middle class has triumphed, Shelley

[1] *A Philosophical View of Reform*, p. 51.   [2] Ibid., p. 70.

demands its dethronement. The merchant is as good
as the noble : then the day-labourer is as good as the
merchant.

It is thus not entirely true that Shelley's views on
politics and religion became more conservative as he
grew older. He did, indeed, come to regret the publication of *Queen Mab*. But that was because he thought it
bad poetry and because its unguarded frankness seemed
to him more likely to harm than to benefit the cause he
had at heart. There is no suggestion that he has wavered
in his devotion to Liberty, Equality, and Fraternity.
It is true, also, that weariness and doubt creep into his
later work. The moral cataclysm that is to usher in the
new Age of Saturn grows more remote and mysterious.
Peterloo and the Congresses have made this bitter world
of ours more bitter ; and that other and perfect world
where he could always take refuge has receded, and is
not free from pain.

It would seem that, in the unfinished *Triumph of Life*,
Shelley had really begun to doubt this romantic belief
that ' Gefühl ist alles '. But this fragment is not enough
to change the impression, produced alike by *Queen Mab*
and by *Hellas*, that he was ever awaiting a moral and
political miracle, seeking the blue flower of a personal,
yet vicarious happiness, striving to live at once in heaven
and on earth. He was ever consistent with the para-
doxical spirit of a remarkable phrase of his extreme
youth—a phrase that sheds a light on the whole romantic
movement. ' In a short space of time the high-souled
and noble Wolfstein, though still high-souled and noble,
became an experienced bandit.' [1]

With Shelley the antinomian spirit reaches its height
in English literature. He took over from Godwin the
anarchical principles that must logically follow the assumption that all men are potentially capable of guiding their
actions in accordance with a perfect, rational justice.
Into these principles he breathed an emotion which

[1] *Prose Works*, vol. i, p. 171 (*Zastrozzi*).

transformed them from a speculation into a faith. But
though they became a faith they did not cease to be
a speculation. The heaven of Shelley's faith is not to
be attained by subduing the flesh, not to be won by
labour and sacrifice ; it is entered simply by submitting
to the impulse of the moment, by keeping this impulse
free from the corruption of external circumstances. For
this heaven must be on earth. And since it obviously is
not, the natural inference is that men's good impulses
are prevented from coming to fruition, stifled at birth by
laws and inhibitions. There are no laws in heaven ; away
with them then on earth ! Shelley really believed that

> It is our vice
> Which thus enchains us to permitted ill—
> We might be otherwise—we might be all
> We dream of happy, high, majestical.
> Where is the love, beauty, and truth we seek
> But in our minds ? *And if we were not weak*
> *Should we be less in deed than in desire ?* [1]

Desire far outstrips this world of flesh ; so then, push
and pull the world frantically along after desire. It did
not occur to Shelley that desire could be brought back
to earth. Perhaps it does not often occur to any man.

3

After every reservation is made Byron and Shelley are
left rebels against society. Their lives are a cycle of
rebellion—discontent, struggle, failure. Or are the romantics right, and does the cycle find a fourth and
final term in success ? If so, it must be a success obtained
out of failure, a triumph of rebellious spirit against
conforming flesh ; and the test must lie in their effect
on their enemy, society. The influence of Byron,
especially, has been so carefully studied that one cannot
hope to add much to our knowledge of it. But it is
necessary to resume briefly the relations of these two
poets with their contemporaries in order to mark the

---

[1] *Poetical Works*, vol. iii, p. 113. I must confess to the italics.

place of their politics in their world. Even more than in the case of the Lake poets, we must beware lest we accept as common property ideas that are peculiar to their owner. Some error there must be, for the ideas of no man can quite fit anything so formless as an historical period ; but we can at least find out whether or not there is a rough sort of correspondence.

Byron, at least, has left traces enough of his passage. When he assumed the name of Noel, as the condition of an inheritance, he used to delight in the signature ' N.B.' ; and if a man's importance is to be measured by the amount of printed matter devoted to him, Byron is indeed a worthy rival of Napoleon Bonaparte. Newspapers, periodicals, memoirs of the time are filled with his name. All England read of him, as it now reads of boxers and murderers. His poems sold like novels. He was translated into a dozen foreign tongues. He became involved in a domestic scandal, fled to Italy and led a flauntingly licentious and un-English life. His name only occupied the more space in the English press. Then he died, and after a brief apotheosis as the hero of Missolonghi, was almost forgotten, and sunk as a poet below Wordsworth, Shelley, Keats, and Coleridge. On the Continent he continued to inspire the Liberal revolt against the system of Metternich and was long held in high honour by the patriots of Germany and Italy. In England his influence in politics was never so great as on the Continent ; but his vast popularity during his lifetime has provided rich materials for the study of what he did achieve in politics.

Almost from the first he was a party figure. It is true that the Conservative *Gentleman's Magazine* is very kind to the author of *Childe Harold* :

' We congratulate his lordship and the publick on this maturer demonstration of poetical genius, and, we will add, though foreign to the present purpose, on the fair promise of excelling in the British Senate, evinced by his eloquent maiden speech.' [1]

[1] *Gentleman's Magazine*, May 1812.

But Byron was not long to move in an atmosphere as serene as this. The Tories soon found that he held dangerous views. In 1814, the *Courier* gives a sneering tribute to his importance :

'The Lord BYRON has assumed such a poetico-political and such a politico-poetical air and authority, that in our double capacity of men of letters and politicians, he forces himself upon our recollection.' [1]

On his separation from his wife in 1816, however, this partisan dislike was outspoken. He was almost uniformly attacked by Tory, and defended by Whig papers. An obscure reactionary journal, the *Anti-Gallican Monitor* was more than usually ingenuous in confounding poetry, politics, and marital misconduct. It concludes that, ' if everything said of Lord Byron be true, it would appear that the Whigs are not altogether so immaculate as they themselves would wish the world to suppose.' [2] The *Morning Post*—now its familiar Tory self—was able most virtuously to reproach Byron with oriental ideas of caste, and with spreading sentiments unworthy of a citizen of a free country.[3] The *Champion* significantly concluded that there was an obvious connexion between the conduct of the noble lord and his *politics*.[4]

On the Whig side, however, the *Morning Chronicle* defended him in a dignified way,[5] and the *Independent Whig* grew eloquent in his cause. ' Than Lord Byron ', it ran, ' who has a higher or a juster claim to public esteem and admiration ; whether we regard him as a Poet or a Patriot, now charming our souls with the magic powers and magnificent harmonies of his immortal lyre, and now standing up the Champion of a Free Press, the advocate of Public Independence, and a Nation's invaded rights—whether our hearts thrill responsive to those animated pictures of Nature whose kindred is recognized by the metaphysical agents in every bosom,

---

[1] *Courier*, 5 Feb. 1814.   [2] *Anti-Gallican Monitor*, 21 April 1816.
[3] *Morning Post*, 23 April 1816.   [4] *Champion*, 28 April 1816.
[5] *Morning Chronicle*, April 1816.

or the lethargic energies of liberty and patriotism are wakened by the loftier numbers of his harp ;—who will refuse to his transcendant talents the just homage of public reverence and wonder ? ' [1]   A few weeks later, this same journal in a leader on ' Lord Byron and the British Press ', points out how much political hatred had inspired the outbreak against Byron's morals.[2]

The quarrel soon passed into the periodical press.   The *Gentleman's Magazine* rashly copied Byron's sonnet on Lake Leman into its pages.   It soon received an indignant protest and some verses to act as an antidote to the Byronic poison from ' One who, though of gentle blood, is not a blasphemer of his God, a libeller of his sovereign, or an enemy of his fellow creatures '.[3]   Another correspondent of this magazine is glad that Byron has taken his dangerous greatness off to the Continent, and consecrates a few couplets to the fallen poet :

> Yes, hapless Bard ! thine errors I deplore—
> Rich were thy talents, but thy morals poor ! [4]

The pamphleteers did not fail to make use of the opportunity afforded them by public interest in Byron. *Childe Harold's Monitor, A Layman's Epistle to a Certain Nobleman,* and others appeared in bad verse.   Some flourished in prose, under such titles as *The Radical Triumvirate ; Infidel Paine, Lord Byron,* and *Surgeon Lawrence ; Cato to Lord Byron on the Immorality of his Works ; Paradise Lost vindicated from the Charge of exculpating Cain ; A remonstrance to Mr. John Murray ; The London Liberal,* an *Antidote to the Liberal ; A Critique on the Liberal.*   Few of these pamphlets can add much to our knowledge of Byron's relations with his fellows. They are mostly protests from shocked Englishmen of traditional English morality.   Some object to the ' wildness ' of his taste ; but most make a distinction between

---

[1] *Independent Whig,* 21 April. 1816.   [2] Ibid., 5 May 1816.
[3] *Gentleman's Magazine,* May 1816.   [4] Ibid., Feb. 1818.

the virtues of his poetry and the vices of his private life. Cato (George Burges) goes somewhat deeper. He couples Shelley's name with Byron's—this in 1824—and reproaches them with furthering the dissolution of social bonds in a time ' when authority, duty, obedience, devotion, are daily more and more losing their hold on the hearts and affections of men '.¹

Perhaps the most far-reaching statement of Byron's influence on English life is to be found in the pages of the *New Times*. A man named Thurtell had committed an unusually brutal murder, and had preserved during his trial the most cold-blooded calm. Lord Byron's works were obviously at the bottom of it, said the *New Times*.

' It may be that Thurtell never read the blasphemies of Lord Byron's *Cain*—perhaps he may not have met with those disgusting stanzas of *Don Juan* (unparalleled in the annals of brutality) which convert the killing *and eating* a man into a subject of loathsome and appalling merriment. But Thurtell lived in an age which had been disgraced with these demoniacal publications, which had sucked in their poison, and wilfully suffered them to corrupt and degrade the moral sense of the community. We cannot wonder, therefore, that he was brutal and unfeeling in the perpetration of the murder, or easy and careless after he had committed it.' ²

This is literally quite as absurd as Harriet Shelley's attribution of her husband's profligacy to the reading of *Political Justice* ; but like that delightful bit of *naïveté* it reminds us that books, too, have lives, and sometimes do tangible and most unbookish things.

At Byron's death the Tory journals relented somewhat. The *New Times*, indeed, continued implacable, and coldly remarked that ' it is most painful to record the extinction of genius, when we cannot soften our regret by remembrance of its usefulness '.³ *The Times*, however, rejoiced that ' that noblest of causes, the deliverance of

¹ *Cato to Lord Byron on the Immorality of his Writings* (1824), p. 119.
² *New Times*, 12 Jan. 1824.   ³ Ibid., 15 May 1824.

Greece, employed the whole of Lord Byron's latter days
—of his pecuniary resources and of his masculine spirit.
It was a cause worthy of a poet and a hero '.[1] The
Morning Chronicle said :

' Thus has perished, in the flower of his age, in the
noblest of causes, one of the greatest poets England ever
produced.' [2]

As a pamphleteer remarked, the general opinion of the
Liberal press was that ' Lord Byron was one of those
characters from whose existence new ideas date their
commencement ; that fresh career of society, which is
beginning in Europe, wanted the stimulus of a mind
like his to carry it onward to happiness and glory '.[3]

Byron, in fact, had never been in England the pariah
he liked, from Venice or Ravenna, to think himself. In
the first place, with the exception of a few very second-
rate critics who mistook the forms of literature for
literature itself and were not to be separated from the
lifeless remains of the eighteenth century, those who
attacked his morals and his politics conceded his greatness as a poet, which is to make no small concession.
But there were many to whom he was a hero and a
prophet. Some clung about his greatness as men must
who come under the influence of that quality which
those who lack it have cheapened into ' personality '.
His Whiggism was sufficiently official to command the
approval of the *Chronicle* and the *Edinburgh*. Finally, he
seems to have been admired by many humble people, to
whom he held hope of a fuller political future. Among
the papers of that desperate character, the Jacobin
Thomas Hardy, there is a yellowed clipping of Byron's
lines on *The Prince Regent standing between the coffins of
Henry VIII and Charles I at Windsor.*

> Charles to his people, Henry to his wife,
> In him the double tyrant starts to life ;

[1] *The Times*, 15 May 1824.
[2] *Morning Chronicle*, 15 May 1824.
[3] Gordon, C., *Life and Genius of Lord Byron* (1824), p. 68.

> Justice and death have mixed their dust in vain,
> Each royal vampire wakes to life again.
> Ah, what can tombs avail!—since these disgorge
> The blood and dust of both—to mould a George! [1]

Carefully cherished among the relics of the State Trials of 1794, these lines must have brought to the old man a second youth of hope. Of these same lines, Moore wrote from Wiltshire to Byron that, though still in manuscript, they ' circulated with wonderful avidity ; even some clods in this neighbourhood have had a copy sent to them by some ladies in town '.[2] Then there is the album at Hucknall Torkard where Byron was buried. Bowring, one of Bentham's most faithful servants, himself not unknown to the Muses, presented the album to the church, and began it with an inscription in which he calls Byron ' the greatest man of our age '. To this little Nottinghamshire village came many admirers of Byron and recorded their sentiments in the album. Many of them were tradesmen and mechanics, and some could hardly spell out their praises. The political sympathies of the writers are almost always evident, as in the entry :

' 1826 Sept. 25. Jonathan Thomas Sleap, of the Middle Temple London visited the tomb of Lord Byron, the greatest poet of his day ; and was induced to do so from the great respect he felt for his memory, he being (in the opinion of the writer) an example for all men (worthy of the name) to follow in his efforts to release from the bonds of slavery (of the most debasing kind) his fellow men.' [3]

The Mirror, a miscellany with a large circulation among the lower middle classes, called Byron ' this guardian spirit of liberty '.[4] But again it was reserved to his enemies to pay the greatest tribute to his success as a political leader. What have the continental monarchs so maligned by the Liberal press done after all, asks

---

[1] Hardy, Papers, B.M. Adds. 27818, f. 700.
[2] Byron, *Works*, Letters, vol. iii, p. 57 *n*.
[3] Album at Hucknall Torkard, quoted in *Byroniana* (ed. J. M. L., 1834).   [4] *Mirror*, 21 June 1828.

Blackwood's, and answers its own question : ' They have crushed their Benthamites and Byronites, knocked up Liberalism, and restored tranquillity to the whole continent.' [1] Nor was it perhaps entirely absurd to speak of Byronites in English politics. Certain it is that the gospel of Bentham needed the aid of such a vague, but thoroughly social, emotion as was Byron's love of liberty ; and it is probable that his poetry helped to keep up the spirits of many Liberals who must have pined away on the work of Dumont and the elder Mill.

This dissemination of Liberal sentiment—and ' sentiment ' is a much better word for it than ' ideas '—is probably Byron's greatest political work in England. In another way he did become the patron of the discontented minority who thought this sort of Liberalism hypocrisy. But in the main he is represented by his good friend Hobhouse, who died, deservedly, a peer. It is true that on the Continent he became, as the Portuguese minister Palmella wrote to Canning, a *nouveau Tyrtée*. To trace his influence in the affairs of Italy, Germany, and Poland, however, would require a volume in itself. In England he was not, politically, the symbol of a cause ; and the chief reason why he was not is just this : he can be taken, as we have seen, in two ways. In one, he is the poet of liberty and equality, modified by social experience into the faith of an orderly, but rapidly growing middle class society, who found wildness and sentiment in literature and nationalism and Liberalism in politics a necessary recompense for the routine of home and business. Ever since the Civil War and the Revolution, England had been steadily approaching such a state of political society ; since the Wartons it had been approaching such a society in its artistic and literary standards ; since Wesley it had been approaching such a religious society. Canning's European policy, the Reform Bill, the poets and prose writers of the new romantic school, and the Oxford movement, very soon

---

[1] *Blackwood's Edinburgh Magazine*, Oct. 1824, p. 451.

brought this society to its perfection. There was no need of a poet-prophet to usher in the Victorian Age. But, in another sense, Byron was the poet of the nihilism that is simply the new faith in natural impulse stripped of religious, social, aesthetic control. We have seen how Byron turned against the public that had delighted in the harmless, and even decent, melancholy of *Childe Harold*. The happy middle class found out that the Byron of *Don Juan* was threatening all the props of its happiness, and it repudiated him. Many a continental admirer of his must have done the same, had Byron been to him more than the poet of national unity and of emancipation from the system of Metternich. Treitschke would hardly have thought so highly of him, had his poetry seemed to threaten the foundations of Prussian ' liberalism '. But why did not Byron become the poet of those who were discontented with the new order in England? He did, in some degree, as the album at Hucknall Torkard, the poem among Thomas Hardy's papers, and the large circulation of various *Lives* of Byron would indicate. In general, however, he was not accepted as a poet of social revolt after the Reform Bill. Cast out by one party, he was not taken in by another. This was due partly to the failure of his works to maintain their literary reputation, partly to the obscurity of such poems as *Manfred* and *Cain*, partly, too, to an old distrust of the proud aristocrat. But chiefly it is due to the fact that Byron had no positive programme, no gospel of social reform. He railed much at kings; but genuine Radicalism in nineteenth-century England was concerned with far more serious matters than royalty— which may largely explain the persistence of royalty. This failure of Byron to see that the real problems of politics are economic was clearly in the mind of Karl Marx when he said :

' The real difference between Byron and Shelley is this : those who understand them and love them rejoice that Byron died at thirty-six, because if he had lived he would have become a reactionary bourgeois; they grieve that Shelley died at twenty-nine, because he was essentially a revolutionist and he would always have been one of the advanced guard of socialism.' [1]

Shelley's name has indeed continued on the banners of social revolt. Even while he lived it was inscribed there in letters large enough for the enemy to discern. The *New Times* warned its readers:

'We speak our sincere opinion in saying, that if we desired to bring a poetic sanction to the basest passions of the human heart, or the most odious, revolting, and unnameable crimes of human society, we should seek it in the works of certain poets who have lately visited the Lake of Geneva.' [2]

That Byron and Shelley were meant was clear enough to the good reader, for scandal had long been rife on the meeting of the two poets in Switzerland. The *Quarterly* in its review of *Prometheus Unbound* finds that Shelley is a bad poet because he is inspired with a hatred of the Tory Government; and it thinks it strange 'that such a volume should find readers, and still more strange that it should meet with admirers'.[3] 'Hibernicus' writes to the *Morning Chronicle* that *Queen Mab* exercises an influence as noxious as that of the *Age of Reason* or Hume *On Miracles*.[4] We are told that *Queen Mab* was published in a pocket edition for the use of 'Radical mechanics';[5] and Cuthbert Southey found 'cheap editions of *Don Juan* and *Queen Mab* lying in the cottages of his rural flock'.[6] Hunt published some of Shelley's poetry in the *Examiner*. Hazlitt referred often enough to him,[7] and characteristically, as when he wrote, 'No one (that I know of) is the happier, better, or wiser, for reading Mr. Shelley's *Prometheus Unbound.*' *Blackwood's*,

---

[1] Aveling, *Shelley and Socialism*, in *To-day*, April 1888.
[2] *New Times*, quoted in *Gentleman's Magazine*, 1819, Supplement, p. 625.
[3] *Quarterly Review*, October 1821.
[4] *Morning Chronicle*, 14 January 1823.
[5] Forman, H. B., in *Notebook of the Shelley Society*, 1886.
[6] Southey, C. C., *Life and Correspondence of Robert Southey*, vol. v, p. 75.
[7] Hazlitt, *Works*, vol. x, pp. 259, 266; vol. vi, p. 149; vol. vii, p. 246.

in the face of the *Quarterly*, called him ' a true poet ',
and praised *Alastor*.[1] All this came while Shelley was
alive. Soon after his death, the author of a sermon on
Lord Byron's works, commenting on the instructive
value to good men of lives of bad, asks, ' Why does not
somebody, competent to the undertaking, write a life of
Percy Bysshe Shelley ? ' [2]

That sentence must be left untouched, stark in its
irony. For Shelley has become the subject for what
a French critic calls ' la hagiographie romantique '.
As early as 1828 there is in the *Athenaeum* a passage that
points the way for the rehabilitation of Shelley.

' We will venture to assert that those of his (Shelley's) doctrines
which are at first sight the most awfully pernicious, are uniformly
objectionable from the form rather than the feeling. It is, on
the other hand, undeniable that his sympathies are the fondest
and the best, his aspirations the purest and most lofty.' [3]

For Shelley soon became a great poet to many who did
not at all share his republicanism, his hatred of the
Christian Church, his Radical faith in humanity. His
contemporaries had made him an outcast for the very
qualities that endeared him to posterity. Only, posterity
did not have to live with him. The difference between
the old generation and the new in their feelings toward
Shelley is well illustrated by a conversation Wordsworth
had with the young Gladstone. Wordsworth remarked
that the discrepancy between Shelley's creed and his
imagination was ' the marring idea of his work ' ; ' in
which description ', says Gladstone, ' I could not concur.' [4]

This adoption of Shelley by respectable people is
worth consideration. Many undoubtedly sought a pure
aesthetic pleasure in his poetry, and no more found
moral ideas in it than in music. But the number of
those who seek in poetry sensations utterly detached

---

[1] *Blackwood's Edinburgh Magazine*, June, November 1819.
[2] Styles, J., *Lord Byron's Works* (1824), p. 19.
[3] *Athenaeum*, 1828, No. 5, p. 70.
[4] Morley, *Life of Gladstone*, Bk. II, Chap. III.

from the rest of the tissue of their lives is far smaller
than the cant of modern art would have it. It is surely
not unfair to assume that most of Shelley's readers
found that his poetry fell into their own scheme of
things. His unrest and striving, his swelling emotion, his
desire to project himself into all things are the common
dreams of humanity. All that he wrote was a product of
that affective disposition that is for ever pushing man
on to enlarge the boundaries of his experience. He
shared to the full the acquisitive spirit of the Revolution.
' The vital truth Shelley everywhere enforced ', wrote
George Henry Lewes in 1841, ' although treated as
a chimaera by most of his contemporaries, and indulged
as a dream by some others, has become the dominant
Idea—the philosophy and faith of this age, throughout
Europe. It is progression, humanity, perfectibility,
civilization, democracy—call it what you will, this is
the truth uttered unceasingly by Shelley, and universally
received by us.' [1] This rather alarming series of synonyms
puts very clearly the common basis of Shelley's thought
and Victorian civilization : a faith in the goodness of
human instincts asserting themselves in a ceaseless
struggle to obtain a richer and more varied life—in a
dynamic rather than a static society.

Lewes, indeed, was on the very edge of respectability,
and certainly subscribed to more of Shelley's political
doctrines than was usual. Professor Dowden, one of
Shelley's most distinguished biographers, is in this respect
more the true Shelleyite of the 'eighties ; and Dowden
has always for the politics of his hero the patronizing
toleration of the good citizen for the fanatic he does
not fear. As Shelley felt, he wrote, and, what is more,
acted. But most of his readers could not act as their
feelings demanded ; that was why they read Shelley.
His poetry, like the British flag, the Church of England,
and many other loyalties, gave scope for the flow of their
feelings. In so far as these feelings were not prodded

[1] Lewes, G. H., in *Westminster Review*, vol. xxxv, p. 321.

into unquiet and discontent, but soothed and stilled by
Shelley's poetry, he may be said to have been a force
working for moral stability. And, like the Lake poets,
he was doubtless for many just such a force. He still
continues to be, for a recent writer goes so far as to say,
' What Wordsworth said concerning his own poems is
true of the works of Shelley. " They will co-operate
with the benign tendencies in human nature and society,
and will, in their degree, be efficacious in making men
wiser, better, and happier." ' [1]
Yet Shelley was also a force working for social discontent and revolt, and as such has always had disciples
who refused to permit this gentle expurgation of his
work by time and sentiment. So, too, there were those
who could not forget the unpleasant things he managed
to do. The clearer minds saw Shelley as the demon or
the angel of revolt ; it required some befuddlement to
see in him a prop of the virtuous feelings that support
the citizen, the husband, the father, and the state.
Matthew Arnold's opinion need hardly be repeated
here. Jowett wrote to Miss Tennant (Mrs. Asquith,
later Countess of Oxford) : ' I think they had better
have left him where the late Mrs. Shelley left him, for
it is impossible to convert him into a decent or honourable man.' [2] Such was the opinion of many nineteenth-
century Liberals. They felt that Shelley set Liberty
above Liberalism.

And so he did. He never set on his own affective
impulses, on his own emotional and physical expansion,
the limits that the average citizen of romantic inclina-
tions sets on his ; or more accurately, he could never
centre his emotions in a corporate loyalty that auto-
matically controlled them. In his writings there is no
trace of this control, this necessary limitation exercised
by institutions, tradition, and experience on human
beings striving to find finite gratification for infinite

---

[1] Macdonald, *The Radicalism of Shelley* (1912), p. 138.
[2] *Life and Letters of Benjamin Jowett* (1897), vol. ii, p. 318.

desires. The reader has to discover those limitations for himself: he will not find them in Shelley. And if the reader be seeking to escape their control, to free his instincts and not to rule them, to let his feelings run out like water and not to direct their course, then will he find that Shelley preaches a gospel of revolt. Stanley, of African fame, once told a member of the Shelley Society, an organization by no means revolutionary in its constitution:

' You are a funny people, you Shelleyites: You are playing—at a safe distance yourselves may be—with fire. In spreading Shelley you are indirectly helping to stir up the great Socialist question—the great question of the needs and wants and wishes of unhappy men, the one question which bids fair to swamp you all for a bit.' [1]

From the way Stanley speaks, it is probable that both ' Shelley ' and ' the great Socialist question ' meant to him rather vague and general symbols than precise ideas; but that is the fate of all men, and of all principles, that become part of the political consciousness of the people. Such a symbol Shelley has become.

For he is one of the accredited poets of Socialism.

' Whence, for example, came the first stirrings of idealism, of enthusiasm within the men and women, old and young, who in every town and village form the growing points and enriching stems of the Socialist movement—the most portentous political movement in the world's history? Assuredly not from the million fold paragraphs of newspapers or the bewildering twinkling of picture shows. No, not from these, but in most instances from Isaiah and the Gospels, from Burns and Shelley, from Ruskin, Morris, and Whitman.' [2]

Shelley, that is, is one of the poets of the men who are seeking to carry out the humanitarian principles of the democratic revolution to their logical conclusion, and achieve a proletarian revolution. His faith in the natural goodness of man has persisted as a social faith through

[1] Quoted by H. B. Forman in *Publications of the Shelley Society*, Extra Series, No. 4.
[2] Glasier, F. B., *Socialism in Song* (1920), p. viii.

all the trials of science and experience; his belief in the coming miracle of a bloodless revolution, divinely guided by that divinity which is in common men, has been strengthened by the influence of writers like Marx. One of Shelley's humanitarian followers writes :

' By the very nature of the case, it is not to the learned and cultured classes that Shelley's gospel will appeal, but rather to those whose conditions and surroundings have not incapacitated them for that most vital learning and only true culture—a conception of the essential equality and brotherhood of mankind. The ideal anarchism of which Shelley is the herald is a state of equality founded not on the competitive or baser element of human nature, but on the higher and ultimately more powerful element which is love.' [1]

This, however, is most temperate enthusiasm. To some of his disciples, only the language of religion is fit for his praise :

' Immortal amid immortals, his spirit in communion with the Most High, fully conscious in its individuality—immortal amid philosophers and the regenerators of the race, with Buddha, with Moses, with Socrates, with Mahomet, with Christ ' [2]

is Percy Bysshe Shelley !

All the elements of the old eighteenth-century creed are thus to be found in these modern exponents of Shelley—the natural goodness of man, his corruption by civilization (' culture '), the domination of man's affective instincts (' love ') over reason in all its forms, social and individual, the leadership of the divinely inspired poet-legislator, who is a leader precisely because the expansive energies of his emotions are not checked by fear of social consequences. Modern socialism, like any great movement for reform, rests on a gospel which can command the hearts as well as the heads of its followers. It must contain an element of mysticism ; that is, it must provide itself with a superhuman justification, with a common

[1] Salt, H. S., *Shelley's Principles : Has Time refuted or condemned them ?* (1892), p. 65.
[2] Sotheran, C., *Shelley as a Philosopher and a Reformer* (1876), p. 50.

something from which each individual believer can draw strength. There can be no doubt that socialism, for most of the faithful at least, rests at bottom on the dogma of the natural goodness of man. The so-called lower classes are really οἰ ἄριστοι. They have never been corrupted inwardly by nineteenth-century competitive civilization. They are better by nature than the upper classes who have been so corrupted. But what is most natural is also most divine, and therefore the struggling proletarian finds in his own cravings the high justification of faith. Socialism has a hold on men precisely because through it self-interest is made socially operative in the only way possible—as a mystic attachment to a corporate reality which has a sanctity not conferred upon it by the mere fact of association, but by the nature of things, by divinity.

All this is in Shelley, and in modern socialism. But it is, as far as politics is concerned, all that there is in Shelley. It is not all that there is in modern socialism. At least, there are hopeful signs that intelligent leadership is slowly applying the lessons of reason to the control and guidance of the vast energies aroused by the spread of the modern spirit of expansion into the proletariat. It is not impossible that a proletarian revolution may be effected in England with as little harm to the stability of English life, and even to the cultural heritage of its civilization, as resulted from the middle-class revolution. And in that case will Shelley's poetry and Shelley's ideas cease to provoke unrest, and become a source of calm and content? Or do they carry for ever the germs of revolt, of discontent and striving rendered hopeless by despair? This is the problem to which we must return. For the present it is sufficient to repeat that Shelley was a rather obscure but not unknown fanatic to his contemporaries, that since his death he has been made for many the respectable poet of the family circle, and that for others he has become a prophet of social revolution, even as he had hoped.

4

Byron and Shelley are linked in rebellion against the England of George the Fourth. And, in spite of Byron's fitful efforts to act like a good Englishman and to write like Pope, the two outcasts have a great deal in common. They share with Hazlitt and Scott and almost all the great writers of their age a characteristic view of Nature. That is, they demand space to grow according to an inner impulse; and that space is provided by what they call Nature. But Scott's common sense taught him the very narrow limits of that space in modern society, and his fortunate disposition allowed him to find contentment in loyalty to institutions which human experience had established as space for common emotional ranging. Hazlitt, though fiercely demanding to be let alone in his own little field, was quite willing to respect those of his neighbours, and to keep his own growth within bounds. Byron, at times, shows a similar feeling for the necessary limitations of civilized life. But in general he and Shelley will be content with nothing less than boundless fields. They will never stop growing, and they must not be stinted for room. To drop the metaphor, Byron and Shelley are both dissatisfied with the social and political state of England because they can conceive a better state: that is, they are unhappy and discontented because their England is not the England of their desires. But Nature taught them that their desires were good, and the true guides to action. They will live in the natural England of their desires, not in the unnatural England man has made. Yet this unnatural England is the land which a whole generation, sharing with Byron and Shelley a common ethical belief in the goodness and sufficiency of the universal, uncritical desire of men for self-expression, had been labouring to convert to its desire. Men like the Lake poets were, on the whole, satisfied that they had succeeded; or at any rate they had come to believe that this self-expansion had gone far enough. Byron and Shelley, in the name of the very faith in Nature for which Wordsworth and his fellows had struggled, revolted against the compromise their elders had made with society, law, convention, and constraint. Change was the only law they could accept, and change meant revolt, since most men are ruled by this evil power of convention that stifles desire—and life. The end of their revolt was nihilism and despair.

> Out of the day and night
> A joy has taken flight
>   Fresh spring, and summer, and winter hoar
> Move my faint heart with grief, but with delight
>   No more—Oh, never more!

And yet perhaps not quite. For in their philosophy, if despair is the end of revolt, it is the beginning of thought.

V

ROMANTICISM AND THE PRESS

I

MANY other men of letters were involved in the political strife that led to the Reform Bill of 1832. It is to be presumed that a trace of political ideas could be found even in the works of Henry Pye. Blake wrote a poem on the French Revolution ; but Blake was mad, unprofitably mad. The historian of political ideas, more fortunate than the historian of letters, can neglect him. Then there were Samuel Rogers, banker, Whig, and poet, in whose salon men of letters met men of the world ; Thomas Campbell, another poet now become minor, who helped to found the University of London, and whose *Gertrude of Wyoming* is an interesting example of the survival into the nineteenth century of the notion of an American Arcadia ; Thomas Moore, poet of fashion, love, and Ireland, whose satirical and patriotic verse gave him no little political influence in his day— though his patriotism was too exclusively lyrical to satisfy Irishmen like O'Connell and his followers ; Landor, one of England's long line of aristocratic re- publicans ; Leigh Hunt, who bravely forsook belles lettres and the fresh green fields of Canning Town to write on politics in *The Examiner*. The political thought of these men—especially that of Landor—is often in- teresting ; but it can add little to what we have already learned from their contemporaries. It will be enough to note that they were all concerned with politics, and in a measure possessed political influence. Moore was offered a seat in parliament for Limerick ; Hunt's *Examiner* was long the most important Liberal weekly in the country ; and Rogers and Moore were at least within the periphery of such important circles as those of Holland House and Bowood.

2

We are still faced, however, with the difficulty of relating the political ideas of the romanticists to the ideas that were current among their fellows. Some rough checking-up has been already attempted, and some estimate made of the degree of seriousness with which the world took the political activities of the Jacobin poets and novelists, the Lake Poets, Scott and Hazlitt, Byron and Shelley. It will be worth while to go a little further into this matter ; for too much attention can hardly be given to the difficult task of following an idea at its work among the crowd.

Were we to weigh the importance of these men of letters in the eyes of contemporary politicians the results would be of the slightest. For Tories like Pitt, Wellesley and Canning, and Whigs like Fox, Holland, and Melbourne, had been brought up in the traditional eighteenth-century way, and never quite accepted the new school of romance. We read that Pitt's study at Walmer Castle was strewn with Greek and Latin classics,[1] but no mention is made of the presence of *Lyrical Ballads*. Fox tried to keep an open mind, and did have romantic tastes to the extent of preferring Euripides to Sophocles and Aeschylus. But with the youthful romantic literature of his age he does not seem to have been impressed. *Pizarro*, he sensibly remarked, was ' the worst thing possible '.[2] Men like Wilberforce took life too seriously to read ; men like Creevey took it not seriously enough. Finally, the good old king himself had no sympathy for the new attitude toward Nature. He told George Rose that ' he had no taste for what

[1] *Diaries and Correspondence of George Rose* (1860), vol. ii, p. 292.
[2] Rogers, *Recollections*, p. 16.

was called the fine *wild* beauties of Nature ; he did not
like the mountains and other romantic scenes of which
he sometimes heard much '.[1]

Without doubt, however, an attempt to find in the
words and deeds of statesmen not a direct connexion
with the romantic writers, but a similar attitude on
certain problems, would be less unsuccessful.   In the
generation of Disraeli and Gladstone it would produce
much.   Even in that of Pitt such an investigation would
have some interesting results.   We can here merely
indicate how one might go about it.   Romilly, for
instance, owed much to the sentimental belief in natural
goodness that produced—and destroyed—the Enlightenment.   He rejoices at the neat valley-farms near Aber-
gavenny :

' They bespeak a happy equality of property, and transport one
back in idea to the infancy of society.' [2]

In Stirling he sees an almshouse founded by a tailor,
and notes with feeling the inscription, ' Forget not,
reader, that the shears of this man do more honour to
human nature than the swords of conquerors.' [3]   Fox,
too, was all his life a defender of the under dog, a lover
of liberty and a hater of constraint.   Byron might have
written as Fox did about love of liberty :

' If it be an illusion, it is one that has brought forth more of
the best qualities and exertions of the human mind, than all
other causes put together, and it serves to give an interest in the
affairs of the world which without it would be insipid.' [4]

Finally, Canning himself gives evidence that English
politics were being penetrated by the same philosophy
of expansion and democracy that inspired the Revolution
everywhere.   In the *Anti-Jacobin* he had disposed of the
silly cant of Southey, Coleridge, and the other friends of
humanity with gratifying finality.   He himself, however,

---

[1] *Diaries and Correspondence of George Rose*, vol. ii, p. 183.
[2] *Life of Romilly* (1840), vol. i, p. 341.   [3] Ibid., vol. ii, p. 24.
[4] Holland, *Memoirs of the Whig Party* (1852), vol. i, p. 67.

became the first defender of oppressed nationalities ; abroad, at least, he was a Liberal of Liberals. And, on his death, a Mexican newspaper found for this English-man, this Etonian, this urbane scorner of the new religion of humanity, an epitaph :

> HERE LIES THE FRIEND OF ALL MEN
> THE MAN OF HUMANITY
> THE CONSOLATION OF OUR TROUBLES
> IN THIS PLACE OUR HOPES LIE BURIED.[1]

3

It is not, however, to the lives of statesmen that we can go with most profit. In any progressive and demo-cratic society—and modern societies are all, apparently, progressive and democratic—public opinion must have a certain margin of advance over actual political measures. The practical politician, like any other professional man, is usually in these days a bit behind the times. He is a result and not a cause ; one suspects a servant, not a master. Perhaps the real changes are economic ; but at any rate these changes spread through society with a thoroughness made possible only by the rule of what is vaguely called public opinion. Obviously, we now use the words public opinion loosely but significantly to describe the sovereignty of the people ; and that is a product of the Revolution. The sovereign people expresses itself, not merely through the vote, not merely by the inarticulate rule of custom, but vocally through its Press. It is the Press that is the real ' Child and Champion of Jacobinism '. It is there that we must look for a reflection of the political thought of the romanticists. If we find it we may be pretty sure that their thought is near enough to the realities of politics to be worth criticizing.

---

[1] *El Vera Cruzano Libre*, 19 October 1827, quoted in the *Morning Chronicle*, 1 January 1828.

This Press was almost a new thing. The period with
which we are concerned saw a very great increase in the
amount of printed matter circulated in Great Britain.
In 1753 stamps for newspapers were issued to the amount
of seven and a half millions ; in 1792 the amount was
fifteen millions, and in 1821 nearly twenty-five millions
in spite of a large duty which raised the price to 7*d*.[1]
It is estimated that about 1818, when both of the great
literary reviews reached their highest circulation, they
were read by more than one hundred thousand people.[2]
As for books, there is a noticeable increase in the number
of new publications. These had been, for the years
1792–1802, 372 per year ; from 1802–27 the number
rose to 588 per year.[3] Coupled with this increase in the
circulation of all sorts of printed matter is the fact that
politics and letters were combined in an unusually
thorough way. Coleridge was attempting to defend
Southey during the trouble over *Wat Tyler*. ' With
the exception of one outrageously absurd and frantic
passage ', he wrote, ' the thing (*Wat Tyler*) contains
nothing, I can find, that would not have been praised
and thought very right *forty years ago*, at all the public
schools in England, had it been written by a lad in the
first form as a *poem*. For who in the Devil's name ever
thought of reading poetry for any political or practical
purpose till these Devil's times that we live in ? '[4] And
a diarist notes in passing : ' Looked into the New Annual
Register for 1795. The tone of *politics* in the *History
of Literature*, and in the *British and Foreign History*,
materially differ.'[5]

The newspapers were, of course, partisan ; but they
were also more closely connected with literature than is

[1] *Annual Register*, 1822, pp. 350–2.
[2] Moore, *Journal*, vol. ii, p. 40 ; Southey, *Life and Correspondence*,
vol. iv, p. 240.
[3] Knight, *Shadows of the Old Booksellers*, p. 275, quoted in Halévy,
Histoire du peuple anglais au XIXme siècle (1912), vol. i.
[4] *Letters of the Lake Poets to Daniel Stuart* (1889), p. 268.
[5] Green, *Diary of a Lover of Literature* (1810), p. 2.

the modern newspaper. To put it more accurately they
contained, in proportion to their total contents, a greater
amount of original work cast in traditional literary forms,
especially in verse. In the last decade of the eighteenth
century the *Morning Chronicle*, for instance, although
it hardly contained more than two pages exclusive of
advertisements, used to publish something like a half to
a quarter of a column of verse every day. Coleridge's
Sonnets on Eminent Characters found a suitable place here.
Then there were the usual reviews, and a great deal of
literary gossip. Politics found its way in here sometimes
as in the ' O. P.' disturbances at the Covent Garden
Theatre in 1809, when the *Morning Chronicle*, in the
name of Whiggism, sided with those who shouted down
the actors with cries for ' Old Prices ', and *The Times*
and *Morning Post*, as Tory journals, sided with authority
and the management. One reason for this attention to
literature was, of course, the lack of an efficient organization for collecting news. *The Times*, indeed, prided
itself from the first on its sober devotion to the news
as distinct from fluff and padding, but even *The Times*
welcomed political verse. The *Public Advertiser*, the
Sun, and later the *Morning Post*, held up the Tory side
with vigour, and gave their readers much the same sort
of half-literary, half-practical journalism that characterized the *Morning Chronicle*. To the *Morning Post*
probably belongs the distinction of having published
more good poetry than any English newspaper, for
Wordsworth, Coleridge, and Southey all wrote for it.
As time went on those newspapers that survived tended
more and more toward the simple presentation of the
news, accompanied by a few more or less formal leaders
chiefly on subjects political. The part played by imaginative literature grew less and less, though in style
and in the peculiar virtues of journalistic composition
the general literary standard no doubt improved. By
1832 the great newspapers had taken on a form not
unlike that of their more sober successors of to-day.

Imagination had taken refuge in the reviews and
magazines.

This form of periodical publication dates from what
we have agreed to call the Revolution. Before that
periodicals had been limited to essays like those of
Addison and Johnson, in which the periodical form is
really quite accidental and unimportant, and miscel-
lanies like the *Gentleman's Magazine*. The review and
the magazine were in one sense the result of the growth
of a new and very numerous class of readers. For this
class, comparatively cut off from classical traditions,
demanded a more varied choice of reading and a more
definite guidance in matters of taste and intellect than
could be found in existing publications. In another
sense the review and the magazines helped to create
a new class of readers by infusing into letters something
of the same spirit that had produced the material prosperity of that class. By 1820 they had multiplied
incredibly. Peacock, as a good son of the eighteenth
century, distrusted them ; and in one passage he has
managed to introduce most of them :

' Of reviews in the present day we have *satis superque*. We
have the *Edinburgh Review* . . . ; and the *Monthly Review*, which
I believe is tolerably impartial, though not very remarkable either
for learning or philosophy ; and the *Quarterly Review*, a distinguished vehicle of compositions in the Language Politica ; and
the *British Critic*, which proceeds on the enlightened principle
that nothing can possibly be good coming from a heretic or
a republican ; and the *Anti-Jacobin Review*, . . . and the *British
Review*, of which I can say nothing, never having read a single
page of it ; and the *Eclectic Review*, an exquisite focus of evan-
gelical illumination ; and the *New Review*, which promises to
be a useful Notitia Literaria : and the *Critical Review* which
I am very reluctant to mention at all, as I can only dismiss it in
the words of Captain Bobadil ; " It is to gentlemen I speak :
I talk to no scavenger." ' [1]

A few of these demand from us less cursory treatment
than Peacock has given them. The *Edinburgh Review*

[1] Peacock, *Works* (1875), vol. iii, p. 126 n. (*Sir Proteus*).

was the first of these modern periodicals. It was founded
in 1802 by a little group of whom Jeffrey, Brougham,
and Sidney Smith were the chief. As the charming
motto proposed by Smith, *tenui Musam meditamur avena,*
would indicate, its founders were by no means optimistic ; yet they were not long obliged to court the
muse, in their Scottish way, on *a little oatmeal.* The
success of the *Edinburgh* was immediate and complete.
Jeffrey maintained that its success was due to the fact
that its criticism was free and unafraid. It certainly was
not unbiased, or ' scientific ' as the phrase now goes.
It may be doubted, indeed, whether it is worth while
to attempt scientific criticism ; for if the critic's mind is
entirely open when he begins his investigation, the
chances are that it will be quite empty when he ends.
There is something hearty and human and unliterary in
the motto finally chosen for the *Edinburgh*—*judex
damnatur cum nocens absolvitur.* It is true that the
Edinburgh is frequently both judge and advocate in one.
But that is precisely the reason for its success. After
all the *Edinburgh* triumphed over the existing form of
review because it was founded on an idea, its rivals
largely on interest. The reviews which the *Edinburgh*
swept out of existence had been for the most part
dictated by the bookseller, and were mere puffs to
produce a larger sale of their books. At best a Jacobinical
pamphlet or so would be perfunctorily damned ; the rest
was a dull mixture of praise and injudicious extracts.
The *Edinburgh* judged everything by its conformity to
a consistent view of life. It believed that the collection
of lessons from historical experience, of the promptings
of human desire for growth, of the prejudices of birth
and education, of the ideals of several centuries of
corporate effort, which goes by the name of Whiggism,
formed a guide to life, and hence to politics and literature,
that could be trusted far more than the opinions of any
single individual. We cannot do without standards ; and
the value of any standard depends on the use it makes

of the whole course of human history, and of the human faculties of faith, reason, and imagination that have developed throughout that history. The best standard is simply the most universal. It is obvious that Whiggism is a better standard, even for the judgement of literature, than the interests of a bookseller. It is perhaps pardonable to believe that it is also a better standard than the 'impressions' of later critics. If we are to abandon ideas for men one man is as good as another, and a bookseller guided by interest is worth an amateur guided by his sensations : Interest may enlist the aid of intelligence.

The success of the *Edinburgh* soon aroused the jealousy of the opposite party. Walter Scott wrote that since the only honest literary criticism was to be found in that review it had penetrated into Tory families, and was subtly poisoning the firmest of minds.[1] The *Quarterly Review* was founded in 1809 expressly to counteract this influence. Murray published it, and such distinguished politicians as Canning and Croker, as well as George Ellis, who just failed in politics and in diplomacy, played a part in its establishment. The intention of the founders had been to make it a purely literary review, but it very soon fell into political disputes. Each of the two great parties now had its own organ, and literature was definitely harnessed to politics.

In 1824, when a prosperous and not wholly uneducated middle class had begun its final quest of political power, the utilitarians came to believe that literature had its value as an ally, and the *Westminster Review* was set up, with Bowring for its editor. Its appearance was suitably greeted by *Blackwood's* defenders of the proprieties :

' The *Westminster Review* . . . is a book of pith, which must be read, as expressing the opinion of the most blood-thirsty and dangerous crew of political speculators in England. The *Edinburgh* is utterly dished by it. We gave it its knock-down blow—this new-comer has given it the *coup-de-grace*.' [2]

The *Edinburgh* managed to survive the ill bodings of its

[1] Lockhart, *Life of Scott* (1900), vol. ii, p. 40.
[2] *Blackwood's Edinburgh Magazine*, August 1824, p. 222.

Tory rival and the Radical hopes of the utilitarian periodical. But the *Westminster* probably served its purpose in prodding the reluctant Whigs into a more energetic agitation for reform, and in giving the opinions of the utilitarians a circulation among the considerable portion of the public that got its ideas from reviews. Indeed, there could be no better testimony to the political importance of this form of periodical literature than the fact that the positive, wilfully unsentimental, art-scorning utilitarians should consent to such an alliance with imaginative literature as was made necessary by the establishment of the *Westminster Review.*

In the meantime the founding of *Blackwood's Edinburgh Magazine* in 1817 had marked the beginnings of the modern magazine. It was meant to provide more room for original imaginative work than could be found within the bounds of a book review. Poetry, essays, tales, and soon the novel, began to find in these publications a sort of test of their value as books. Yet even here the reader could not escape politics. The young men of *Blackwood's* did not propose to let the Tory cause languish in the hands of the dull and sober *Quarterly.* They contrived to attach the label ' Cockney ' to Hunt and Keats and Hazlitt, and even to that good Tory, Haydon ; and by a kind of assimilation, such men as Bowring, Joseph Hume, Hobhouse, and Burdett became ' statesmen of Cocaigne '. Lockhart, under the signature of ' Z ', attacked this curious miscellany of opponents with a richness of invective, an abandon, a delirium of contempt that is either insincere or uncivilized. Of Leigh Hunt, for example, he writes :

' His patriotism is a crude, vague, ineffectual and sour Jacobinism. He is without reverence either for God or man. . . . His poetry is that of a man who has kept company with kept-mistresses. His muse talks indelicately like a tea-sipping milliner girl. . . . With her, indecency is a disease, and she appears to speak unclean things from perfect inanition. . . . The very concubine of so impure a wretch as Leigh Hunt would be to be pitied, but alas ! for the wife of such a husband ! ' [1]

[1] *Blackwood's Edinburgh Magazine*, October 1817, pp. 39–40.

To find a parallel in scurrility it is necessary to go back to the anonymity of Jacobite pamphlets. There has been nothing like it in modern literary circles of a similar degree of respectability. For literature has played its part in the political and social education of the dominant class in the modern world, and has, to a certain extent, sunk back to the more pleasing task of satisfying aesthetic demands.

The *London Magazine*, founded in 1820, is less saturated with political prejudice than *Blackwood's*, and during its short career of nine years maintained an unusually high standard in all respects. But as it admitted Hazlitt to its pages it could hardly keep politics out. *Blackwood's* soon associated it with the Cockney school, and for better or for worse it was condemned to rest in the Liberal camp. Just before the Reform Bill, *Fraser's Magazine*, destined to have a distinguished career in the next age, was founded. There were hosts of other periodicals, some organs of particular bodies like the Dissenters, others relics of the last century struggling to prolong an old age. The five periodicals we have considered, however, unquestionably had a greater influence than any of their competitors. Before we attempt to find out the nature of that influence a word or two must be said about several publications that escape this classification.

In the first place there is the *Gentleman's Magazine*, founded in 1731 by Cave. All through the years with which we are concerned it preserved its characteristic eighteenth-century form : A miscellany contributed by its correspondents, and ranging over all possible topics from sheep dips to the poetry of the Abbé Delille ; a report of parliamentary proceedings ; a digest of news ; ' original ' poetic extracts ; and brief notices of new books. Its value to the historian consists in the fact that underneath the stability of its outward form there can be traced a distinct change of spirit. It would be difficult to find a more illuminating record of the gradual transformation of English taste between the reign of Johnson and the reign of Tennyson than is to be found in its pages.

Secondly, there is the *Examiner*, founded by the brothers Hunt in 1808. It appeared weekly, and was known as a newspaper. But it approached in many ways to the type of the modern weekly review, such as the *Spectator* and the *Nation*. Leigh Hunt in his *Autobiography* has explained the political tone of his paper :

' The main objects of the *Examiner* were to assist in producing reform in parliament, liberality of opinion in general (especially freedom from superstition), and a fusion of literary taste into all subjects whatsoever. It began with being of no party, but reform soon gave it one. It disclaimed all knowledge of statistics, and the rest of its politics were rather a sentiment and a matter of general training than founded on any particular political reflection. It possessed, however, the benefit of a good deal of reading. It never wanted examples out of history and biography, or a kind of adornment from the spirit of literature ; and it gradually drew to its perusal many intelligent persons of both sexes, who would perhaps never have attended to politics under other circumstances.' [1]

The circulation of the *Examiner* was undoubtedly increased by the picturesque martyrdom undergone by its editor as a result of his conviction for libel against the Prince Regent. Hunt seems to have worn ' the chain for Freedom's sake ' lightly enough, but he clearly gained prestige from his imprisonment. The *Examiner* consistently preached a thorough-going parliamentary reform, but its radicalism was held in leash by a respect for the decencies of middle-class life, and it always evinced a horror of that other Hunt (whom people *would* confuse with Leigh) and Cobbett.

The *Political Register* of this last gentleman is another periodical about which a word must be said. It is not easy to classify this weekly and its writer. It certainly had little enough to do with *belles lettres* : and Cobbett would never have allowed himself to be called by so

[1] Leigh Hunt, *Autobiography* (1850), vol. i, p. 177.

namby-pamby a name as romanticist. Yet he wrote
good loose prose, much too artlessly not to be romantic ;
and his robust independence, his unhesitating, uncritical
energy, his irrational likes and dislikes, his impatience of
mere form for form's sake, his incredible vanity, are all
parts, and by no means the least valuable and least
healthy parts, of the romantic temperament. After
Cobbett had lowered the price of the *Political Register*
to two pence, and so acquired for it the proud title of
' Twopenny Trash ', his influence among artisans, small
tradesmen, and country people—a class almost untouched
by other journalists—became very great indeed. Looking
back now, it is fairly clear that this influence was a conservative one. For Cobbett helped to divert the thoughts
and hopes of a whole class from dogmatic radicalism like
that of the author of *Queen Mab*, from a radicalism that
aimed at economic changes then clearly dangerous, into
a demand for a political reform which really did but set
the seal on changes that had already taken place in the
English body politic. He always thought of the middle
class as a yeomanry, and its accession to power as a
restoration of old England, of agricultural peace and
plenty, of the good conservatism of the soil. Furthermore, he was a strict moralist, and far from urging
abandonment to naturally virtuous instincts, preached
a rigid self-control and an ethical creed on the whole
that of the protestant reform. The sort of life he held
up as an ideal in his *Advice to Young Men* has indeed
something of the harshness and barrenness common
enough in the lives of self-made men ; but it is far
removed from the flabbiness of Shelley's dreams. William
Cobbett had a share in the stability of Victorian England.

   Such, briefly, were the journals that gathered up and
focused the new force of public opinion in England.
In a sense it was not a new force, for England had been
in a measure governed by public opinion for a long time,
and that public opinion had long been able to find
expression in the printed word. But between 1780 and

1832 this reading public had increased so enormously in
size, and what it read had been so profoundly modified
that it deserves to be considered a new force. Proportion is everything, and the historian especially must be
willing to treat a great change in degree as a change in
kind. This force of public opinion was by no means
a simple one. Within it were all sorts of oppositions
and cross currents. Jacobite and Owenite were to be
found giving voice to their faiths ; lovers of ancient
Greece and lovers of modern Germany were not to be
denied a public wooing. Yet even in this confusion of
thought traces of order can be discerned. Certain
qualities are common to English journalism of the period.
It must be repeated that it is always a question of pre-
ponderating influences, and no generalization worth
making can hold over every case. A Gifford and a
Southey collaborate in the *Quarterly* ; and hardly anything can be said of one that is not contradicted by the
other. Yet there can be little doubt that Southey has
more in common with what ultimately prevailed in
England than Gifford. Thus cautioned we may attempt
to distinguish how English journalism indicates the
currents that gave a general direction to public opinion.

In all that pertains to national culture the trend of
periodical publications of all sorts was overwhelmingly
toward romanticism—to an aesthetics founded on common
instincts alone, and almost devoid of intellectual elements ;
in other words, it was a tendency away from aristocracy
and toward democracy. This statement may seem too
sweeping to those who see in the *Edinburgh* and the
Quarterly alike firm opponents of the romantic poets.
But it is possible to conclude too much from the fact
that Jeffrey ridiculed Wordsworth in one review, and
that Croker persecuted Keats in the other. To take
first the case of the *Edinburgh*. Everything that Jeffrey
has written shows that he sought in poetry the magic
and the colour of words that are somehow more than
words, that have a power greater than their meaning.

Now this inexplicable power of words, whether it come from sound or from association, is to be found in the *Ode to a Nightingale*, and is not to be found in the *Dunciad* ; and Jeffrey in 1820 reviewed the poems of Keats in a most sympathetic manner. His dislike for Wordsworth can be explained without in any way making him an enemy to the new school of poetry of the heart, without making him a belated apologist for poetry of the head. He disliked Wordsworth's politics, and in those days that was a very powerful motive. He disliked Wordsworth's metaphysical tendencies because his own delight was in clear bright colours, and not in the grey of speculative poetry. But his chief objection to Wordsworth's poetry was that it was too often a pedantic attempt to carry out a preconceived theory of the author's. Where Wordsworth succeeds, says Jeffrey— and he has often succeeded—he writes at the command of passion, fluently and lyrically ; where he fails—and he has still more often failed—he attempts to exemplify a theory of poetic diction, devised and carried out in the empty, rational, simplifying manner of the last century.[1] That is surely not the judgement of a man who has set his face against literary innovation of all sorts. As a matter of fact it is very close to the opinion of Wordsworth's poetry held by Hazlitt.

The *Edinburgh* on Wordsworth goes far to prove the hold romanticism had on the English people long before the Reform Bill. But a review of Scott's edition of Swift in the September number of 1816, also by Jeffrey, is final. If any one doubts that one of the two foremost periodical publications in the England of the Regency held views on English literature that would have passed unquestioned in 1870 let him read this review. The wits of Queen Anne's reign, we are told, are not of the first rank in English literature. They have ' no glow of feeling, no blaze of imagination, no flashes of genius. . . .

[1] Jeffrey's reviews of Wordsworth in the *Edinburgh Review*, October 1807 ; November 1814 ; October 1815 ; November 1822.

They never pass beyond the visible diurnal sphere or
deal in anything that can either lift us above our vulgar
nature, or ennoble its reality.' Dryden, it seems, long
balanced between old English traditions of spontaneity
and wildness and the new French formalism, and at last
succumbed to the ' evil principle '. The age of Elizabeth
was ' intrinsically romantic ', and so is the present age.[1]
We have here the modern belief that there have been
two great periods of English literature, one in the
seventeenth century and one in the nineteenth century,
and that in between all is darkness.

The *Quarterly*, as was fitting to a Tory publication,
was somewhat more hostile to the culture that had
refused to honour such poets as Pope, Prior, and Addison.
John Wilson Croker, as his whole life shows, was entirely
immune to plebeian contagion, as proof against Macaulay
as against Keats. Gifford maintained to the last a stub-
born adherence to the dullest followers of Augustan
tradition. But there was a leaven of the popular—or at
least of the *bourgeois*—in the *Quarterly*. Southey, with
the sin of nearly half a dozen irregular epics on his head,
was a regular contributor ; and Southey had a hearty
contempt for the eighteenth century and all its works.
He had read Spenser through some *thirty* times, but
could not read Pope through *once*.[2] It is perhaps not
worth while resisting the temptation to make the pert
addition that Southey died of softening of the brain.
For the rest Scott and Byron were well received in the
pages of the *Quarterly*. And in the 'twenties, Lockhart,
nourished on Spanish *romanceros*, a devoted friend of
Scott, and thoroughly in sympathy with those who
loved Nature more than Art, became its editor.

In the pages of the *Gentleman's Magazine* this change
in the cultural ideals of Englishmen is distinctly marked.
In 1790 Art was nearly supreme ; in 1832 Nature had

[1] Jeffrey, review of Scott's edition of Swift, *Edinburgh Review*,
September 1816.
[2] Rogers, *Table Talk* (1903), p. 159.

usurped her place. This is the more significant because
the circulation of the *Gentleman's Magazine* was confined chiefly to the landed gentry, to the clergymen,
who were really a part of the landed gentry, and to
those who wished to assimilate themselves to that class.
In the volumes of the *Gentleman's Magazine* we have
a clear example of the workings of a process that was to
end in the conversion of a large part of the gentry to
a culture that certainly was not ' gentle '. This levelling
of the taste of the English gentry is a fact not without
political importance ; for it meant that when the middle
classes had been admitted to a share of political power
they found themselves in full cultural sympathy with
those with whom they were to share political power.
Even in 1790 the ideal of Nature was opposed to the
formalism that was all that remained of the good sense
and urbanity of better days. Perhaps the most interesting example in this magazine of devotion to Nature as
the nurse of our better passions is afforded by a long
series of letters from ' An Architect ' on Gothic architecture, begun in the last years of the century. The
writer, an amateur named Carter, is a confirmed lover of
Gothic diversity, and, of course, can find little beauty in
Renaissance architecture. Under the title of ' The Pursuits of Architectural Innovation ', he defends the
venerable monuments of the Middle Ages from the
desecration of restorers like Wyatt. He insists on the
conformity of Gothic irregularity, warmth, and invention to the true spirit of England, the spirit of the age
of Elizabeth. He contrasts Gothic aspiration, the heaven-
scaling spire, and the soaring pinnacles, to the dull, flat,
grovelling and earthly character of classic architecture.
And what is still more significant for our purpose he
finds in the Gothic cathedral a focus for patriotic feelings, a symbol of the power of England, ever mounting,
ever in visible alliance with God. In his zeal the writer
oversteps the bounds of archaeology, and suggests that,
since the style was obviously invented in England, the

derogatory epithet, 'Gothic' be dropped, and the majestic piles of the Middle Ages be invested with a new charm as edifices in the 'English' style. Carter was a Tory; but he was much more akin in spirit to the Tory of 1870 than to the Tory of 1770.[1]

There are many traces in the *Gentleman's Magazine* of the humanitarian spirit of the Enlightenment which is so nearly that of Romance. The terms 'nature' and 'humanity' are freely bandied about,[2] often in a sense closely approaching that used by Rousseau. The original poetry is often strongly tinged with irrational and expansive emotion. The social tear, so frequently shed in the society of the time, is shed here. There are complaints of the poor reminiscent of Wordsworth's *Salisbury Plain* manner. Of these *Humanity : An Ode* may stand as a type; and one stanza of that will be quite enough.

> Nor let thy legal rage pursue
> The wretch, already beaten low
> By dire Misfortune's undeserved blow!
> Affliction's sons are brothers in distress;
> A brother then relieve; and God the deed shall bless.[3]

Letters abound with the signatures of *Benevolus, Humanitas*, and in one case with the Spartan eloquence of *A Human Being*.[4] As early as 1794 there is a poem lamenting the evils of the industrial revolution:

> The plenteous stream, that spread its fruitful course
> In many a channel, through the spacious vale
> Freshening the tender herbage as it sprung
> And faded flowers that hung the languid head,
> Is stopped—and its collected force applied
> To move one vast machine.[5]

Then too, there is a tightening of the restraints of prudery; and prudery, whether a vice or a virtue, is

---

[1] Eastlake, *History of the Gothic Revival in England* (1872), has a brief account of Carter.

[2] *Gentleman's Magazine*, October 1793, p. 930.

[3] Ibid., August 1794.   [4] Ibid., October 1804, p. 907.

[5] Ibid., Supplement, 1804.

peculiar to a middle class. Perhaps the most convincing
indication of this increase of prudery is afforded by the
letter of a gentleman who objects to the Westminster
play on the ground that the words, Latin though they
be, are too indecent for English schoolboys and for
English audiences.[1]

There is, however, even in 1800, a preponderance of
the old school among the contributors to this miscellany.
The heroic couplet is still in fashion, modern times are
distrusted, enthusiasm suspected and deviation from tried
standards condemned. The plays of Kotzebue find no
defenders. Wordsworth and his school are neglected at
first, and when, somewhat later, Byron made an apology
in a note to the *Siege of Corinth* for an apparent plagiarism
from Coleridge a contributor could remark that none of
the classical readers of the magazine could have accused
the noble lord of plagiarism from so obscure a writer.[2]
Byron and Scott, however, were accepted from the first.
Mountain scenery is described with the true romantic
fervour in the original poetry. Later in the century the
heroic couplet begins to lose its predominance. By 1819
Kotzebue has been quite forgiven, and has become a distinguished dramatist, partly, no doubt, because he had,
as a good Conservative, fallen victim to a political assassination. But no such reason can be adduced for the
approval given to Goethe,[3] who in the last century had
been simply another German barbarian. Admission was
actually given to a letter from ' Christianus ' defending
the radical propositions of Owen, and displaying a love
of benevolence and philanthropy as warm as if the French
Revolution had never occurred. Such, for instance, is
this qualified statement of the natural goodness of man :

' There is not, Mr. Urban, any inherent depravity in human
nature which a Christian education, in a society formed upon
the basis of Mr. Owen's true and unerring principles of political
economy, cannot overcome.' [4]

---

[1] *Gentleman's Magazine*, April 1794, p. 361.   [2] Ibid., April, 1819.
[3] Ibid., August 1824, p. 140.   [4] Ibid., Jan., 1818.

But the final capitulation of the *Gentleman's Magazine* to the spirit of the new age would seem to be in a little poem, 'The Broken-Hearted Thrush', published in 1825, and beginning :

> If Pity ever touch'd your heart,
>   Or Mercy taught to save
> The parent birds deplore with me
>   Brought to untimely grave.[1]

The poem continues in this way to tell how a pair of thrushes died of grief on seeing their young killed by wanton schoolboys. It is signed *Britannicus* !

English journalism is then, on the whole, favourable to the development of popular romantic standards in art. Beauty came less and less to be seen in order, form, and proportion, and became more and more attached to picturesque profusion, colour, and extravagance. Mrs. Raffarty, in Maria Edgeworth's *Absentee*, sought in all her buildings ' a studied crookedness ' ; ' yes, she said, she hated everything straight, it was so formal and unpicturesque. "Uniformity and conformity ", she observed, " had their day : but now, thank the stars of the present day, irregularity and deformity bear the bell, and have the majority ".'[2] That such tastes must have an effect on the social structure of England seemed obvious to the supporters of the old order. One of them (Francis Hodgson) hoped to stem the tide of innovation with couplets like the following :

> If youthful tastes from Gothic models draw,
> No right obedience follows faulty law ;
> But tinge them early with the classic creed,
> And orthodox the fruit that springs from such a seed.[3]

The victory, however, has rested with the Gothic models. The political consequences have not been as disastrous as some timid Conservatives feared, but they have been marked. We have seen that English journalism

---

[1] *Gentleman's Magazine* June 1825, p. 546.
[2] Edgeworth, *The Absentee, Works* (1832–3), vol. x, p. 127.
[3] Hodgson, F., *Childe Harold's Monitor* (1818), p. 27.

of the forty years before the Reform Bill records a gradual change of taste as the reading public became more numerous. A similar change is to be expected in the political temper of these publications, and does indeed occur. Here again it must be repeated that the change is but a change in proportion. And in politics, which is so largely dependent on things outside the minds of man, it is less complete.

It appears chiefly as a change of tone. Hazlitt, writing of Horne Tooke as the last representative of the generation of Wilkes, remarks with surprise that the political views of the old man seemed to have no roots in his emotions. ' It was curious ', wrote Hazlitt, ' to hear our modern sciolist advancing opinions of the most Radical sort without any mixture of Radical heat or violence.' [1] It is not that English politics had previously been conducted with the unemotional calm of a chess match. But when almost every one who took an interest in politics had also a part in them, emotions were the emotions of those who play a game—keen, but always centred upon an immediate action, always firmly under the control of an intelligence seeking a practical end. When, however, there came to be a great mass of spectators, and when those spectators came to act in a measure as umpires and judges of the game, it is obvious that the quality of emotion centred upon the game changed. Doubtless the figure of speech breaks down here. Or is democracy as absurd as a game decided by the spectators? At any rate emotion was spread among far greater numbers, and ceased to be translated directly into action. It became more vague, more vicarious, and partook more of what, for lack of a better word, we have been forced to call mysticism. Politicians came more and more to have to appeal to popular ' sentiment '. That is why Hazlitt was surprised at Horne Tooke's coolness; and that is what is behind this passage from the *Examiner* :

' And what is it, after all, that has given to our men of the

[1] Hazlitt, *Works*, vol. iv, p. 232.

world the security and enjoyments they possess? What is it that enables them, in common with better Englishmen, to breathe the free air of opinion, and to live and move, and have their being to themselves—but something which this very " enthusiasm " or " romance " has produced—something that has occasionally risen up to admonish injustice or stimulate virtue, at one time in the grosser form of war, at another in the more ethereal form of philosophy—at a third, in the eloquent and outspoken voice of domestic patriotism? . . . Thus romance and enthusiasm, or in other words, a farsighted generosity opposed to a winking selfishness, have established for us the right of taxing ourselves ;—romance and enthusiasm saved us from that very faith when it was in full power, which dotage and worldliness are now protesting against when it has grown harmless :—romance and enthusiasm rid us of our invaders, created us a navy, bequeathed us trial by jury, and in short, instead of a set of paupers, friars, and slaves, enabled us to be a rich, an intelligent, and a free people.' [1]

From this introduction of ' enthusiasm '—that is, an expansive, contagious, mob-emotion—into English politics it was impossible to escape. It is the only way in which a democracy can be brought to deliver a decision. But it need not be, and in England it was not, unmingled with more rational elements.

In yet another respect is there an underlying political unity to be found in English journalism of the time. The same spirit that has touched politics with a new emotion has given them a new faith. This is a belief in change. And few there are, even among the Tories, who have not accepted it. Society has become an evolutionary process, change is accepted as inevitable, and the only dispute is concerning the rate and extent of change in the present. The cruder forms of the theory that environment is all are not lacking in the newspapers, especially in the early days of the French Revolution. The *Gazetteer* is confident that

' Experience proves that the character and spirit of a people change with the form of government, and that a different government gives by turns to the same nation a character, noble or base,

[1] *Examiner*, 10 January 1813.

firm or fickle, courageous or cowardly. In every nation, its
character either changes on a sudden, or alters by degrees, according to the sudden or insensible alterations in its form of government.' [1]

Progress was, of course, the ideal of the utilitarians and
their press. But not even the *Quarterly* could escape
drawing from the incredible material transformation of
England the conclusion that all the conditions of human
life, too, must change. The numerous social essays of
Southey, mutilated by Gifford though they were, are
filled with the idea of progress, and with the humanitarianism that is the spiritual parallel of material expansion. *Blackwood's* is itself a result of Progress, and its
pert confidence in the world around it inspires even its
attacks on Radicalism with a Radical character. When
George Henry Lewes strung together those sonorous
synonyms for the spirit of England—'progression,
humanity, perfectibility, civilization, democracy'—his inspiration, if not his phraseology, must have received the
approbation of all but the most irreconcilable of Tories.

Faith in progress and domination of politics by the
vague emotions of the people are the most important
common characteristics of the English press of the time.
They confirm what we have already learned from the
romantic writers. They are a part of that deepest
stirring of something human or inhuman, and certainly
incomprehensible, that produced the Revolution. They
have a connexion, remote though it be, with the dogma
of the natural goodness of man. But, just as in the case
of most of the romanticists, there has been imposed on
this expansive revolutionary spirit a certain vague form
that helps to moderate it. Periodical and daily press
alike are careful to observe the proprieties of middle-
class life. They are never revolutionary in a social sense.
They are champions of the compromise between the
desire for expansion and the necessity for contraction
that resulted in Victorian civilization.

[1] *Gazetteer*, 9 July 1790.

One other fact may be added. The contents of the periodical press are another indication of the conversion of the English gentry to the tastes of the middle class. The conversion was not complete. There were doubtless many in the nineteenth century to whom taste meant what it had meant to the patrons and friends of Swift, Pope, and Prior. But they were not numerous enough to have influence on manners and letters and art through the press. It is true that long after the Reform Bill the same ' governing classes ' continued to govern ; but this governing aristocracy had largely abandoned aristocratic standards in art, letters, morals, thought, and had become thoroughly sympathetic with *bourgeois* ideals. It certainly could not afford to jest about the middle class ; Twiss was once forced to apologize humbly in Parliament for seeming ' to ridicule the middle class '.[1] The genuineness of this conversion is another matter, and not for us. One wonders, however, whether the British upper classes desired the Albert Memorial, or merely connived at it. At any rate, there it stood ; there were *The Princess* and *Rabbi Ben Ezra* ; and the Russells were as important as ever. Surely in this triumph of *bourgeois* tastes lies one of the reasons for the becoming moderation of English political reform, and the large toleration it observed toward an aristocracy that had ceased to possess an aristocratic culture.

Of the spirit of revolt of Shelley and Byron, however, the regular press shows little trace. The literature of proletarian revolt is not very evident on the surface of things. But, in a subterranean fashion, the less restrained emotions and beliefs which lie behind this revolt find expression in the ephemeral writing of the day. Radical publishers like Hone, Eaton, and Sherwin printed many pamphlets, doggerel rhymes, and periodicals in the cause of social revolution, republicanism, and natural religion. We hear of the steady circulation of Tom Paine, and of how *Queen Mab* and *Don Juan* have been

[1] *Parliamentary History*, Third Series, ii, p. 1144.

added to the slender literary stock of the extremists. No doubt English society rejected the less rational aspects of the great ferment that made the Revolution. But those aspects are none the less real. We cannot, after all, escape Shelley, the Shelley who tossed Radical pamphlets from the balcony in Dublin. There are traces—slight ones, it is true—of his spirit in the lesser writing of his own time. He remains the crucial test of romantic ideas in politics.

VI

CONCLUSION

'THE minds of men were excited to new enterprises; a new genius, as it were, had descended upon the earth, and there was an erect and outlooking spirit abroad that was not to be satisfied with the taciturn regularity of ancient affairs.'

This is entered under the year 1788 in Galt's *Annals of the Parish*. It gives a greater reality to the state of things from which we must start than could any abstract summary. For everywhere in the England of the latter part of the eighteenth century there was an outbreak of human energy. In a thousand parishes men were attempting to lead a different sort of life from that which their ancestors had led. They were clearing new lands, building new houses, constructing mills to make more cloth of brighter, newer patterns, sending out bigger ships, acquiring a more respected place in society, doubting old religions and inventing new ones, seeking novelty and adventure, exploring all things, 'voyaging through strange seas of thought alone'. Into the difficult question of the origins of this outbreak of expansive energy, and the reasons why it occurred at this particular point in time, we cannot go. It is sufficient that men did protest against 'the taciturn regularity of ancient affairs'. Where old ways were a hindrance to this delightful new life of changes and growth they had to be abandoned. But old ways were common ways, and to abandon them was to revolt from the commonwealth. The new movement was necessarily individualistic. Freedom was a means, not an end; for freedom was but a condition of growth. Under this freedom a man could follow his nature, whether it led him into cotton manufacturing or into pantheism. Ruskin would not have cared to admit it, but the industrial revolution he detested, and the 'iridescence, colour-depth, and morbid mystery' of things he loved, had the same historical origin.

One caution is suggested by this last remark, and a few words must be devoted to it before we continue. It is obvious that to a psychologist the feelings and impulses centred around this expansion of human energy must be infinitely complex, and that all sorts of shades and distinctions exist for him in the conduct of the artist and the manufacturer ; nor is it reasonable to maintain that such differences are unimportant to the historian. But it would be impossible to come to any conclusion if the minds of men in their social relations were to be as minutely distinguished as is the habit of the psychologist to distinguish them. Moreover, idiosyncrasies disappear in large bodies of men ; and, to the analyst of human conduct, men doubtless differ less in their broad relation to the state than in their more intimate relations to the immediate objects of their desire. It may indeed be urged that the psychology with which we have approached our problem is too simple. It is really nothing but the very old belief that most men follow, guided quite as much by instinct as by reason, what they take to be their interest in the struggle to prevail over their fellows, and to survive among the fit ; it is, if long names must be given, an *irrational utilitarianism*. The answer to the reproach of simplicity is this ; in attempting to understand the actions of great numbers of men, the only safe thing to do is to accept the lessons of experience, and assume that men act from selfish motives. The weakness of this point of view is its failure to take account of religion. But true religion is less a projection of desire into another world than its annihilation in this, and has always been a very rare thing. Surely if the historian cannot understand this religion neither can the psychologist.

After this apology to an outraged science the matter in hand can be renewed. Life was quickened toward the end of the eighteenth century, and every man found himself impelled to crowd into his life more of something, more action or more feeling or more dreaming. Institutions, which have something of the immobility of things as well as of the mobility of men, did not feel all this quickening. Men therefore turned from institutions and relied on themselves alone. The spirit of expansion prevailed through individualism. So successful has been the thing named that the name, for all its erudite and Latin past, has become a part of popular speech. Individualism, as every one knows, explains the origin of the modern world. Yet justice is not always done to the speculative basis of individualism. There was no attempt to pulverize society. There was no aim to destroy the state in order to set up an anti-social collection of separate individuals. What individualism really did in theory was to appeal to the individual to abandon one society and join another, to give up a bad discipline and assume a better one. Man under this new discipline, so stood the dogma, will be a member of a higher society, and will yield a higher obedience to a stricter law, the law of Nature. The individualist commonwealth is a natural society as opposed to an artificial society; it is not, however, a disordered society as opposed to an ordered society.

Thus, the individualist theory sets up its claim to accord with the eternal fact of the individual's dependence or a strength that is not his own. It too is a common thing, a *res publica*, and gives men the strength that comes from union; and since this is a union with Nature, with the greatest and most omnipresent force in the universe, it is clearly the most desirable union of all. Now the natural—and hence perfect—state will solve the old antithesis between liberty and authority. The state should be a personality common to the persons who compose it. If that which is *naturally* common to all men is made *politically* common in the state the antithesis is solved. Submission to authority will be

freedom, because that within us which demands freedom
is Nature; and Nature will be authority. Rousseau said
no more than that.

Strange as it may seem to our faithless age this apparently naïve faith has a profound justification in human
nature. Let us assume a man attempting to live his life
to the fullest extent of his desires. However successfully
he may gratify most of them he cannot avoid discontent
in some form, through satiety or through failure. But
his desires have the astonishing complexity of the world
we live in; and to secure consistent gratification they
must be reduced to the simplicity of the world we build
for ourselves. It is no doubt a fitting judgement that,
after condemning Coleridge for bringing epistemology
into politics, we should ourselves approach dangerously
near a theory of knowledge. Perhaps we can avoid the
worst by a confession of ignorance. Somehow from the
confusion of our sensations we slowly build up recognizable objects. Now desires are no doubt born of these
confused sensations, but they must be directed toward
objects that possess the comparative simplicity of that
which is known. Through this miracle of knowing desire
can find satisfaction, if not extinction. For all knowing
is an abstracting, and all things known are in a measure
abstractions. Rousseau's 'pervenche', alas! was an
abstraction else it could never have lived in his memory.
So, too, the British Empire, Uncle Sam, and virtue are
all abstractions. Indeed, the distinction between abstract
and concrete nouns is much more grammatical than real.
The real distinction, as ever, is a matter of proportion,
and lies in their relative nearness to or remoteness from
the primary confusion. In proportion as our desires are
directed towards objects remote from this confusion—
that is, towards objects of a high degree of abstraction—
is it easy to gratify them. It is much easier, and in some
ways more satisfactory, to love virtue than to do a
virtuous deed. It is easier to succeed as an Englishman
or an American than as a carpenter. If we return to

the man who is attempting to live his life to the fullest extent of his desires, we shall find that, baulked of more finite gratification, he is forced to satisfy these desires in his relations with church, with state, with class or group. Now in these relations his desires do not receive the more intense requital that comes from a fuller sensual gratification. Perhaps they are not even as completely stilled. But they are vastly less liable to failure and disappointment in this abstract world than in the confused world of the senses ; and they are less in need of discipline.

For the man who attaches himself to an abstraction secures not only a means of gratifying his desires, but also an ally that can make the whole course of his life smoother and more expansive. The savage who sees in a tree not merely a tree but a superhuman power, and who therefore guides himself in his relations with it by certain rites destined to secure its aid or propitiate its wrath, is at once making a generalization and entering into a mystic relation. The civilized man who sees in his country not merely a tract of land characterized by certain natural features, buildings, and inhabitants, but a superhuman power which he can love, and which will in turn protect and cherish him, is doing exactly as the savage does, creating an abstraction and making it an influence on his own life. The metaphysical problems in this connexion are infinite, but they need not concern us. It may be true that any generalization is an act of faith. But for practical purposes the test whether faith enters into the relation between a man and his generalizations is the existence in his mind of the belief that he is in alliance with a superhuman power. That power need not be called a god ; it is necessarily superhuman only in the sense that it cannot be completely contained in any one human being.

It is plain that to speak in this sense of a political faith is no mere figure of speech. No amount of pragmatic denials of the existence of the ' group-mind ' or the 'corporate soul' can alter the fact that men do believe that every association possesses a soul and a power that is not possessed by any one of its members by himself, that is not a mechanical addition of the qualities of its members. And after all, though any group may be merely a certain number of warring individual wills, it does *act* as one will. That ought to be enough for the pragmatists. The real task of a mind politically sceptical should be to examine into the workings of these political faiths, to ask whether the organizations and dogmas through which they are obliged to work really provide a good life for their devotees. What we must ask about the revolutionary faith in Nature is just this : Did it successfully transcend its narrow but firm base in the appetites of the individual, take to itself the wider experience of the race, and make good its claims to be not a chaos but a discipline ?

To judge from the political development of the Lake poets—and if our premises are correct, this is not a reck-less and unwarranted proceeding—the first and simplest form of the revolutionary faith in Nature was inadequate. To state that faith is not easy. All sorts of men and ideas went into its making, and gave it a greater hold over men than any forced historical summary can explain. Voltaire, for instance, gave it far more common sense than Englishmen, at least, have generally been willing to admit. But in its simplest form it is something like this : Nature is the ultimate thing common to all men, and loyalty to Nature is loyalty at once to one's self and to a far greater power. But in the society of the eighteenth century it is clear that institutions are not a part of Nature. For Nature is goodness, happiness, purity, simplicity. It is that for which we yearn. But since that for which we yearn is good our yearning must be good. That within us which is good and natural is our desire for happiness. The true link between men and men, and between men and Nature, is feeling, emotion, instinct. This is the doctrine of the natural goodness of man. It is forced to realize itself, however, in institutions upon which the emotions of men can be focused. What the eighteenth century called reason played a large part in the devising of these institutions. They are chiefly based on universal suffrage, the separation of powers, written constitutions, bills of rights, codes of law, and similar democratic machinery. Sometimes, as in the case of Godwin, the machinery becomes so perfect that it eliminates itself, and the natural goodness of man is translated directly into anarchy. But whether Sieyès or Godwin or Bentham provide the scheme under which this revolutionary society is to work, the thing that gives men such faith in it that they are willing to forsake or to undermine established society is just this vague belief in the natural goodness of man. This belief is no more than the aspirations of thousands of common men pooled into a faith. It is Liberty, Equality, Fraternity.

The revolutionary faith of the Lake poets failed them in the face of events. The French Revolution had been natural enough ; but they could no longer find it good. Evidently, their aspirations needed some centre other than the simple institutions of revolutionary democracy. So the Lake poets turned aside to find a new set of institutions. But they could not entirely give up their old faith in Nature ; they must provide in some way for the desire for expansion in which they had grown up. They could not return to the loyalty of their fathers. Their problem was, in Coleridge's own words, to find rest in unrest. To a very surprising extent they succeeded. Any summary of their attitude must be inaccurate because of differences in details. But, if we look rather to the spirit than to the letter, they arrived at a conclusion which is on the whole representative of the English middle-class view of life. First of all they maintain the idea of progress, of growth ; and faith in progress is intimately connected with their earlier faith in Nature. Progress is simply another form of that expansive energy in man which is perhaps

what we mean by Nature. A man wishes a better
position in the world ; but his present position is a part
of what he is, and in a measure prevents his attaining
any other. To this old problem of environment the
revolutionary had a simple answer. Man's wish can
immediately modify his environment, and then his
environment will strengthen that within him which
formed the wish. Now, this notion that a man has the
ability, by controlling his environment, to achieve a
perfection which is *natural*, existing *in potentia* in every
one of us, is at bottom a good and hopeful one. But the
followers of Rousseau and of Godwin propose a short
cut to this end by eliminating the environmental differences which civilization has built up, and falling back
on what is apparently more fundamental than civilized
differences, the energy that drives us to expand. They
did not see that, far from solving the problem, this is
but clearing away all that historical experience has contributed towards its solution, as if to state the problem
in falsely simple terms were in itself a solution. There
is certainly an energy within men that tries to make the
outer world like the inner, the inhuman world human.
But this energy is wasted if it tries to use as its instru-
ment the desire that is its source. It must work through
instruments the race has built—instruments that are of
the same material as the world they are used to transform. Otherwise, this energy is as useless as so much
steam in the open air. The notion of progress, as the
more moderate thinkers of the nineteenth century came
to conceive it, retains the hopeful belief that man can
partly control himself by controlling his environment,
and rejects the wildly mystic belief that this control can
be achieved merely by desiring it. Progress, in this
sense, attempts to reconcile man with nature, not to
emancipate him from her nor to enslave him to her. It
is clearly the notion of progress brought forward in
Coleridge's *Church and State*.

The difficulty that faced the repentant Jacobins, however, was not so much to allow for this spirit of expansion in the individual as to control and direct it. They had seen in the French Revolution how men act when they are freed from the control of institutions and delivered over to their own instincts. They had ceased to believe in the natural goodness or reasonableness of man. They could hardly persuade themselves, however, that it was possible to suppress the awakened energies of men, although Wordsworth in his old age seems almost to have come to this degree of absurdity. What they had to do was to devise suitable social restraints. These they partly constructed from the very aspirations they sought to satisfy, and partly took over from existing institutions. Wordsworth's own philosophy of Nature is an example of this first activity. Nature became in his poetry a source of repose, a healer, a restraining power. When this conception of Nature is compared with Byron's, where the rebel passions find strength, but neither repose nor content, the full extent of Wordsworth's achievement is clear. His poetry brought to the vague, excited, struggling, discontented spirits of his emancipated generation a purpose and a faith. In a way more directly political, the Lake Poets helped to turn some of the emotions of a people in full social revolution into a love of country that was new in extension if not in depth. Patriotism was brought back in the *Convention of Cintra* to ' the sentient, the animal, the vital ', where it has remained ever since. In another way the service of humanity became a social bond capable of uniting those who served under it. Southey's services for the poor, his constant insistence in the *Quarterly* on the value for rich and poor alike of a wise humanitarianism, will be recalled. Religion, too, received a new life from the romantic feeling for mystery. In this way, in their relations to Nature, to their country, to their fellow men, to religion, the Lake Poets are but striving to do what their whole generation was striving to do—to find beliefs, men, institutions, any object of loyalty upon

which the desires of many men, not very well educated,
not very critical, and recently freed from age-old restraints, can be centred. As a result, all in life that was
not action became sentiment. But in a sense the end
was achieved. Many of the old restraints were kept, or
formed a basis for the new sentimental loyalty. In particular, a strict Protestant code of morality was retained,
and no touch of licence was admitted into manners. In
this way the peace of the Georgians, which was also the
peace of the Victorians, was secured.

It was a peace that permitted within itself an extraordinary turmoil. One who studies the chaotic development of English industry in these years must come to
understand with a new sympathy Burke's conviction that
civil society is a miracle. It has become the fashion now
to condemn the excessive individualism that then prevailed in economic life ; the historian will be content
to wonder at it. Economists believed in Liberty and
a kind of Equality, if not in Fraternity. This dogmatic
faith in liberty, rejected with scorn by practical English
politicians as the dream of a weak, vain people like the
French, took its revenge by transforming the whole
fabric of English society ; and this was inevitable, for
Nature, having made the English Channel, had no
difficulty in crossing it. The classical economists, indeed,
were pessimists, who owed their views of human nature
rather to Hobbes than to Rousseau. But their method
of reasoning brought them to conclusions astonishingly
like those of the optimistic revolutionists. Men are bad
and selfish ; but let each man strive for his own ends ;
provide an entirely open field for competition ; and then
the play of jealousy and desire will result in a neutral
good, in a fair market price. Organization is always an
organization of evil, ever aiming at monopoly and unfair
prices. The individual is, then, to be trusted, the society
to be distrusted. Orthodox economic theory is purely
anarchical ; Nassau Senior is a peer of Godwin. It is
true that all this applies only to man as an economic

animal, and that the political, moral, and religious speculation of the age is a constant search for means of limiting and controlling the expansion of the individual. It is also true that industrial conditions never measured up to the standards set for industry by philosophers, for not even economic life is as good or as bad as the theories about it. Yet it is hard to conceive how this incredible expansion, this making over of the slow old world, could have been achieved had not art, literature, morals, religion, and in a measure politics, provided a compensating quiet, a sense of something finished, stable, permanent. Society was forced to protect itself from the anarchy that is always threatened when men believe that life must afford them much more than it did their fathers. England made heroic efforts to confine this belief within institutions—to reconcile progress with experience.

In a measure the effort succeeded; yet the very measure of that success meant that it could not be permanent. It now seems likely that the Victorians achieved but a partial and incomplete peace. The Victorian Age is indeed so near us, and so much a part of the controversies of our life, that we cannot claim to judge it impartially. Yet surely history, so well tried in controversy, ought not prudishly to shun the present merely because it is controversial. It is at any rate worth while attempting to understand the very evident modern abandonment of Victorian standards in art, letters, politics—in almost all things.

The striking thing about Victorian civilization is the persistence, under the control of forms borrowed from wisdom and experience, of faith in Nature, and in the natural goodness of man. The good life was the simple, common life of the emotions, uncorrupted by any critical reservations. Reason was suspect, as not being English in origin, and as inhuman in its methods.

> Our meddling intellect
> Misshapes the beauteous forms of things;
> We murder to dissect.

The sign-manual of membership in the community was, be it repeated, the possession of a spirit of ' Gemütlichkeit '. This was inevitable, for—crude though the generalization seem—feeling is common to mankind, while critical intelligence is a rare gift, and one which can only be developed through long apprenticeship. Such intelligence was not uncommon in the Victorian Age, but it was shut out from its best contacts with mankind in art and politics.

All this is perhaps an exaggeration. The truth at the bottom of it ought, however, to be plain enough. Matthew Arnold was not tilting at windmills in his innumerable essays on the lack of the critical spirit among his contemporaries. Tennyson was too much read not to have had some influence ; and Tennyson's politics, like those of the last of the Victorians, Mr. Kipling, are more expansive than critical. Such a rule of the more readily communicable human desires and aspirations is perhaps a necessary condition of democracy. It prevailed almost as much in the clear-thinking France Arnold admired as in England. A minority in France, as everywhere, continued to believe that experience interpreted by intelligence is the best guide in all human activities. But democratic France was not to be controlled by these, but by the ' citizen-king ', the Napoleonic legend, the Third Republic, and other irrationalities. In view of the long years that had gone into building the French and the English nationalities, the parallels between them in the nineteenth century are amazing. The subject would lead us astray now ; yet in letters and in politics it ought to be possible to collect many facts like this : Meredith is a refinement of much that is purely English, just as Stendhal is a refinement of much that is purely French ; yet the elder Dumas surely had more English readers than Meredith and more French readers than Stendhal.

Art in Victorian England was thus in all its forms saturated with sentiment. Intelligence, condemned in art and letters to pander to the emotions, was for the rest abandoned to itself. It threw itself into science; and scientists, no longer in healthy contact with all human activity, became inhuman. When they had built up a body of scientific knowledge outside human life, man's affective instincts, with characteristic perverseness, embraced it, and it became a religion. Art and science alike contrived to flatter man's desire to snatch at infinity. The true symbol of England was indeed the Gothic church.

Now, this faith in progress has an obvious relation to the Utopias that strengthened the revolutionary hopes of the Rousseauist. Like them it preached the doctrine that men ought to be happier on this earth than they now are, and that if they will but make an effort, not of self-denial but of self-indulgence, they can achieve this happiness. Put as simply as this, injustice is doubtless done to Victorian beliefs. But the presence among them of a strong materialistic optimism based on the expansive tendencies of human nature is incontestable. Such an optimism is highly dangerous. We can all of us conceive a life so much better than that we actually lead that we must be pessimists of a sort in order to be happy. Christianity, which has for so long determined men's outlook on life, is profoundly pessimistic as regards this world. The mysticism of Nature, and to a less degree the Victorian belief in progress, is optimistic beyond all bounds. Like men's dreams it promises more than it can fulfil. As long as this optimism is tempered by a recognition of the immediate limitations of things worldly it may bring content. To those who are already beyond the pressure of poverty it probably affords no more than a necessary stimulus to action. In spite of the excesses of commercial speculation the English middle class was not violently aggressive, and even its enthusiasm for imperial aggression was not wholly severed from a respect for fact. But for those who are not comfortably established it is difficult to rest content with the sentimental compromise the Victorians had made with Utopia. What had been a philosophy of social content for the middle class was almost bound to become a philosophy of revolt for the proletariat.

For there is no way to make faith in Nature a complete discipline in itself. If men are taught that their aspirations towards a fuller, more materially comfortable existence are good they will scarcely put up with physical suffering. If they are taught that all men are roughly equal in their most truly human characteristic, feeling, they will not long be willing to suppress their feelings. The middle class did rise to power on some such doctrine as this, and it did commit itself in print to many radical theories about perfectibility. Given popular education, and those vague and powerful words—liberty, progress, democracy—must come to the ears of those to whom they meant something to be achieved, not a vicarious achievement. The lower classes, too, might have been content with the Victorian faith had they possessed a worldly competence which permitted the indulgence of desire through sentiment. But vicarious delight in anything demands a stomach not vicariously filled. The prosperous England of the last century might well have provided all her citizens with the decencies of life. But it could not be. Neither intelligence nor experience guided the course of English industry as a whole, but Nature ; and Nature is blind, improvident, prodigal. Nothing could be more natural and more inhuman than the growth of the great manufacturing towns. It was idle for a Macaulay to insist that everybody in England was physically better off than his ancestors in 1685 ; to those who suffer misery is never comparative in point of time. Or again, the lower classes might possibly have remained contented under a faith based on earthly limitations, denying earthly progress, questioning earthly happiness, and demanding sacrifice, not indulgence, from its devotees. Christianity was such a faith. The mixture of Christian ethics, belief in progress, and patriotism, which was the faith of the Victorian middle class, was not such a faith. It was a source of contentment to the satisfied of this world ; to the dissatisfied it was not a consolation, but a spur. Disraeli saw clearly that the lower classes needed another faith if they were to be content with subordination. *Sybil* and *Coningsby* are a search after such a faith. It is one of the tragedies of the last century that the search was to end at Suez.

Through this new imperialism the England of the middle class has no doubt contrived to retain a measure of loyalty from great numbers of the lower classes. A way out may yet be found in that direction. But it is undeniable that more and more of the lower classes, and many serious people of other classes, have come to accept a philosophy of revolt, a philosophy that has much in common with Shelley's. Alone among the great English romanticists he carried out rigorously the common romantic philosophy to its logical political conclusion. He is the prophet of a pure faith in nature and in reason ; Rousseau and Godwin unite in him. Many of Shelley's most desired measures have been realized—universal education, universal suffrage, complete religious toleration. He is to-day honoured as one of the founders of a great political movement. More than any of the other great romanticists Shelley is now politically alive. Yet surely his political ideas are not in themselves less visionary than they were a century ago. His Utopian faith is in itself as unmixed with the lessons of experience as ever. It is not necessary here to go over Shelley's ideas. It may be recalled that his central principle is simply revolution by miracle, the conquest of the promised land by a mere sounding of the trumpets of desire. Shelley wants to achieve earthly happiness without earthly suffering. Even those who wish well to socialism may suspect it of entertaining an analogous desire.

It is tempting, after a survey of the doubtings, the miseries, the uncertainties, the failures that have accompanied the transformation of society under the impetus of the Revolution, to wish the whole process at an end. It has occurred to many besides Henry Adams that the progressive speeding up of civilization must be approaching a limit. How can we continue to have as many styles of architecture as we have architects? How can art be more independent than the independents? Who will innovate on Mr. James Joyce and the Dadaistes? Must man move faster and faster, be ever the victim of a new megalomania? It is not astonishing that men have thought that the only cure for the evils of progress is to have no progress. In this respect the attitude of so distinguished a Radical as Mr. Bertrand Russell towards China is interesting. It is possible that the popular movement may be turned into a general renouncement of the whole revolutionary philosophy of expansion. But to give up the fight seems a sorry way out. The zest of western life has come from the struggle between the intelligence that sets limits and the instinct that breaks beyond them. From that struggle have sprung many precious things, not the least precious of which is that romantic literature we have sought to criticize. Nor need we fear that the fine classic tradition of order, harmony, and repose which has survived so many outbreaks of mystic enthusiasm among those who shared neither its discipline nor its freedom, will be destroyed by this new movement of the people. Already there are signs that within the proletarian movement the lessons of experience are being engrafted on the emotional qualities of a faith that gives the movement its empire over its followers. Shelley's thought is in itself a pure mysticism, a counsel of the impossible and a source of discontent and revolt. But intelligently handled by capable leaders it can be made a genuinely social belief. There is no reason why social democracy, profoundly irrational though its foundations be, should not be a discipline as well as a faith. The real service of those who cherish the wisdom of the past is to apply that wisdom to the present. Doubtless it is very little to state so evident a necessity in such general terms. But it is something. For there is a tendency among those who love order and the classic tradition to believe that they can best serve their ideals by holding to principles and institutions that once preserved order, and have fallen into general neglect. But order and repose are wasted on the dead. The living need them ; and to-day democracy alone is living.

For it must be apparent to any one who has studied some part of the social history of the Western world in the last century that democracy is after all what its founders claimed it to be, ' natural '. It is natural because it is a social assertion of the eternal restlessness of the man of appetites, who is the man of politics. And just because this man is a political animal it has become a faith. The ' religion of humanity ', in one form or another, has set itself up everywhere. To many good men the phrase ' religion of humanity ', as well as the faith it expresses, seems an unqualified evil ; and well it may, for it neglects the noblest of human experiences, which have always been outside of humanity in the mass. We have insisted throughout this study on the mystical character of the social creed of the romantic writers, of the Conservative Lake poets and of the Radical Shelley alike ; and we have quoted from them in vain if it has not been clear that they often make use of a quasi-religious terminology. It is not that the movement we have called the Revolution was entirely religious. To call it so would be misleading. But theology and politics meet in ethics, and any great human effort must take on social forms. The Revolution of the last century was simply a freeing of human energies. It has certain analogies with such expansive movements as the development of Roman dominion, the Germanic migrations, and the crusades. It has other likenesses with outbreaks of curiosity like the Renaissance. Finally, it has distinct analogies with the institutional development of early Christianity and of Protestantism.

Now, if one considers the history of Christianity, it must be apparent that the form eventually taken by the Church was the result of a long struggle between the wisdom and conservative good sense of those who directed Church organization and the irrational mysticism implicit in certain aspects of the faith, a mysticism which would deny the facts of life. Upon the existence and nature of this mysticism it is hardly necessary to dwell. It reached its height in the ascetic fury that drove men into the deserts. And in all ages rebels have never failed to seek justification in the word of the Gospels. Shelley and Rousseau could refer to the teachings of Christ. Yet from this overreaching insatiable mystic fervour the Catholic Church achieved its own miracle of organization. A striking instance of this imposition of rational bounds on essentially rebellious, centrifugal, anarchic emotions is afforded by the history of the most recent of the great Protestant sects, the Methodists. The process is not otherwise in politics. Everywhere in modern France public buildings carry the inscription, ' Liberté, Egalité, Fraternité '. It is an arresting thing to come in some quiet village upon a school inscribed with these three words. Though their past is the past of the terror and the guillotine, their present is peace. Not quite complete yet, for the Revolution has not exhausted itself; and no one would suggest the Third French Republic as a model for the political organization of democratic emotion. Yet the instance is valuable. It shows clearly how some of the most explosive of democratic doctrines can be robbed of their dangers and converted into objects of social loyalty that do not stand in the way of intelligent administration. Imagine a school really conducted on the principles of ' Liberty, Equality, Fraternity ' ! To borrow again the vocabulary of religion, what really happens is the formation of a ritual that can satisfy the demands of a faith.

Victorian civilization was almost such a ritual for

democracy. Perhaps it could not have achieved more to appease the restlessness of the many. And yet one feels that it failed to make use to the utmost of the highest of human faculties, intelligence. Only very pert and ignorant young men of the present generation will dare maintain that the Victorians were unintelligent. The great men of that age were many of them very great, and far above their critics. Yet intelligence was too often separated from life, diverted into a barren Science, dried up within the individual, unsubordinated to a common standard and a common purpose. Such a standard, such a purpose did exist, but it had been completely sentimentalized, cheapened by a vulgar contempt for reason, overwhelmed with democratic unrealities, choked with mysticism. Possibly classical reason has no higher place in modern life. Yet there are signs of change. Mr. Strachey must be the first Englishman since the eighteenth century who could praise Racine in a popular essay. So good a Radical as Mr. Wallas has written : ' Thought may be late in evolution, it may be deplorably weak in driving power, but without its guidance no man or organization can find a safe path amid the vast impersonal complexities of the universe as we have learned to see it.' This is encouraging. We are no longer to rely on the ' impulse from the vernal wood ', even in politics.

The fact is that Western humanity has lifted itself by its bootstraps ; but it can hardly hope to maintain itself by the same method. The Revolution, in order to free men's energies, was obliged to maintain that all men are roughly alike. It has succeeded in giving them at least political equality. Energy in the service of faith in a fiction has gone far to make that fiction truth. But there are signs that both the energy and the faith are dying out. We can only maintain our gains—if gains they are— by carefully distinguishing what is real in them. Men, after all, are the only political realities. Under an aristocratic government, what humble men were like did not much matter, for such men led unpolitical lives.

Every one counts now. Yet the old Benthamite myth that all men are alike, once so useful to the cause of the Revolution, still survives, attacked only by the Conservatives and the psychologists. It deserves a better fate. Critical intelligence can still use it as a myth should be used, to satisfy and restrain men by giving them a faith. But this faith must never promise men much more than it can give them on this earth. That is, it must be controlled and given institutional form by intelligence, reason, common sense, or whatever it is that teaches men the meaning of limitation. In politics certainly, as Burke saw, our ultimate faith must be a faith in experience. He did not, however, except in the closing words of the *Thoughts on French Affairs*, foresee that democracy was to be a part of human experience. Now that it has become so there is no reason to believe that it can be completely destroyed. The necessary task is to give it institutions which satisfy men's irrational aspirations, and yet are controlled by men of wisdom and experience.

Perhaps the task is impossible. If men would only make of Equality a philosophical and religious truth, as Mr. Belloc would have them, democracy might attain stability; but the acceptance of such a truth demands a power of abstraction beyond the ability of many men, especially when every-day experience contradicts the truth. It is easier to believe in equality before God than in equality before the law, if only because, to our simpler selves, the law is better known than God; so, too, it is easier to believe in the fraternity of the faithful in the next world than in any earthly brotherhood. But the Revolution was not concerned with the next world. ' Le bonheur est une idée neuve en Europe ', said St. Just. It was indeed; not new perhaps in heaven, but new in Europe. None of the abstractions, none of the faiths and loyalties set up by the nineteenth century —nationalism, middle class morality, liberalism—were able to withstand this dissolving desire for happiness.

Democracy, then, has not yet become a formula, a ritual. Men are still seeking to make it a reality. Western politics are still a struggle. Prophecy in such a matter is dangerous and futile enough; but prophecy is only the last term of any critical endeavour, and can hardly be avoided. Economic democracy may be achieved by a development of the abstract modern nation-state. A bureaucracy may come to rule over a population removed from want and devoid of envy as well as of imagination. The Socialist state may find a way to satisfy the natural man, if only by feeding him. Or success may come to the many groups that are attacking the modern state, and the proletarian revolution be accomplished through syndicalist decentralization. To those who are convinced that a man is more likely to be reasonable in the conduct of affairs of which he has personal experience than in the judgement of affairs about which he knows nothing, there is much that is hopeful in this possibility. It is tempting to think that man is better found in his parish than lost in the modern state, and that many a citizen can be trusted to administer a town's highways who ought never to cast a ballot on a question of foreign policy.

Whether the modern world reach a stable socialist equivalent of the *pax romana*, or whether it become a collection of syndicalist bodies struggling together as profitably as the city-states of Greece, or whether it remain much as it is, the place of critical intelligence in it will probably be higher than in the last century. The art of the present day, at least in its more serious forms, is surely not sentimental. Even popular art is less sure that virtue is its own reward than it was fifty years ago. The American comic supplement, indeed, is at times almost cynical; and jazz has a clarity, a directness, an intellectual honesty, not to be found in the work of Ethelbert Nevin. Political studies, too, have become less assured, less emotionally optimistic. The mass of conflicting facts about human beings accumulated by straightforward research has become so large that hasty conclusions, supported only by sentimental fervour, have become less common. The social sciences, having acquired a sceptical turn, are perhaps on the point of becoming genuine sciences at last. Reformers are studying the ways of bosses and common men. The age is critical and humble; for the critical spirit, so misunderstood and misapplied by the Victorians, is really a kind of humility.

There is then the possibility that intelligence, which does after all seem to have been most useful to the race, may survive a further democratic change. The present lower classes, never having been subject to the restraints of middle-class respectability, may perhaps learn other than vicarious indulgence in art and politics. Their present leaders, never having been taught that feeling is the best thing in life, may perhaps value thought more highly. In the worst case history warns us that humanity is too much for the cynic. The greatest of societies has survived for two thousand years with sweeping revolutionary dogmas incorporated in its faith. 'How hardly shall they that have riches enter into the kingdom of God!' 'If any man desire to be first, the same shall be last of all, and the servant of all.' The United States have endured, though founded on certain self-evident truths, such as 'that all men are created equal' and 'that they are endowed by their creator with certain inalienable Rights, that among these are Life, Liberty, and the pursuit of Happiness'. The civilization of Western Europe has always thrived on heresies; it need not fear democracy.

SELECTED ANN ARBOR PAPERBACKS

works of enduring merit

For a complete list of Ann Arbor Paperback titles write:
THE UNIVERSITY OF MICHIGAN PRESS / ANN ARBOR